ACTING AS FRIENDS

After a career in journalism Michael De-la-Noy served as press officer to the Archbishop of Canterbury from 1967 to 1970. He has since written biographies of Elgar and Denton Welch and contributed articles and reviews to the *Guardian*, *Books and Bookmen* and the *Spectator*.

By the same author

Elgar: The Man
Denton Welch: The Making of a Writer
The Honours System

Michael De-la-Noy

ACTING AS FRIENDS

The Story of the Samaritans

Collins
FOUNT PAPERBACKS

First published in Great Britain in 1987 by
Constable & Company Ltd
This edition first published by
Fount Paperbacks, London in 1989

Printed and bound in Great Britain by
William Collins Sons and Co. Ltd, Glasgow

For FREDO DONNELLY and
SHEILA COGGRAVE
Repraesentativus
and in loving memory of
CAROLYN and ERNEST MOSSNER

'We are not professionals. We are acting as friends.'
A deputy director in the Midlands

CONTENTS

INTRODUCTION

Without the unreserved co-operation of the Samaritans, no comprehensive book by a non-Samaritan could ever be written. Nevertheless it is necessary to emphasize that although the executive committee of the Samaritans satisfied themselves initially of my essential empathy as a writer, and the general secretary was kind enough to read a draft manuscript in order to have the opportunity of correcting factual errors and commenting upon value judgements, total editorial control has always resided with the author and the publishers. This is not another official handbook about Samaritan principles or codes of practice; it is an independent account and assessment of the history, purpose and practical functions of the Samaritans and of the scope of their work and potential usefulness in the context of society at large, written by an interested outsider. The ultimate responsibility for opinions, judgements and errors of fact is mine alone.

It is also essential to emphasize that on a wide range of matters there is a lack of uniformity between branches. To remind readers continually of this fact would be tedious, but it needs to be borne in mind that there is no definitive method of running a branch (the existence of a ratified set of principles and practices is another matter) any more than there is an archetypal Samaritan or one entirely typical caller. Those who work as Samaritans will find plenty here with which to disagree, facts that do not coincide with their own branch procedures and opinions that differ, perhaps radically, from their own, gained from years of personal experience. This book can only be read as one person's objective view of a national organization which bases its aims and modes of operation on a standard code of conduct and then leaves thousands of voluntary helpers a measure of freedom and responsibility in which to implement that code to the best of their human endeavour.

Initially, it was envisaged that in order to facilitate research I would be allocated a sort of liaison officer at the general office in Slough, through whom arrangements would be made for me to visit centres, attend training courses and so on. But so immediate and spontaneous were the flood of invitations and offers of unrestricted co-operation which I received from individual Samaritans on behalf of their branches that in the event the necessity for any sort of clearance through 'official channels' became almost entirely superfluous. Alas, because of the essentially confidential nature of the work of the Samaritans and the need to retain a large measure of anonymity it is, however, impossible for me publicly to thank an incredible number of people to whom I am indebted, not least to former callers who have talked to me of their need for help and the extent to which they felt they had received it. But I hope they will all know how much they have assisted me, and how grateful I am. With the exception of a handful of instantly identifiable people, mainly present or past full-time employees, who have given permission to forego anonymity, it can be assumed throughout that the names of every Samaritan and caller, and, when appropriate, the location of branches referred to, have been disguised. So far as the staff at the general office are concerned, I can only say they have consistently made my task an easier one, and turned the pleasure of their company into a privilege.

In 1986 I was granted an Authors' Foundation Grant by a panel chaired by Lady Antonia Fraser and nominated by the Society of Authors, which considerably eased the financial burden of research.

Michael De-la-Noy
London, 1987

·1·
A BENEVOLENT DESPOTISM

'I first went to the Samaritans when my marriage was cracking up. My husband's drinking had been very serious. He'd left me, and I was very lonely, and I had the complete responsibility for my son, who by this time was a drug addict. Then my mother died. I was left without any relatives except my brother, and he always kept himself pretty well detached. He is frightened of involvement, and yet he's a Samaritan! As a Samaritan he might be quite good, because he mustn't get involved with the callers. Perhaps he's a very good Samaritan. Perhaps he's good with people who are not related to him, people he feels he can escape from.

'I rang the Samaritans a lot, nearly always because of my son. I didn't know how to cope. I was completely and utterly and solely responsible. Sometimes, hysterically, I felt like killing myself, because I didn't know where to turn, but by the time I actually picked up the phone to ring the Samaritans I usually said, "Is it all right to ring, because I'm not going to commit suicide, but I don't know what to do and I feel very miserable and I don't know who to turn to?" And they'd say, "No, no, that's perfectly all right, fire away." Or I might burst into tears, or something, and then talk. Or put the phone down and ring them back. Sometimes I'd try to ring them and couldn't get through because the phone was engaged, and try three or four times, and in the end give up and then recover anyway.

'If the Samaritans knew I'd rung several times recently, they'd ask me to come in. If I went in immediately, or if I went in, which occasionally I did, without ringing them, I'd get to see anybody, and sometimes it wasn't very helpful. Nearly always it was helpful over the phone, for some reason, but when I went in, once or twice I felt worse when I came out, because I felt that the Samaritan I'd met wasn't very understanding. But if they already knew something about me, because I'd met them before, they would be very concerned, and listen well, and make me feel sort of welcome. But once or twice I felt I was being a nuisance. I know they don't give advice, but after talking at some length on the phone I usually felt better, it clarified my mind. You see, the worst thing when you're living alone is having no one to talk to, to clarify what's going on in your head. Sometimes writing it down helps, but it's a slower process, and if you're feeling very emotional it's not so easy to write down. It's easier to talk it out, having some response of nods and smiles and "Yes" and "Go on" and "What does that mean?"

'But I remember on one occasion a woman being slightly aggressive and interrupting me and saying, "Well, that's not so, you've contradicted yourself." She sounded as though she was tensed up herself, irritated. I mentioned this to my brother, and he asked who she was, and I gave her Christian name, and he said, "Oh, I know her, she does get rather sharp at times." Which I thought might have tipped the balance for somebody who was feeling worse. I could take it in the sense that I didn't kill myself. But after seeing this woman I went away crying, when usually they had put my problems in perspective, or sorted out that I should come and see someone regularly. I was in fact befriended twice. I went back because I had experienced better results previously.'

It seems that every decade or so, one obscure, previously unknown person is liable to come up with a brainwave, a simple idea that captures the public imagination or fulfils a commonplace need that no one else has catered for. It may be double-glazing, or the invention of cats' eyes. In 1953, the year of the Queen's coronation and the conquest of Everest, it dawned upon an Anglican clergyman, the Revd Chad Varah,[1] that if people who needed to summon the police, ambulance service or fire brigade in an emergency were accustomed to dialling a telephone number, those in emotional distress might be encouraged to call for help in the same way. He had been led to this basic proposition partly through his experience as a parish priest, more particularly by an almost obsessive interest in the social and religious history of sexual harassment. 'I am not particularly modest,' Chad Varah admits, and he records that since 1935 he had been regarded 'as one of the chief exponents of the theology of sex'. In 1935 he was ordained deacon. He was twenty-four, and still a bachelor. Nevertheless, 'as a young priest', Dr Varah has told countless audiences throughout the world, 'I had attempted to teach youngsters about sex in my youth club, and I had started giving marriage guidance to young couples. As a result, I became very knowledgeable and practised.' It is this self-taught knowledge, and practice acquired at vestry level, that has formed the basis of his public platform ever since, and in large measure has been used to justify and underpin the philosophy and mode of operation of the Samaritan movement that developed from it.

Many children destined to head a large family need to achieve at an early age an enviable degree of self-assurance. Born in 1911, at Barton-upon-Humber, Edward Chad Varah was the eldest of nine children. Varahs – almost certainly Ukrainian in origin – had lived in Yorkshire since at least 1537, and Chad himself was named after the seventh-century saint who converted the Midlands and founded the church in Lincolnshire where his father was parish priest. He was educated at Worksop College in Nottingham, gaining an Exhibition in Natural Sciences to Keble College, Oxford.[2] From there he went on to

[1] He was appointed a prebendary of St Paul's Cathedral in 1975.

[2] In 1981 Keble College conferred upon Chad Varah an honorary Fellowship.

study for the ministry at Lincoln Theological College, where one of his teachers was the sub-warden, Michael Ramsey, later Archbishop of Canterbury. After serving three assistant curacies, Varah was inducted, in 1942, to his first living, Holy Trinity, Blackburn. He remained there until 1949, and for the next four years he was vicar of the Church of St Paul, Clapham Junction.

Not content with exploring the theology of sex in the course of his parish work, Chad Varah had begun to supplement his stipend by writing articles on the subject. 'So when, in 1952, the editor of *Picture Post* got no reaction from a dreary series of articles about sex, I was the natural person for him to ask to write something exciting,' he has recalled.[3] 'I contributed what was probably the first article ushering in the "permissive society".' He received letters from 235 readers, fourteen of whom he thought were suicidal. The 'dreary' articles to which Chad Varah refers in fact appeared in 1951, supervised by a 'panel of experts', which included the poet Charles Madge, one of the inventors of Mass Observation and at that time professor of sociology at Birmingham University. They were introduced by one of *Picture Post's* star journalists, Fyfe Robertson, and included pieces with riveting titles like 'What Should You Tell Your Children?', 'The Roles of Men and Women' and 'Some Common Worries, Real and Imaginary'. After courtship, marriage and divorce had all been dealt with, Chad Varah's 'exciting' contribution appeared, on 10 November 1951, under the banner headline, 'A Parson Puts His Case', but far from ushering in the Permissive Society, the advent of which is generally reckoned to date from the Profumo Scandal in 1963, it read like a perfectly responsible, indeed highly orthodox, Christian commentary, and contained the pithy remark, 'The solution to marital unhappiness is not easier divorce but harder marriage.'

After four years in Battersea, and inevitably already aware of

[3] 'Why and How I Started the Samaritans', the *Samaritan*, special issue 1976.

the tragedy of suicide through his work as a parish priest, Varah read that in Greater London alone three people killed themselves every day, and it occurred to him that 'the kind of counselling I had been giving to people anxious or depressed about their sexual problems might well be applicable to people with other problems.' It further occurred to him that if you were feeling suicidal you needed to talk to somebody about it there and then, and the best way you could speak to somebody was by picking up a telephone. Varah's awareness in 1953 of suicide statistics in Greater London coincided with an offer of St Stephen Walbrook, a magnificant Wren church in the City, closed for thirteen years after being bombed early in the war, a benefice he has held ever since. In addition to a verger aged ninety-seven, who lived to be 102, it was blessed, in those days, with the fortuitous telephone number MANsion House 9000.

Varah told the patrons, the Worshipful Company of Grocers, that if he did move in as rector he would want to set up an emergency telephone service for people tempted to commit suicide, and they agreed to the experiment. It was started in such an *ad hoc* way that no serious consideration was given to a name by which it was to be known. Within days, Chad Varah was being quoted in the press as referring to 'Good Samaritans', and 'The Telephone Good Samaritans' became an instant if temporary sobriquet. Within a matter of four or five weeks the word 'Good' had thankfully been dropped from the official title, and for the next ten years 'The Telephone Samaritans' became the forerunners of the Samaritans. Yet so potent is the imagery of the New Testament that when speaking to the *Daily Mirror* in December 1953, Chad Varah was still apt to explain that 'If a case is sufficiently urgent, a Good Samaritan will dash to the caller and try to comfort and help him or her.'[4] And so carried away with enthusiasm did he become that within a month he had told the *Daily Mirror*, 'I want to spread the organization so

[4] Samaritan, *n. & a.* Native or language of Samaria (*good* – genuinely charitable person, w. ref. to Luke x: 33 etc.). *The Concise Oxford Dictionary*.

that there are at least two Samaritans for every four square miles of Greater London and the suburbs.' At this time, the 'organization' consisted of precisely four volunteers, two of whom were Chad Varah and his secretary. Neverthless, journalese already had the upper hand, the *Sunday Chronicle* breathlessly reporting on 13 December that 'in desperate, anxious undertones' a man on the run from the police had 'pleaded with the kindly-voiced priest who answered his call to grant him sanctuary in his church.'

'Telephone Samaritan No. 2, pretty twenty-four-year-old Vivien Prosser of Wimbledon' (the *Sunday Chronicle* again), Chad Varah's secretary, had taken the first call herself, because the rector was out. During the first twelve months, about 100 callers were spoken to on the telephone or interviewed in the vestry. Although an average of two such pastoral consultations a week would constitute a very small proportion of the total numbers of parishioners to whom a parish priest in a busy inner-city area might be expected to minister, they had at least three factors in common which made them unusual and newsworthy, time-consuming and often emotionally draining; the majority had arrived from outside the parish, all were feeling suicidal or in despair, and those who had already attempted suicide were guilty of a criminal offence. Furthermore, by having contemplated suicide they had attracted to themselves a social stigma, for in 1953 the subject of death still remained – as it does today – one of the last taboos in our society, and suicide in particular was regarded as antisocial and irresponsible to a degree.

Those two callers a week clearly represented merely the tip of the iceberg, for although suicide rates may fluctuate, sometimes quite irrationally, today 13,000 new callers a year contact the central London branch of the Samaritans alone, and there is no reason to imagine that a similar number of distressed or desperate people were not walking the streets of the capital in 1953. Had they all converged on St Stephen Walbrook at once, the fledgling operation would have been squashed at birth. As it was, within a matter of months the two callers a week were swelling by geometrical progression, assistance from voluntary helpers was needed to interview them, and a good deal of initial help was actually being offered by fellow sufferers. 'Chad saw that a lot of clients waiting to see him were befriending each other,' John Eldrid, an Anglican priest who joined the Samaritans in 1958 and is now the full-time director of the central London branch, has recalled. And Chad Varah himself has said that his small band of initial helpers were doing more good than he. 'They had no qualifications at all but great human qualities. They were simply listening to callers and making coffee, providing just what the clients mostly wanted, a listening ear, with no advice or preaching, just a great deal of warmth, tolerance and acceptance. They did not necessarily approve of everything the callers had done, but they offered acceptance of them as suffering human beings.'

There were, in the earliest days, perhaps some dozen helpers. By 1956 there were still only twenty, but in three years they had dealt with 350 callers. Recruitment tended to be by word of mouth, and of course, for a variety of reasons, the earliest volunteers, like so many of their successors, tended to leave. Originally they were known not as volunteers or Samaritans but as 'rector assistants'. The first Samaritan volunteer to be enrolled immediately after the founder and his secretary was Mary Meikle, who rejoiced in the number 3/1. A volunteer who can remember being referred to as a rector assistant as late as 1955, the year he drifted into St Stephen to offer his services, was Roger Martyn (44/1), who eventually became the Samaritan's first honorary legal adviser. With no training or experience of any kind, he was sent within minutes of volunteering to see if he could be of assistance to a man in distress at Wimbledon Station. Because the numbers of callers were initially quite small it was possible, even with a small staff, to devote a considerable amount of time to individual cases, although when the vestry was in use interviews might have to be conducted in the church in competition with the organist. Roger Martyn's recollection of his first night duty, on New Year's Eve 1956, places in perspective the level of activity at St Stephen

Walbrook thirty years ago compared to that of almost any Samaritan branch today: absolutely nothing happened.[5]

Roger Martyn's mercy dash to Wimbledon Station may have furnished Chad Varah with the case history he wrote up for *Picture Post* on 30 June 1956, in 'the first of the *Picture Post* reports on the desperate men and women the Suicide Samaritans have SNATCHED FROM DEATH.' London, even then, was described by Varah as the 'biggest, loneliest city in the world'. The article is remarkably orientated towards religion, and it is written (ghosted, perhaps, in the office) in a journalistic style impossible to parody. A workman reading a newspaper, and a man waiting to jump under a train, meet, providentially, on the platform. As the 'impatient man' leapt forward, the workman caught him roughly by the collar.

'"You silly fool!" he hissed.

'After what seemed an interminable delay, the doors closed again and the train moved grindingly on. The workman pushed a newspaper under the nose of his companion, who was drawing deep, sobbing breaths. "Read that," he ordered, stabbing at a paragraph with a calloused forefinger, "and if you'll ring these Samaritans I won't hand you over to the police, which is what I oughter do. Funny, I was reading about 'em just before you tried to do yourself in, and thinking it was a lot of rot. But I'd say they're just the people you need."'

'Gradually I found my senses again. They even encouraged me to find a job,' the reformed suicide reported from the caption beneath a photograph of himself driving a van. This picture, like all the others liberally illustrating the thrilling adventures of the Suicide Samaritans, taken during heart-to-hearts on station benches and frantic phone calls from telephone boxes, were shamelessly faked. They do not write articles like that any more, but no wonder some potential volunteers still harbour the notion that being a Samaritan

[5] The fact that in 1956 a new volunteer had been allocated the number 41 does not mean there were at that time 41 volunteers; when a volunteer left, their number was not reallocated. In 1956 there may in fact have been only twenty volunteers *in situ*.

involves the glamour of rushing around seeking souls to save.

'Befriending' was the therapeutic term Chad Varah soon gave to 'the listening acceptance and personal caring' that he estimates was all that was required by seven out of eight of the people who called at the vestry or telephoned, and there are still Samaritans today who regret that the term Befrienders was not officially adopted, as it has been in some places overseas, instead of Samaritans, with its obviously Christian connotations, derived from the parable of the Good Samaritan. For the word 'Samaritan' is one reason why, although the Samaritans are now forbidden to proselytize, a good deal of identification with religion has undoubtedly rubbed off on to the movement. The early core of 'rector assistants' actually banded together into a Company of Samaritans, holding special services of dedication and admission. Not only was the founder a priest but the first two full-time assistants at St Stephen were clergymen, and for ten years only clergy were appointed, by Chad Varah, as branch directors. 'It added tone,' the present general secretary, the Revd David Evans, suggests. For an organization staffed by amateurs to be dabbling in sex and suicide was considered by many in the medical profession, the police, the Church and the social services to be foolhardy, to say the least, and certainly the wearing of a collar back to front was felt by society at large to confer an aura of respectability. A more positive advantage in recruiting clergy as local directors lay in their vocational understanding of confidentiality.

'It was very difficult for someone like a doctor to be a Samaritan,' says Mr Evans. 'There are ethical problems over the possibility of appearing to treat somebody else's patient. On the whole, the role of doctors has been as consultants.' A faint atmosphere of religiosity may linger, but nowadays women outnumber men as directors by just over two to one, there are four medical directors and precisely three clergymen. As for the term 'befriending', this does now have a firm place in Samaritan terminology. From the moment a caller contacts the Samaritans he or she is regarded as in some sense being befriended, and support offered to a caller after initial contact, and for a limited length of time, is officially known as 'on-going befriending'.

Even while vicar of St Paul, Clapham Junction, Chad Varah had regarded himself as 'possibly the busiest parson in the C of E.' The setting up of his experimental emergency telephone line had of course been work undertaken in addition to routine duties as a parish priest which at St Stephen Walbrook involved a certain amount of ceremonial, for St Stephen is the parish church of the Lord Mayor of London, and within three months he decided to disengage from befriending (but not from counselling, 'which I was quite capable of giving') in order to concentrate on administration and on enquiries from well-intentioned innovators overseas. 'I shall never again pick up the emergency telephone,' he told his rector assistants. 'But I will answer letters, and I will select you, instruct you, deploy you, discipline you and, when necessary, sack you.' Not for nothing did some of his recruits refer to him as the Boss. 'It was,' recalls Jean Burt, who became a Samaritan volunteer in 1958, 'a sort of benevolent despotism. He gave very firm direction. And we needed this, because we were so inexperienced, and there were no national standards of training to fall back on. So we used to have our own training classes, and every Monday, at lunchtime, Chad used to hold a meeting of all the volunteers, and there was practically a one hundred per cent turn-out, because we were all so frightened of making mistakes. People brought their sandwiches and the meeting used to last about an hour. We learned a lot about the callers, and about ourselves.' A volunteer who offered his services within the first six weeks has said that 'in those days, the only way you were trained was by doing the work, meeting the clients and learning from your mistakes.' Undeterred by the despotic atmosphere, however, in 1971 Miss Burt quit a civil service post in the Cabinet Office to become assistant general secretary to the Samaritans, being made an MBE in 1979 for her work. She later served as joint general secretary, resigning in 1984. After thirty years she is still a volunteer at the central London branch.

Eight years after the war the condition of St Stephen Walbrook remained deplorable. One outside wall of the outer vestry consisted of nothing but plywood, and the room itself was heaped with builders' rubble and old organ pipes. All this mess had to be cleared up, but even after the church had been restored, Jean Burt remembers conditions at St Stephen as being 'remarkably cramped and sometimes bitterly cold,' an impression echoed by another volunteer who joined a year later than she, who has written, 'Almost my first impression of the Samaritans when I joined in the autumn of 1959 was an engaging atmosphere of rather dotty scruffiness. We were herded together in the outer vestry which continued to retain a distinct air of the war damage it had sustained. This not over-large room had to contain the volunteers, the staff, the clients, an assortment of tables, desks and chairs of varying age, the all-important telephones, and, almost as important, the tea and coffee-making impedimenta. Although we were totally untrained in any psychological or sociological disciplines we were soon made aware that there were certain cardinal principles to be observed, the breach of which would involve instant dismissal; absolute obedience to one's superiors in the branch, complete discretion, no false sentimentality and above all the knowledge that the client's needs were paramount.' But although they were dealing in matters often literally of life and death, the prevailing atmosphere, he says, seemed primarily to be one of laughter, friendship and a certain openness.

The two volunteers on duty at night slept on bunks in a tiny room in the tower, with telephones on a shelf opposite the bunks, and cold linoleum in between. A hoaxer took to telephoning on a regular basis to inquire if the volunteers were awake, and one night a lady rang to say she had chucked her cat out of a fifth-floor window, and what was she to do with the body? John Eldrid was one of those who slept in the tower when on duty at night; it was not until 1964 that the crypt was converted, at the expense of the patrons, to ensure that permanent Samaritan premises would always be available when the living changed hands. Eldrid's arrival heralded a nucleus of full-time support beginning to gather around Chad Varah, including a second priest, the Revd Eric Reid, and Mary Bruce, a psychiatric social worker who came over from St Bartholomew's Hospital in 1958 to help consolidate the experience of the past five years and to set up properly structured training classes. She remained with the Samaritans until 1965. 'One of the significant things about the Samaritans,' says Mr Eldrid, 'is the way it has changed so little in essence from the early days. Of course, thirty years ago people were not as permissive as they are now. Not only was attempted suicide still a crime, but so was all homosexual activity, and in withholding information from the police Samaritans were not protected by law. Some of the volunteers used to get worried about not giving information, and two things Chad Varah had to fight hard for were the necessity for volunteers to be open and non-judgemental about sexual matters, and the absolutely overriding necessity for confidentiality. These days a lot of the things he fought for are considered quite normal, but even to offer befriending rather than counselling was an entirely new concept. One of the people who helped us gain acceptance among statutory and other voluntary bodies, and also enabled us to understand certain psychological and psychiatric problems better, was Richard Fox, the doctor in charge of the emergency clinic at the Maudsley Hospital on Denmark Hill. He became consultant psychiatrist to the Samaritans. Most branches will now have a psychiatric consultant – not to interview the callers, unless they wish it, but as a consultant to the director.' Dr Fox was in fact appointed consultant psychiatrist in 1963, and he was soon being telephoned by the Samaritans for permission to send callers who were obviously in need of psychiatric care to the Maudsley for admission. 'I was impressed by the quality of the referrals for admission,' he says, 'and eventually I even referred a client back from the hospital to the Samaritans for befriending. At that time the Samaritans were held in great suspicion by the medical profession, and Chad Varah had been searching hard for respectability.'

Eric Reid was thirty-seven when he arrived from Ireland,

with a training in psychology and philosophy (he had been ordained into the Church of Ireland), and along with John Eldrid he was appointed a deputy director. His Samaritan number was 332, which would indicate that over the first six years one new Samaritan had been recruited, on average, every week, although of course by no means all of them had remained as volunteers. He was attracted to the work on a full-time basis because, he says, 'I liked the whole idea of befriending by ordinary, down-to-earth people, and I had always been interested in social work within the Church. Although I did my stint of parish work for twelve years, I'm not a parish man.' One of the most remarkable rescue missions Reid got involved in during the ten years he worked at St Stephen occurred on receipt of a letter from a man which read, 'By the time you receive this I shall be dead.' The only hint of an address was a hotel room number in the five-hundreds, and a London postmark. Reckoning there were few hotels in London with more than 500 bedrooms in those days, he and Chad Varah exercised some rapid detective work, and tracked down the writer of the letter, who was rushed to hospital suffering from an overdose.

'I would say about thirty per cent of the clients – a word we always used then and one I prefer to callers – were, in our opinion, suicidal,' he recalls. He also remembers 'many a good set-to' with the founder. 'We argued about all kinds of things, but he admired you if you stuck to your guns. One of my faults was that I wasn't always prepared to let go of clients that easily, and finish off befriending. So much of our work was still experimental that I don't remember any rules or regulations being laid down in writing, other than the sacrosanct rule of confidentiality. Much of our time was spent devising preparation classes – not training classes; you can't train someone to be a Samaritan, you can only prepare them. Chad generally took the classes in sexual problems, and it was very noticeable how high the drop-out rate of new recruits was after those. I suppose it was the shock! I remember one volunteer was horrified at the thought of anyone having oral sex.' Eric Reid resigned from the Samaritans in 1967 to become chaplain to a psychiatric hospital.

In 1979 he was appointed an honorary canon of Newcastle Cathedral, and in 1987 he retired after twelve years as secretary to the Hospital Chaplaincy Council.

Despite Chad Varah's initial dream of spreading to the suburbs, for six years the church of St Stephen Walbrook seemed likely to remain the single centre for the Telephone Samaritans in the United Kingdom, the one address and telephone number available 'to help the suicidal and despairing'. 'I don't think the idea of expansion outside London ever occurred to Chad Varah in the early years,' says Jean Burt. 'He was too busy seeing callers and corresponding with people from all parts of the world who wrote to him about their problems.' Looking back on an era of almost unbelievable expansion that eventually did take place, she remembers that when new branches got started in the austerity of post-war Britain it was never easy. 'There was an acute shortage of everything, premises, volunteers and money, and as always, as soon as you advertised for new volunteers to man a centre you induced a disproportionate influx of new callers.' But in 1959, the year that was marked by a six-year grant from the Gulbenkian Foundation, Edinburgh, under the ecumenical leadership of Presbyterians, Roman Catholics and a Presbyterian minister, Professor James Blackie (henceforth known as James 1/2), achieved the distinction of becoming the first of a galaxy of branches eventually destined to cover every essential catchment area in the United Kingdom. Looking back on the decision to open a branch in Edinburgh, one of the original Scottish volunteers has written, 'I tremble at what had to be done. There were no models on which to build, except St Stephen, and London was so different. It is interesting, first, to note that Chad let us be different, indicative perhaps of the Samaritan spirit to improvise and to be flexible, and secondly the warmth and commitment of ordinary people who worked for hours – cleaning, scrubbing, painting, training, fixing rotas, doing duties. To a schoolteacher, sadly accepting so many of the restrictive practices of that profession, finding kindred spirits – bus drivers, university lecturers, chars, housewives – willing to get stuck in and try to do something for other people was an eye-opener.' Despite the apparent lack of models, within twelve months three more branches had been established, one of them in Liverpool, the first English branch outside London and the third formally to be recognized, set up by a future suffragan-bishop of Buckingham, who became Christopher 1/3, and who managed to acquire from the Postmaster-General the eight-millionth telephone installed in Great Britain. The other two branches were in Scotland, in Glasgow and Aberdeen. Another half-dozen centres took root in 1961, in Bradford, Bournemouth, Hull, Jersey, Portsmouth and Belfast, where, of all places, a Presbyterian director joined forces with Anglican, Roman Catholic and Methodist colleagues. A former Lord Mayor of Belfast chaired its finance committee, and the branch was opened just ten weeks after an exploratory meeting had been held in the Chapter House of Belfast Cathedral.

'There was a good deal of evangelical religious fervour in the early branches,' a former member of the executive committee recalls, 'and the setting up of the earliest branches was often a bit chaotic. You'd get a group of ten Methodists sitting round a table saying "We ought to have a branch", and the next week they'd started one. Hence there was no systematic recruitment, and very often people weren't selected or trained. Anybody who turned up was put straight on the telephone. But as branches spread, new branches were able to draw on previous experience and disasters.'

Press publicity had by now taken hold of public imagination overseas, particularly in Europe, South Africa and India, and centres supposedly based on Samaritan principles of befriending had come into existence in Salisbury in Rhodesia, in Karachi, Bombay and Hong Kong. They tended, however, to depend upon professionals to the exclusion of volunteers and to be strongly orientated towards denominational religion, and sometimes also they were based on psychiatric hospitals. In 1960, in order to try and steer a good deal of misplaced enthusiasm in the direction of his own concepts of 'listening acceptance and personal caring', Chad Varah organized a conference of overseas branches in Switzerland. 'Imitations of varying inadequacy' was how he later described the earliest attempts at forming Samaritan-style branches overseas, and he admitted that efforts to let the 'Samaritan ideal' influence the work of other organizations had not, at this stage, been successful. In the United States, needless to say, 'students of suicide' emerged, and even an American Association of Suicidology, from whom, in 1974, Chad Varah was to receive an award. But a good deal of flexibility in approach by countries with traditions different to the British occurred. Istanbul produced the Comrades in the Spirit; Israel, the Helping Hand. The simple word Friendship was chosen by the Parisians, the Belgians opted for Tele-Welcome, and *Telefonseelsorge* (Pastoral Care by Telephone) was the rather appealing name adopted by the Germans.

But before the 'Samaritan ideal' had taken a firmly rooted hold throughout the world, a major breakthrough in social attitudes, destined to alleviate the task of the Samaritans at home, was about to be accomplished. For some years, attempts had been made behind the legal and political scenes to have the felony relating to attempted suicide removed from the statute book, and one influential campaigner had been a remarkable woman, Dr Doris Odlum, who became an inspiration to three generations of Samaritans. A child psychiatrist, who had served from 1954–58 as president of the European League for Medical Hygiene, she was born in 1890 and educated at St Hilda's College, Oxford. In 1916 she had stroked the London School of Medicine for Women's eight in the first women's race ever rowed, against Cambridge University. She was also a national fencing champion. Having already been consulted over the 1958 Mental Health Act, which altered radically the status of patients in psychiatric hospitals, Dr Odlum was now recruited to help draft the 1961 Suicide Act, and in the same year Chad Varah invited her to become consultant psychiatrist to a newly formed branch in her home town of Bournemouth. From then on she devoted a vast amount of her time to Samaritan work, contributing to the movement's magazine and in 1974 being appointed president for life, a role in which she played an active and stimulating part until her death eleven years later, at the age of ninety-five.

By the start of 1963, with attempted suicide no longer a crime, the total of Samaritan branches in the United Kingdom, including branches still on probation, had risen to twenty-three, a dozen new centres having been set on their feet the previous year, in Birmingham, Cambridge, Croydon, Derby, Dundee, Guernsey, Halifax, Nottingham, Manchester, Reading, Salisbury and Stoke-on-Trent. This was the year the suicide rate for England and Wales (the rate for Scotland is always calculated separately), having slumped in 1941 to 9.0 per 100,000 of the population, was to reach a peak, 12.2 per 100,000 of the population. (It is currently 8.2 per 100,000.) Also in 1963 the existing twenty-one fully recognized branches became incorporated into a company limited by guarantee, with the name 'The Samaritans'. Those twenty-one founding branches were Aberdeen, Belfast, Bombay, Bournemouth, Brighton, Cambridge, Dundee, Edinburgh, Glasgow, Hong Kong, Hull, Jersey, Karachi, Liverpool, London, Manchester, Portsmouth, Reading, Salisbury in Rhodesia, Stoke-on-Trent and Woolwich. For the next four years they were to be served only by a full-time secretary and an honorary bursar.

A Memorandum of Association spelt out the object for which the Samaritans had been established: 'to assist persons who are suicidal, despairing or in distress and thus reduce the incidence of suicide by providing a service in each area where a branch is formed to enable such persons to receive immediate help, compassion and friendship from members of the Association selected and prepared for the purpose, working under direction; and also, in accordance with normal procedure, counselling or referral for treatment or advice from members or non-members of the Association having specialist or professional skills.' A precept clearly enshrined in the Articles was that 'the business of the Association shall be managed by the Council', and no longer could the Samaritans be charged with being run from a church in the City by a benevolent despot. In particular, the Articles granted to a council of management the right to recognize and to close down a branch, and forbade members of a branch that had been closed down to form a separate association of any kind having a name incorporating the word 'Samaritan'. Thus by becoming a company (licensed by the Board of Trade to omit the word 'Limited' from its title) the Samaritans were enabled to lay claim to copyright in their name and, by implication, in their activities. A very distinctive and beneficial feature of the Samaritan movement was clearly laid down, too. 'A director of a branch', one of the Articles read, 'shall be given wide powers in the management of the branch to the intent that the primary objects of the Association may be pursued without undue restriction; and in particular when, in the opinion of a director there is a possibility that a client may commit suicide, he shall be empowered to take such steps as he reasonably thinks fit to avert that possibility.' It is interesting to note that in 1963, those who called upon the Samaritans for help were officially referred to as clients, and continued so to be called for some considerable time; today such terminology is generally thought too clinical, and anybody currently telephoning or visiting the Samaritans is usually (although not invariably) referred to as a caller.

In addition to assuming responsibility for endorsing or closing branches, the council of management was empowered to appoint branch directors. Initially the council was to consist of no fewer than twenty members, and the first council was elected by the subscribers to the company. There were thirty of these, all but three of them men (one of whom described himself as a gentleman); two were bishops and another twelve were clergymen, one of whom later became a bishop. Membership of the council was restricted to Samaritans, any one of whom might be removed from the council 'if he becomes of unsound mind'. There is no recorded instance of such a disaster, but the condition of someone's mind is often difficult to determine. Just as difficult to ascertain is whether the Samaritans have achieved their stated objective of 'reducing the incidence of suicide'. If suicides fell to zero there would be no conclusive proof that the Samaritans had achieved such a miraculous event, and even if a caller were to report back – and many have – that through support received from the Samaritans he had refrained from killing himself, such testament would only amount at best to circumstantial evidence. The argument about prevention is presented early in order to dispose of it early, for in a way it is irrelevant. Because, from empirical evidence, it is impossible to prove that the Samaritans have ever prevented a single suicide, no argument follows that they should not try, and most Samaritans would regard one life saved in thirty years as a worthwhile achievement. In any event, the aims of the Samaritans extend far beyond the explicit attempt to prevent suicide – to the alleviation through compassion of distress at every level, and even to the comforting of a caller who they believe may be dying of their own free will. In the face of such a harrowing experience as that, semantics about statistics and evidence tend to pale in importance.

Nevertheless it has been claimed that the decline in the suicide rate after 1963 was attributed to an increase in the number of Samaritan branches, and hence the number of callers. This may be so, although unfortunately saturation coverage of the country by Samaritan centres did not prevent the suicide rate from creeping up by 0.7 per 100,000 of the population between 1975 and 1985. However, there was certainly an undeniable correlation between the expansion of Samaritan activity and a decline in the rate of suicide between 1964 and 1975, a rate which may look small and seem to reflect little fluctuation as between, say, 11.5 per 100,000 of the population in 1959 and 12.2 in 1963, but a suicide rate of 11.5 per 100,000 in 1959 represented about 5,250 deaths, and a suicide rate of 12.2 per 100,000 in 1963 meant that almost 5,750 people had killed themselves, an additional 500 per annum, or a rise of around ten per cent. While the Samaritans were slowly getting underway between 1959 and 1963, by which time they had established (by the end of 1963) thirty-five branches, the suicide rate, as indicated, had risen to 12.2 per 100,000. But between 1963 and 1970, during the greatest period of Samaritan expansion, it fell steadily and consistently – to 11.7 in 1964, by which time there were forty-eight branches, to 10.8 in 1965, when there were sixty-five branches, to 10.4 in 1966, when there were seventy-three, to 9.7 in 1967, with eighty-eight, to 9.4 in 1968, with ninety-six, to 8.9 in 1969, with 107 branches, and to 8.0 in 1970 when, by that time, there were 117 branches. By 1975, with 165 branches in existence, the suicide rate had fallen to 7.5, the lowest level ever recorded.

The decade of the sixties saw an avalanche of new centres, among them, in 1964, Leicester, where for the first time a non-clerical director (a solicitor) was appointed as one of a team of co-directors. With the arrival of every new branch there arrived, also, an inevitable proportion of volunteers who turned out to be less than suitable, for nothing resembling a uniform procedure for selection and training had yet been established. 'There was trouble sometimes in the early branches,' Jean Burt remembers. 'Directors could become a bit too dictatorial, or just unable to cope. You also had unruly volunteers. Not everybody can work under direction, and a lot of people came into the Samaritans in the early days thinking it was going to be terribly glamorous, with a lot of rushing about and drama, and some of them wanted to do their own thing, which would have been far too dangerous. Mistakes were made also in opening branches which were not really viable, in small catchment areas, where there was perhaps more enthusiasm than real need.'

For better or worse, between 1961 and 1969 no less than 102 Samaritan branches came into existence, just over half the total achieved in the period 1959 to 1986. On average one branch was established every four weeks in 1963, in Bedford, Cheltenham, Doncaster, Guildford, Hastings, Havering, Ipswich, Oxford, Southampton, Stafford, Weybridge and Worcester. A similar rate of progress was maintained the following year, with thirteen branches appearing, at Leicester, Bristol, Colchester, Coventry, Exeter, Folkestone, Grimsby, Macclesfield, Norwich, Reigate, Scunthorpe, Shrewsbury and Torbay. The busiest year of all was 1965, when seventeen branches were opened, at Bath, Bolton, Cardiff, Chelmsford, Crewe,

Dumfernline, Eastbourne, Harrow, Kilmarnock, Leatherhead, Leek, Maidstone, Newcastle, Northallerton, Orpington, Sheffield and Wolverhampton. The next twelve months saw a further eight branches established, in Falkirk, Leeds, Lincoln, Lowestoft, Luton, the Medway, Northwich and Southend. Fifteen more centres got going in 1967, in Basildon, Basingstoke, Brent, Chester, Darlington, Newport, North Devon, Redbridge, Rochdale, Slough, Swansea, Swindon, Tunbridge Wells, Whitehaven and York. Another eight branches opened in 1968, in Brighton, the Chilterns, Kingston-on-Thames, Huddersfield, King's Lynn, Northampton, on Teesside and at Ware. This remarkable decade closed with a fine flourish, eleven more branches opening in 1969, at Bexley, Blackburn, Canterbury, Carlisle, Great Yarmouth, Lewisham, Putney, Walsall, Warrington, Watford and Worthing.

But this almost reckless enthusiasm led to some bizarre events. One branch was actually run single-handed by a clergyman who, it was alleged, would cheerfully leap from the pulpit on a Sunday to answer the telephone. A Non-Conformist minister managed to split his branch in two by having sexual relations with some of his volunteers, and engaging in psychotherapy with the callers and then making a charge for his services. An Anglican clerical director was so incompetent he handed over the day-to-day running of *his* branch to a semi-recovered alcoholic, who photocopied four case records and sent these off to the *News of the World*, who declined to publish them. One of the first members of the new executive committee recalls, 'The whole of the administration in the early days was done by a lady with rheumatoid arthritis and an old gentleman who had a background in accountancy. They kept all the records in the loo at their little home in Oxted. But they did it magnificently, organizing conferences and writing to people, and they kept the whole thing ticking over until it just got completely beyond them.'

The branch in Manchester, the seventh to be established, had been launched, in 1962, largely under the leadership of an Anglican priest, the Revd Basil Higginson (Basil 1/7), and in

1967, the numbers of branches having already trebled since Incorporation four years previously, he was appointed the first general secretary. Much of his seven years in office (he was compelled to resign through ill health in 1974, and died two years later) was spent travelling the country, offering advice and practical help to local citizens intent on starting a branch in their own town. He inspected premises, ensuring that the need for adequate financing was understood, and that potential volunteers realized the kind of commitment they were taking on, especially in terms of hours of voluntary service required to man a branch. It was said after his death that his memory about branches had been phenomenal, that he was able to recall precisely 'their history, troubles, triumphs, premises, personnel and clients'. Trouble of a major order arose in 1972, when the opening hours of one branch located in a seaside holiday resort became so haphazard that the matter had to be discussed by the council of management. 'It took the council four hours to arrive at a decision,' Jean Burt, by then assistant general secretary, recalls. 'And a decision to close the branch was only made after there had been numerous attempts to get the volunteers to maintain the high standards necessary. The thing was played right out until it became obvious that with the present people in control it was not viable at all. So the council decided to close it, which was very traumatic. The honorary solicitor and I had the awful job of actually going personally to do it. We called one evening to collect the keys, and to place the assets in a separate account. Eventually the lease had to be wound up, too. We took away all caller records, and lodged them with another branch seventeen miles away, who had agreed to do a holding operation. I'm happy to say that a very good branch rose from the ashes eight years later.' This was the only occasion when a branch has ever been closed through misdemeanour, although another was at one time reduced to probationary status, an act, says the present general secretary, 'which concentrated their minds no end'.

Branches tend to run so smoothly today, with a degree of dedication that often involves volunteers undertaking many more duties than they originally committed themselves to, that it is a salutary reminder of times past to recall how novel and unexpectedly difficult some of the early enthusiasts found it to establish a routine and a set of essential guidelines for operating. In 1973, two years after the Ealing branch had been founded, one of their members was writing to the *Samaritan*, a quarterly magazine founded the year before, to bewail the difficulty of welding into a team 130 volunteers, 'few of whom regularly meet more than one in ten of their colleagues'. Support for branch meetings aimed at further training had been disappointing, he said, and when a meeting was convened to discuss the lack of support, only half the branch membership turned up. One vital matter thrashed out was a policy over temporary closures during summer holidays, when the numbers on duty might be down to two, the telephones were ringing and half a dozen clients were waiting to be seen. It was agreed that in those circumstances a 'Closed' notice had to be exhibited, giving the telephone number and the time of re-opening. Just two years into the life of the branch, two perennial problems all too familiar to Samaritans young and old received an airing: 'How long must we suffer the minority who telephone us several times a day?' and 'Why has the branch not given directions on sex calls?' Another ominous question on the agenda was, 'How should we deal with a client carrying a weapon?' By the end of December 1973, out of 143 branches being manned by 17,285 volunteers, ninety-two were in fact already offering a twenty-four-hour service at the branch premises, and the forty-six still unable to achieve this ultimate goal were having calls transferred to volunteers at home or in other branches. The practice of volunteers taking calls at home would be severely frowned upon today.

An atmosphere of inspired chaos and improvisation can stimulate and strongly appeal to the pioneer spirit, and a former vice-chairman, who joined in 1969, got some of his frustration at the way the Samaritans had developed off his chest when he resigned in 1985. He had joined the movement, he explained in the *Samaritan*, because 'it was something I could do where I could give of myself, that the giving was of value to someone else. The Swinging Sixties swung to a halt, and all the open, challenging, optimistic things which were there for us retreated into the drab Seventies and the fearful Eighties, and with the changes the Samaritan movement became middle-aged before its time. It became necessary to justify one's existence, to be more accountable, so there was more control, organization, measuring. The Samaritans became semi-professional, confused by the worst of both worlds.' He went on to regret the modern need for organization, training, hot-lines, standing orders, manuals and directives, 'all the paraphernalia of a recognizable organization'. What he described as 'Chad's Little Army' used, he said, to be a guerrilla movement in an uncaring society; now it was more like a pillar of NATO. A colleague from Teesside responded in a letter by saying he could understand the disillusionment displayed, but somewhere, he felt, there was wrong thinking. It was only natural to look back with nostalgia at the movement as it had been in the beginning, but any organization which did not adapt would die. 'We *have* to evolve,' he wrote, 'as we and our task grow bigger. Only our refusal to succumb to disillusionment may stand between our callers and the abyss. Our nostalgia is a luxury they can't afford.'

By contributing articles to *Forum*, a magazine devoted to sex under the banner of education but whose correspondence columns were sometimes so erotic as to verge on the pornographic, Chad Varah had risked being cold-shouldered by the Establishment, but in 1969 the mantle of respectability fell upon the Samaritans when its founder was made an OBE. Presumably the civil servant known as the Ceremonial Officer, whose job it is to compile the prime minister's honours lists, had, like a volunteer named Susan, writing in 1972, 'missed the highlight of Chad's sex lecture'. These spicy performances lingered long in the memory of those volunteers he trained personally. 'Tonight I'm going to talk about sex, about heterosexual sex, homosexual sex and abnormal sex,' an Australian Methodist remembers the rector of St Stephen Walbrook beginning a training session. Again, 'All keyed up for the Kingdom of Heaven, we got Chad on sex,' a founder member of the branch in Edinburgh has recalled. 'In our cold climate we didn't have problems of sex – at least, not until Chad arrived.' Sex, for Chad Varah, has remained something of a speciality. In a book called *The Samaritans in the '70s*[6] he contributed sections on *Befriending the Sexually Frustrated* as well as *Befriending the Homosexual*, and one of his more esoteric publications was titled *Telephone Masturbators and How to Befriend Them*.

'In my view, the Samaritans actually started as a sex counselling agency, with suicide prevention growing out of that, and Chad's attitude towards sex has always been a threat hanging over the organization,' says one of his admirers. 'He once wrote a book on sex in which he insisted on writing all the words in their original Anglo-Saxon, so it was "fucks" and "cunts" all over the place, and Doris Odlum was the only person who was able to persuade Chad not to publish this bloody book. If it had been published it would have caused a furore, in and out of the Samaritan movement. When he went to branches to give talks on befriending people with sexual problems he deliberately went out of his way to shock as many people as he could, with, I think in part, the laudable purpose of removing from the organization people who were going to be shocked. But the consequence of this was that we had branches all over the country threatening to leave. The first job I did when I was elected to the executive was to visit a branch in Surrey to close it down, because Chad had given them a talk on sex and they were so outraged they were threatening to leave the movement. We decided they were really rather a nice lot and didn't deserve to be closed down. Wherever he went we had to send people to damp things down afterwards. I'm sure Jesus Christ would have made a terrible pope, and in Chad Varah we had a brilliant, charismatic, creative person who started something quite new but, as his creation expanded, he proved not at all to be the person to carry out the bureaucracy.'

[6] Constable, 1973.

Three years after Chad Varah had featured in the honours list his adolescent offspring received its most influential flood of publicity: eleven episodes of a television series called *The Befrienders*. Based on archetypal case histories, it went out, in 1972, at peak viewing time on Saturday evenings, and was seen by an estimated eight million viewers. The result was a heavy response from young callers and youthful volunteers. Some branches recorded a two-hundred per cent increase in calls during transmission, but commenting at the time on the quality of the programmes, a volunteer from Reading who was also a television producer wrote to the *Samaritan* to say that many fellow Samaritans had found the series unreal, and many television professionals had found it trite. Left only with a relationship between client and volunteer to explore, he thought the programmes lacked dramatic content, for a Samaritan was essentially a passive listener. The clients, too, he thought unconvincing and uninvolved, but he concluded that the series had probably been good for the Samaritans. Quite apart from the bonus of free publicity on television, it has always been the case that in the United Kingdom, volunteers have been easier to recruit than overseas, for in this country there already exists a tradition of charitable and voluntary service, which perhaps is one advantage of the existence of a distinct and clearly identifiable middle-class. It was soon recognized by the Samaritans that the poorer the country overseas the more difficult they would find it to recruit volunteers prepared, or with the time available, to offer their services free of charge. In many developing countries it is common practice for people to take two jobs, when the work is available, just to make ends meet, and – again, when the work is available – whole families tend to seek employment from a very young age. Often, too, when a Samaritan branch did get established, there were no social services to back it up. Nevertheless, by the mid-seventies there were branches, in addition to Hong Kong, Bombay and Karachi (and excluding branches in Europe and affluent countries like Australia, Canada and the United States), in Zambia, Brazil, Malaysia, Singapore, South Korea, Calcutta (where one of the volunteers was Jacob de Mel, Bishop of Calcutta and Metropolitan of India), Delhi and Sri Lanka, with many more in the course of preparation. In 1974 twenty-two delegates from branches all over the world met at St Stephen.[7] The result was the setting up of an entirely independent organization called Befrienders International, The Samaritans Worldwide, and on 2 November 1974, twenty-one years to the day since establishing the Telephone Samaritans, Chad Varah resigned as director of the London branch to become the president of Befrienders International. He resigned from this post, together with the honorary presidency of the central London branch, on 2 November 1986.

So far as setting up new branches in the United Kingdom was concerned, the years 1970 to 1973 remained as busy as the Sixties had been. The first year of the new decade saw ten new branches, in Barnsley, Bognor Regis, Coleraine, Dublin, Hartlepool, Perth, Peterborough, Sunderland, Truro and Weymouth. In 1971, the year the Duchess of Kent became patron, a further eleven branches followed, at Barrow, Chesterfield, Durham, Ealing, Kirkcaldy, Mansfield, Preston, Wakefield, Weston-super-Mare, Yeovil and in North Hertfordshire. In 1972, still at the rate of one a month, branches or groups were appearing in Bracknell, Bury St Edmunds, Cork, Hamilton, Hereford, Lancaster, Pendle, Plymouth, Scarborough and Wigan. The other two branches set up that year marked a dramatic widening of Samaritan horizons: a Scottish Correspondence branch and a branch specifically designed to befriend in the open air, at Festivals. This was also the year Chad Varah received the Albert Schweitzer Gold Medal. Yet a further thirteen branches were founded in 1973, in Ashford, Bangor in Northern Ireland, Bridgend, Brierley Hill, Elgin, Gloucester, Hillingdon, Horsham, Inverness, Milton Keynes, Newry, Retford and Taunton. Although by this time the scope for further expansion was inevitably shrinking, thirty-seven

[7] A decade later the numbers of branches overseas had reached ninety-nine, no less than forty-three of them situated in Brazil.

more branches remained to be born. Five appeared in 1974, at Derry, Enfield, Grantham, Rhyl and Solihull, seven in 1975, in Aberystwyth, Ashington, Ballymena, Craigavon, Limerick, Omagh and Telford, and another half-dozen in 1976, at Galway, Harrowgate, Haverfordwest, Tamworth, Waterford and Winchester. Buxton, Rotherham and Southport were equipped with branches in 1977. The Scottish Borders and Farnborough were covered the following year. In 1979, Blackpool, the Isle of Man and Stockport each acquired a branch, and so, in 1980, did Dumfries. Bury followed in 1981, Matlock (since closed) the following year, and in 1983 Banbury became independent. Bangor in North Wales and Gwynedd became operative in 1984, Sligo and Shetland followed in 1985, and in 1986 Ennis, Caithness, Newbury and Newport, Isle of Wight brought to an astonishing total the establishment of 198 centres in twenty-seven years, a rate of progress which averages out at nearly one new branch every eight weeks over an unbroken period of a quarter of a century.

·2·
CARING FOR THE CARERS

One of the salient features of the Incorporation of the Samaritans in 1963 was the degree of autonomy granted to branches, so as to enable the movement to serve national needs at local level without the handicap of a top-heavy bureaucracy, one of whose functions might well have been to distribute funds from central sources. The reverse became the case. Each branch was made responsible for financing its own centre, and for handing over to the general office a proportion of its annual income, raised by itself, as a contribution to central running costs. That proportion is currently seven and a half per cent. According to the present general secretary, between 1963 and 1969 the general office consisted of a few boxes filed under somebody's bed, and later on of 'a couple of rooms in a vicarage out in Iver, for some reason'. It was not until 1969, by which time 100 branches scattered all over the British Isles were clamoring for advice and administrative support, that the Pilgrim Trust contributed £5,000 towards the purchase of a six-room semi-detached house in a residential area of Slough. It was going cheap because a road development scheme, which in the event fell through, was scheduled, and the house had been earmarked for demolition. Into these rather unpromising premises Basil Higginson moved eighteen months after taking up his appointment as general secretary.

Eventually two extra rooms were added, and today, the general office is staffed, in addition to the general secretary,

David Evans, by an assistant general secretary, Simon Armson, an administrative officer, Mrs Vera Feeney, who started work as secretary to Mr Higginson, three secretaries, a bookkeeper, an accountant and a publicity assistant. Funds have recently been supplied by British Petroleum for the employment for two years of an assistant to build up a data base. It was while he was chaplain to University College, Swansea, from 1969 to 1971, that Mr Evans first became a Samaritan volunteer, and eventually director of the Swansea branch. In 1971 he was appointed chaplain for social work in Birmingham, and again became director of the local Samaritans. Between 1972 and 1975 he was area representative for the West Midlands Region. Following Basil Higginson's resignation, Evans became joint general secretary, and since 1984 he has been designated general secretary. In the same year, Simon Armson was appointed assistant general secretary. He came to full-time work with the Samaritans with administrative experience in health service management, allied to personal knowledge of no less than four Samaritan branches, Birmingham, Shrewsbury, Telford and Oxford, in each of which he worked as a volunteer.

In 1975, David Evans inherited a movement receiving one million calls a year, of which 210,000 were coming from first-time callers, a situation that meant that one family in forty now had a Samaritan caller in their home. A survey that year carried out by National Opinion Polls, based on a random sample of 2,125 people picked from the electoral register in England, Scotland and Wales, was designed to gauge public awareness of the Samaritans and the likelihood of someone calling them. Ninety-two per cent of all those questioned had heard of the Samaritans, and the majority were reported to have a correct idea of their purpose, the level and accuracy of knowledge being highest among the younger age-levels sampled. Only seven per cent overall thought the Samaritans concerned themselves exclusively with suicide, a remarkable discovery for a movement which by that time might well have become almost wholly synonymous with suicide prevention. Equally satisfactory was the finding that only one per cent thought of the Samaritans as a religious organization, but it was a disturbing revelation that three out of five people questioned entertained the notion that the Samaritans were some kind of welfare agency. The report contained 10,000 statistics, hopefully more accurately compiled than a return sent in that year from a branch which reported fourteen unwanted female pregnancies and one male.

In so far as the Samaritans have evolved a hierarchical structure, it consists, at the top, of the council of management, who meet three times a year, and are ultimately responsible for the work and conduct of the Samaritans in the United Kingdom and the Republic of Ireland. As each branch is represented on the council usually, but not always, by its director, the size of the council is too unwieldly to deal with detailed business, and this is normally undertaken by an executive committee, meeting eight times a year and consisting of the chairman and three vice-chairmen, thirteen regional representatives, medical consultants and holders of a number of honorary posts – the bursar, solicitor, publicity officer and youth officer. The local branches are grouped into regions, each with a representative, elected annually by the regional branch directors. On a day-to-day basis, the branches are supervised either by a team of deputy directors or by 'leaders'. Once a volunteer has been accepted by their branch they automatically become a member of the Association, and they cease to belong to the Association – in other words, they stop being a Samaritan – when they resign from membership of their branch, or endure the disappointment of being asked to leave. There is no such thing as a Samaritan floating around in suspended animation. On moving house a volunteer must apply to join his new local branch, and there is no guarantee that he or she will be accepted without a period of retraining.

At the core of the Samaritan operation there resides a set of seven principles and seven practices, established by the council of management in 1981. For some volunteers, they read like a second revised version of the Bible; for everyone they serve at the very least as a basic yardstick for conduct, and by a careful if not perhaps too rigid adherence to them it is felt that every Samaritan everywhere, despite that element of autonomy the branches like to retain, can be assumed to be acting at any time of the day or night in accordance with one another and in the spirit of a quite definite philosophy. The council regard their set of fourteen cardinal principles and practices as a contract with the public. Among other things, they enshrine the necessity for preserving confidentiality, and they absolutely forbid a Samaritan to impose upon a caller their own convictions with regard to politics or religion. They make it plain, too, that in contacting the Samaritans a caller never loses his freedom to make his own decisions, including the decision to end his life.

It is interesting to note that there is a major difference of emphasis regarding confidentiality as between the Samaritans and the Church. No priest, Anglican or Roman Catholic, is permitted to reveal any information imparted in the confessional, even with the permission of the penitant, but the fourth Samaritan principle lays down that everything a caller says in asking the help of the Samaritans is completely confidential *within the organization*, and goes on to stress that a Samaritan volunteer is not permitted to accept confidences if a condition is made that not even the branch director should be informed of them. In order to be able to discuss a situation within the centre, the Samaritans in fact exercise a kind of collective confidentiality. But the Samaritans will refuse to reveal the fact of a telephone call or visit having been made to them, even by a child, without the caller's permission, and they will not disclose, again, unless they have permission, facts relating to a crime. This point was dramatically stressed in 1975 when the West Midlands police were hunting Donald Neilson, a notorious kidnapper who became known as the Black Panther. The director of the Stafford branch said at a meeting that if the Black Panther contacted the Samaritans their code of confidentiality would prevent anyone informing the police, and he was taken to task by the chief constable, who accused the Samaritans of neglecting their public duty. But in fact many gruesome crimes attract imposters, and the Birmingham branch had no less than two Black Panthers, neither of them Neilson, checking in. There is one exception in law which obliges disclosure of information to the police; receipt of information relating to an act of treason or terrorism, so that if someone telephoned a Samaritan centre threatening the life of the Sovereign, or to say that they had planted a bomb (as indeed they did in 1983, when the central London branch was alerted to the bombing of Harrods), the call would be reported immediately, whether the volunteer taking the call believed the threat to be a hoax or not. If a Samaritan was subpoenaed to appear in court as a witness in a criminal case he or she would be obliged to attend, but they could decline to testify by trying to seek the same protection accorded by custom to a priest, who would never be expected to break the seal of the confessional.

When it comes to setting up a new branch, the first criterion has always been not whether the area it is proposed to cover still remains uncatered for but whether, in terms of population, it is large enough to justify a twenty-four-hour emergency service staffed by unpaid volunteers in premises they must raise their own funds to run. There is nothing more demoralizing for a volunteer who has undergone eight weeks of intensive training and geared himself up to cope with some fairly grim situations than to sit around for four hours at a stretch with nothing to do. 'Now that the coverage of the country is so complete we are getting enquiries from groups of people in places too small to carry the commitment,' the general secretary says. 'A branch can open with about seventy volunteers, on the basis that publicity will bring in the other forty you need, but what many people don't realize is that to do even this you have to receive something like 350 applications, so as to allow for people who drop out of their own accord and the loss of people you regard as unsuitable. And they don't realize the boredom factor. It's not right to mount that sort of operation where the usage is going to be so slight that there will be a lot of blank shifts. Our experience is that you more or less know how many callers you will get from a given population.' When it is proposed to open a new branch, or grant full status to an 'associate group', the regional representative is responsible for taking the proposal to the executive committee. If the committee thinks the proposition worth investigating further, a steering committee is formed, headed by a local convenor. A public meeting is then held, to attract a nucleus of potential helpers, to encourage initial financial support and to make sure that the social services are kept informed of possible Samaritan involvement in their area. Contact is encouraged with a neighbouring branch so that they can offer assistance with the selection and training of the first volunteers. When a new branch becomes established, one of its first priorities is to elect a branch committee, to take charge of administration and fund-raising. Once open, the branch is placed on probation for at least a year. By trial and error it has often been found that the first available premises are not necessarily the most suitable. A front door adjacent to Barclays Bank, British Home Stores and the police station may seem conveniently central but it does lack privacy. On the other hand, the ideal Samaritan centre is not too far removed from the bus or railway station, and it needs to be reasonably quiet yet easily located.

In the dozen years since 1975 the numbers of contacts made annually with the Samaritans, by telephone, letter or personal visit, has doubled to around two million, some 380,000 now being first-time callers.[1] The number of volunteers is currently registered at about 21,000, 6,000 short of the numbers required to maintain a really efficient service round the clock in every branch, where ideally at least three Samaritans will always be on duty, two to man two telephones and a third to answer the doorbell. But it is not unknown in the smaller branches for only one Samaritan to be on duty at a time, a practice very much deplored but occasionally inevitable. Even in those branches with a theoretically healthy membership, three volunteers sharing a shift can be run off their feet. 'Although 27,000 volunteers is a realistic figure to aim at,' says Mr Evans, 'in a way, the sky's the limit, because there are always occasions when branch lines

[1] In 1985 the Samaritans received 2,154,233 calls, an average of 5,901 a day.

are engaged. But certainly we need another 5,000 or 6,000. Although in recent years we have opened a few new branches, the numbers of volunteers has stayed steady, which amounts to a possible real decline. We lose upwards of thirty per cent a year. Considering the time we invest in selection, training and support, it's disappointing, although there are other organizations that have an even higher turnover.'

A branch with only two emergency lines really needs a minimum of 130 members, and 160 would be ideal. It has been estimated that if a branch inserts a third line, it immediately requires an additional forty volunteers to complete the rota. 'In some branches, with very large populations, we simply haven't got enough volunteers to cover the third line that we need,' says Mr Evans. 'We are worried about this rejection of people who get the engaged signal. We try not to block both lines with long calls, and sometimes we transfer to an ex-directory line and bear the expense of phoning the caller back. But not all callers want to give their number. At this point we may have two volunteers on two lines and someone at the door as well. It is good to have one, sometimes two, lines in each branch not advertised to the public. We use them, for instance, to ring in with messages, so as not to block the emergency lines ourselves, and if an ex-directory phone is picked up and put down we know the branch is busy and we ring back later. They can be used for fixing up the duty rota, or consulting a leader or a director on call at home, again allowing us to keep the emergency lines open as much as possible.'

It rather seems as if a Samaritan is liable to remain a volunteer for fifteen years – and sometimes much longer – or to drop out after three, often for perfectly practical reasons; pregnancy, enrolling for a degree course in further education, moving home or changing jobs. And Mr Evans placed his finger on one particularly sensitive spot. 'It's hard to cope with a string of sex calls when you have otherwise blank shifts, and you wonder what it's all about. Sometimes you can almost hug a genuinely distressed person.' Women Samaritans take a very large number of calls from men wanting to masturbate while engaged in conversation on the telephone, and not surprisingly, some women feel able to deal with this aspect of their work in a more detached way than others. 'Two of my friends became volunteers,' a member of one of the busy London branches explained, 'and the reason they both left was the number of sex calls they had to deal with. I think a lot of people feel they are going to sort out dramas all the time, and be able to help in a practical way, and even after they've completed their training they still have false expectations. But if you go on duty and for the fifth time in an evening somebody asks you what colour your knickers are, you tend to get a bit cheesed off with it, frankly.' This volunteer, married to a Samaritan and a member of her branch for the past eleven years, cited as another cause of people dropping out the possibility of personality clashes. 'Then, again, some people just find they can't cope, or a crisis comes up in their own life they have to deal with, and they find they can't deal with that on top of their Samaritan work.

'I think you could become stale, or cynical, if you did nothing else except your duties, and you stayed very much within your branch. But because my husband and I both have Samaritan duties outside our branch we've made a lot of friends. If you have a spouse who isn't a volunteer there can be some conflict. Although the Samaritans always insist that a spouse should be happy about their partner's involvement, there can be some uneasiness occasionally.' Mr Evans stressed the opportunities for maintaining interest. 'The average length of time for a volunteer is about three years, but a change of role in the branch will keep up morale. There are lots of roles for keeping up enthusiasm – rota secretary, membership of the committee, acting as a leader or a deputy director. Although it's not a rule, a lot of branches are now leaving people in a post not longer than three years.'

In 1980, a volunteer from Bognor, writing in the *Samaritan*, said she thought that 'in a small branch such as ours, boredom can be a problem. The large city branches probably have calls practically non-stop, whereas we can spend the whole shift chatting to our colleagues, pausing only to seize gratefully upon a long-term caller and reluctantly obey standing orders to limit him to ten minutes. It can be hard to accept the maxim that we joined the Samaritans to be there, not to be busy, but it is something we have to accept.'

Between 1978 and 1980, fifty-seven volunteers resigned from the branch in Reading, twenty per cent per annum of the branch membership. During that period, one of the volunteers telephoned all those who had left to try to ascertain the reasons, and found that fourteen had done so for the perfectly good reason that they had left the district, eleven because of ill health or old age, thirteen because of a variety of changes in personal circumstances, including pregnancy and promotion at work, and three had felt the time had come to leave because of long service. Of the remaining fifteen, the volunteer carrying out the telephone survey concluded that nine had never enjoyed a real commitment, expressing comments like, 'It was not what I had expected', five had felt doubtful about Samaritan methods ('We ought to be able to do something for our clients, not just listen,' one former Samaritan told him), and two were apparently dissatisfied with the leadership in the branch, feeling they could have done a better job themselves.

The image of an organization run by middle-aged, middle-class women, dressed in sensible shoes, twin sets and pearls, to which many female Samaritan volunteers themselves subscribe, is not borne out by the facts. At least a third of Samaritan volunteers are men, most branches outside London and the Home Counties are staffed by local people with regional accents, and many more Samaritans pertain to lower-middle-class status than to middle-class. And, unlike many voluntary organizations, the Samaritans seem to make no appeal whatsoever to the upper-middle-class; among some 175 volunteers elected or co-opted to the council of management in 1984, not one had a title. However, there is still within the Samaritans, in common with most other voluntary agencies, an overwhelming dearth of volunteers from ethnic groups other than white and established British. At a conference of 300 Samaritans drawn from every part of the United Kingdom and Ireland it would be rare to spot more than one coloured face. Mr Evans places the chances of more than five coloured or ethnic volunteers turning up among 1,000 delegates to the annual conference (excluding visitors from overseas) as most unlikely. 'I have no idea why this is. As their situation has been politicized, maybe it is less likely they will volunteer for what they see as a white agency. But then we don't receive many calls from members of ethnic communities, either. Occasionally you do receive a call in a Birmingham or Yorkshire accent and something doesn't add up, and you suddenly realize in spite of the accent you are talking to a West Indian or an Asian. Their expectations tend to be different, towards marriage, the family, parents, grandparents and so on. But no specific training has yet been given to help with this. I think almost any branch would fall over backwards to encourage ethnic volunteers, but they are not coming forward, and in company with many other organizations, we don't know the answer – unless we ran a black branch, but it might be very inefficient in terms of resources.'

A deputy director who did have a coloured volunteer in her branch said she thought he might be one of so few because of 'an image we've got that we shouldn't have. In a lot of voluntary organizations we tend to be middle-aged, middle-class women, people like me, but it's largely a question of who's got the time.' Robert, her West Indian colleague, has got spare time because he is out of work. 'I don't think a West Indian accent, for example, would be off-putting to a white caller,' she said. 'A Sloane voice is much more likely to be. But I don't think people in a crisis really care whose voice they get, quite honestly.' Robert said he had never experienced any problems with people talking to him. 'I even had a caller the other day moaning on to me about coloured people. We have a gay volunteer who's sometimes on duty with me, and he had a caller recently complaining about gay people! When we first volunteered we were both asked what our attitude would be if that sort of thing happened. If you're going to get the hump about it you can't act as a Samaritan.'

The key person in every branch is the director, for he is the man or woman ultimately responsible for the morale of the volunteers, upon whose performance the lives of some of the callers could depend. And one of the most reassuring aspects of Samaritan organization, despite some disadvantages it brings in terms of a lack of continuity, is the way in which directorships turn over every three years or so. A stretch in office of five years is tolerated, but no more. This gives the branch a regular chance to renew enthusiasm under new leadership, and continually reminds all those who hold office that they remain first and foremost a Samaritan volunteer. The chances are that a director will have had several years' experience as a Samaritan. In 1980 a branch in the Midlands chose a local government officer of twenty-nine, but he had been a volunteer since the age of twenty. In 1986, a branch in Yorkshire acquired a director of twenty-seven, who joined the movement when he was only seventeen. A fair proportion of directors are in their early thirties. Anyone taking on the directorship of a branch at whatever age assumes considerable responsibility. A young male director in the Eastern Region, on the point of stepping down after three and a half years, explains how his successor, a woman, came to be appointed.

'I think it's important to remember that the director of every branch is appointed by the council of management, not by the branch, so that the director is the Samaritans's man or woman in a certain branch. The branch only nominates. When a director resigns it is the responsibility of the branch chairman to set up a working party to consider the needs of the branch. Our working party consisted of two committee members, one representative from the leader team, and one representative from the branch. We approached at least fifty per cent of the volunteers to sound them out. We talked to everyone in the leader teams, because they work most closely with the director, and everyone on the training team and the interviewing team.

'We came up with about eight names. But there were not even one or two who were willing to take on the job. Nobody we had considered suitable wanted it. It was too big . . . it wasn't the right time . . . But two names emerged as favourites. One still remained determined not to go forward, so the other woman said she would. The regional representative was consulted. She came down and met Betty quite informally, over dinner, but she did manage to conduct an interview in those circumstances. She then had a meeting with the working party, and said she was prepared to put Betty's name forward to the council of management, and the working party reported back to the branch committee.'

Every one of the 182 directors may see his or her task in a different light, and will certainly bring his or her own gifts and handicaps to the job. A schoolmaster in his late thirties, who professes to shyness but hides a tough interior behind a winsome veneer, gives an account of his own approach:

'As director I'm responsible for the volunteers as well as the callers, and I refuse to be responsible for people I don't know. So I interview each volunteer, and the interview usually lasts anything from an hour to an hour and a half. It's difficult to keep it shorter than that. I want them to get to know me as much as I want to get to know them. They think I'm quite an authoritarian figure, but I'm not! I investigate how, during training, they have experienced asking about suicide. Has it been difficult for them? Have they always asked about suicide? If not, why not? Have they had any calls that they found particularly difficult to cope with? Was there anything about our work that took them by surprise? Was it what they expected? They must have given some thought to being a Samaritan before they came along and volunteered their services, and I do sometimes distrust people who say, "It was exactly as I expected it to be," because I don't think it can be. I really don't think it can. I always ask, "Have we disappointed you in some way? Did you expect that we were going to do wonderful things, wave magic wands and make everything better?" And I'm pleased to say that in almost every case people say it's better than they expected it to be. The thing that makes it better for them is the fellowship and support they get from other volunteers.

'I spend a good twenty-five hours a week on Samaritan work.

I suppose it is a lot, but you don't do any more than you want to do. I do it because I find it rewarding. Make no mistake about it, I get a great deal out of it. And at the same time I'm looking forward to handing over to somebody else!'

With the continual growth of new branches over the years, not necessarily evenly spread across the country, the regional boundaries into which the United Kingdom branches are divided have been altered four times since 1966. Recently it was found that one region possessed seven branches, another twenty-four. For members of the Truro branch, located in the South West Region, to meet up with members from Haverford-west involved a round journey of 600 miles. While Carlisle remained in the North West Region (it has now been reallocated to the North), this branch was separated from its fellow regional branch of Bangor by 400 miles. So at the end of 1985 a major reshuffle took place, leaving only two of the previous dozen regions unaffected. Twenty-five branches changed regional affiliation, and a new, thirteenth, region was established to cover South Wales and the Marshes. The largest region at present is the North East, with sixteen branches. The remaining twelve regions consist, on average, of about four-teen branches each.

Regional representatives are elected annually by the branch directors in their region. Their appointment is ratified by the council of management, of which they automatically become a member, as well as a member of the executive committee. This involves nine meetings a year. In theory it would be possible to combine the job of regional representative with directorship of a branch, but probably ill-advised. Previous experience as a director, on the other hand, is considered almost a *sine qua non*. A regional representative who has only been doing the job for a short time explains how she envisages the job and what she is trying to make of it:

'I was told it was a doddle, that I wouldn't be half as busy as I had been as a director, and then I received a four-page job description. But in fact the task is mainly representing the views of the executive committee to the region – views you may not share – and representing the views of the region, which, again, you may not share, to the executive. It's a very effective way of passing information backwards and forwards. You are consulted when a new director appointment has to be made, and you have to interview the person who may be appointed, and discuss with them all the aspects of being a director, which is why you need to be an ex-director yourself.

'You oversee regional spending, things like the publicity budget, the budget for befriending in the open, and for training in the region, and you help to mount regional training conferences. In my region I have thirteen branches, and I am responsible for support of the thirteen directors. But I never visit a branch unless I'm invited. I'm quite sure that if I said I want to come to a branch they'd be delighted, but I prefer to be invited rather than inflict myself. I also chair the regional directors' meetings, three or four times a year, and put together the agenda. We may discuss callers who are of concern to a number of branches, or any particular aspect of work that's come up at the executive that needs to be discussed with the directors, or anything that the council of management has decided upon which they want to discuss. You have to be re-elected each year, and it's generally for three years, and of course you continue as a volunteer in your own branch.'

One of the most crucial group of Samaritans in any branch are the leaders, a kind of back-up team who form part of the decision-making hierarchy, between the volunteers on duty and the deputy directors, and whose task also is to supply an instant source of comfort and support within the branch. 'Caring for the carers is their most important task,' is how one director put it. 'You don't know what's going to be thrown at you during the course of a duty and sometimes it's quite traumatic.' One branch on the east coast has eighteen leaders, who work in pairs over a twenty-four-hour shift, one as leader and the other as deputy leader. The leader remains on call at home, 'and thus can remain more detached, and defuse any heavy situation in the centre.' If a caller wanted the Samaritans to ring for a doctor, the leader would undertake to do so. Leaders are also responsible for discipline. One explained: 'If I was seriously concerned about the capabilities of a volunteer I would talk to them first, at the time if possible, but failing that I would arrange to meet them and hear what they had to say about the situation. If it was a matter of not following one of the practices or principles, and they felt unable to accept these conditions, then I would take it further, to the deputy or the director. But usually I find that if you just talk to a volunteer about any matter of conscience they manage to work out the correct solution for themselves.'

A Samaritan from one of the London branches recounted her experience of the role of a leader. 'It varies from branch to branch. Some do a twenty-four-hour duty, some a twelve-hour duty. And some branches have leaders who change with each shift. If the leader needs help he will go either to the deputy director or the director. In point of fact, in my branch we don't have leaders as such, we have deputy directors, and we do a seven-day stint. We are on duty as a deputy director from midnight on Sunday until midnight Saturday. You go about your normal everyday work and you carry a bleeper, so that if you are not available at the end of a telephone and the centre needs you urgently, they bleep you. A leader, or deputy director, is in charge of decision-making on the shifts. If a volunteer has a difficult call, someone obviously dying, for instance, they would consult the leader. If a leader has had a disturbed night every night for seven nights, by the end of the week you're feeling a bit shredded, to say the least.'

Deputy directors usually take on a specific task in a centre. At a branch in the East Midlands, one deputy is responsible for initial training, one for on-going training, one for callers and one for volunteers. 'One thing that our volunteers here find very reassuring,' said the deputy director who looks after the welfare of the volunteers, 'is that they are never alone. There's always someone else on watch with them. There is always a leader to whom they can refer, and the leaders are very good at helping them to express their own feelings after they have spoken to a caller. It's my job to speak to a volunteer if they've done something silly, like promising to go out to see a caller when they've finished their watch and going off without reference to anybody else. This sort of thing can all be done in a hurry, with the best possible motives, but really it isn't on. Then there are volunteers who are having a hard time themselves. They won't always ring me, they may prefer to speak to some other friend in the branch, or even outside, but if they want particularly to talk to me, that's fine. If anybody is having a break because of some personal difficulty, or they are ill, I keep in touch.

'But my main task is to support volunteers when they have taken a really difficult call. Things like silent calls. A long, silent call can be very distressing. You feel an absolute failure at the end of it when you've been trying to get someone to talk for half an hour and then the phone goes down. They can really be quite hard to deal with. And then there are the people who ring – we do get them occasionally – who have quite made up their mind they are going to take their own life, and really just want to tell somebody. But they don't want any help, they don't want us to go to them, and that's hard. The caller ends the conversation, usually. We don't have absolutely firm rules about it. Although we respect everybody's right to make their own decision we do not accept that they have a right to involve us in their death. So we will not actually sit and talk to somebody while they die. That's too harrowing for a volunteer, we feel. It used to be that you stayed with them until they were unconscious, then rushed them to intensive care, by which time some vital organ might well have been damaged, resulting in kidney failure or a stroke. So now you do not enter into any contract to stay with someone while they die. If we have a caller on the phone who has overdosed then we would make it clear to the caller that if they passed out on the phone, if they lost consciousness, we would do everything we could to get help. And that's not asking them if we may, that's saying, "If this happens, this is what we shall do." And then the caller has the choice of hanging up or allowing us to help, because we feel otherwise that it's much too heavy for the volunteer.

'If something like this happens, you do need to talk it through afterwards, because you can't take it home. You can't talk to anybody else about what has happened. So we need a very strong support system within the organization. I may go home and say, "I've had a terrible time, it's really been awful," but you can't go into the details at home in the way you can in the centre. And it's hard, sometimes, when you worry about what you've done. You may feel OK when you leave the centre but later you need to ring someone. I think – I hope – that's what we're good at. I think we do support each other.'

To make quite sure that Samaritans *are* supporting one another, and of course that they are providing the most effective service possible to callers within the guide-lines laid down by the fourteen principles and practices, a system of branch visits has been inaugurated. These are conducted, about every two and a half years, by a panel of experienced Samaritans, many of whom will have served as directors, and who will therefore have personal knowledge of the stress involved in running a branch. Regional representatives are encouraged to put forward the names of suitable Visitors, but a final choice is made by the executive committe. All Visitors attend training weekends. The best they can hope to gain during a necessarily brief visit is an overall impression of a branch and its atmosphere, and every effort is made to dispel the impression that somehow a branch is under threat. What the Visitors are most anxious to experience is the relationship that has developed within the branch between callers and volunteers, and they tend to ask themselves two basic questions: would I care to be a caller at this branch? And could I feel happy as a volunteer here? Visitors work in pairs, and always come from two different regions. They attend a branch meeting so that they can meet as many volunteers as possible, and they inspect every aspect of the branch work – funding as well as caller-care.

Samaritans come in every shape and size, and from every corner of the British Isles. Among the 20,000 people at present manning 380 emergency telephone lines, some live in the leafy lanes of Horsham, others overlook the industrial wastes of Gateshead, the slag heaps of Ebbw Vale, the rolling green of the

Lowlands. Yet although the movement embraces geographically nearly as wide a diversity of accents and attitudes as the nation itself, those 20,000 disparate individuals do seem to be welded into some sort of recognizable entity. They possess more in common than a shared philosophy or frame of mind. Some are more modest and self-effacing than others, some better drinking companions, others less unimaginatively dressed, but taken all in all a distinguishable aura of gentle tolerance and patience emanates from Samaritans, a noticeable inner quiet one does not encounter at a cocktail party, where strangers look over your shoulder or try to get into an argument. Like monks and nuns, who consciously but politely distance themselves from personal involvement so as to preserve their emotional chastity, Samaritans create conditions for instant, disinterested contact rarely possible elsewhere in our frenetic age. The contrast between delayed adolescent neurosis let loose at an Open University summer school and the relaxed, mature revelry at a Samaritan conference could not be greater. This temporary, professional celibacy, the peace treaty they seem to have signed in the battle between the sexes, for example, enables the men, especially, to relax. While many Samaritans smoke like chimneys and laugh an awful lot, they disarm criticism by their lack of aggression. They do not try to score points off one another, nor off those they meet outside the circle of Samaritan colleagues, so that when a Samaritan asks quite a personal question, designed to elicit information about your marital status or possible sexual orientation, the question comes after a relationship has been established and as an act of friendship. It never stems from prurient curiosity. They look you in the eye, and make you welcome without overwhelming you with *bonhomie*. These are of course overall and generalized impressions gleaned in the course of restricted research, but they represent very positive impressions, all the more distinctly etched and registered for being, in the normal round of life, such rare experiences.

Somehow or other, the Samaritans also survive, most of the time, their own and other people's grief on a scale almost incomprehensible to an outsider. During a recent annual conference, for an hour and a quarter Mother Frances Dominica, who runs a hospice in Oxford for children, calmly introduced a succession of slides showing boys and girls, babies and teenagers, and just as calmly spoke of everyday life in the house as they and their families and the staff and the Duchess of Kent, who pops in to help every now and again, contemplate the ever present reality of premature death. 'I was all right until the dog came on the screen,' one Samaritan said afterwards. 'That was too much.' After half an hour the hall had become a gently lapping sea of hankies, with men and women quietly wiping away the tears that had become a kind of common denominator of their own voluntary calling. And of course Samaritans are vulnerable to body blows from all sorts of directions. At the same conference, a talk on child abuse resulted in a female volunteer who many years before had been sexually assaulted by her father becoming so suicidal she had to be professionally befriended.

And to say that Samaritans come in every shape and size is no exaggeration. If you meet a Samaritan he may be a handsome young left-wing idealist, with thick black hair and wearing filthy dirty jeans, who rolls his own cigarettes and speaks with flattened-out Midland vowels. Or she may be a cosy middle-aged lady ideally suited to running the local post office. Or a young freckle-faced housewife wearing a mushroom-coloured skirt. He may be a West Country farmer, too young to have begun such a worrying paunch and too busy ever to have cleaned his fingernails. They are the sort of people who nearly always eat well and live in comfortable surroundings but are prepared, like boy scouts from good homes, to put up with any deprivation at a weekend conference, including packeted soup at every meal, served to an unbroken string of announcements about cars parked improperly, claims for travel expenses, orders for Sunday newspapers, requests not to slam firedoors after one o'clock in the morning. And their reading habits, if conference bookshops are anything to go by, are catholic, to say the least; copies of *Adrian Mole* rub shoulders with *So You*

Think You're Attracted To the Same Sex?, *The Body Electric* with *Divorce and Your Money*, *Living With Multiple Sclerosis* with *Father and Son*.

Snatches of Samaritan conversation at conference time, caught on the hoof, can be instructive, too. A rather roly-poly volunteer from Scotland recalls how the Samaritan who had trained him had said that he had found he could only be himself as a Samaritan. 'And I've found the same,' he says. 'I can now talk to anyone about sex, about anything.' A rather earnest young man with a beard, gripping a pint of beer, gets into an argument in the bar with a colleague from the same branch about whether they are there to prevent suicide. 'I am!' she snaps. Someone else can be overheard to say, 'We are neurotic about confidentiality,' which is almost a heresy. Discussing the subject of training new volunteers, one old girl in tweed skirt and brogues, with a twinkle in her eye, says it is important to ask potential Samaritans if they have transport to get to the centre long before you start worrying whether they get upset by homosexuals. 'We don't encourage journalists to join,' comes over as rather an unnerving aside. A young wag called Martin suggests the Samaritans should automatically reject freemasons, too, and everyone looks suitably shocked until he explains it was a joke. Someone really lets the cat out of the bag when she is heard to offer advice on the treatment of new recruits. 'Don't tour the premises and let them see the files and so on,' she suggests, 'not until they've definitely been selected. They'll only find out things they shouldn't know.'

Whether Samaritans are jovial by nature or driven to drink through the stress of their work, they certainly let down their hair at conferences. A gay Quaker turns a corner of the bar into a cabaret; an actress lets off steam about the group to which she has been assigned, every member of which, she complains, refused to admit they had any hang-ups. 'I told them not to be so ridiculous,' she hisses into her soup at lunch. 'We all have hang-ups. Mine's the group I'm in!' A very glamorous volunteer who looks as though she ought to be an actress too, adorned with chunky blue earrings, a silver bangle round her ankle and wreaths of imitation coral round her neck, vigorously makes the point that there is no conceivable way you can dodge rejecting unsuitable candidates; rejection, she says, is rejection: 'You can't wrap it up.' Silently suppressing his mock resentment, a chubby young man with greying hair and piercing blue eyes whispers behind his hand, 'That's my leader over there. I can't *stand* him! He thinks we shouldn't ask new volunteers about personal problems at all!' Suddenly the door of the telephone kiosk bursts open, and a Samaritan mum from Surbiton bursts out. 'My daughter's got a First, my daughter's got a First,' she shrieks, 'I must hug someone,' and she flings her arms ecstatically round the first person she sees.

·3·
AMATEURS AT WORK

Being a Samaritan is not a job for someone primarily seeking a lot of personal contact and direct involvement with other people. The majority of those who approach the Samaritans do so on the telephone, and after spending perhaps half an hour listening to a tale of woe, the volunteer, once that call has been discontinued, may never hear from the caller again, nor ever know for certain what effect their attempt to offer compassion, understanding, sympathy, care and reassurance has had. Yet at a period in our social evolution when, so far as such things can ever be accurately measured, kindness and consideration towards fellow human beings seems to be at a premium, when an atmosphere of alienation, at home, in school, at work and on the streets seems to have become the standard environment, and indifference to the lot of neighbours common practice, the Samaritans, with their deliberate policy of distanced involvement, their exchange of first names only, their use of numbers instead of surnames, their often faceless and always essentially anonymous offer of help, have become the organization towards which millions of people throughout the world instinctively turn at times of acute, sometimes suicidal, crisis.

The way in which housewives and solicitors, farmers and school teachers, accountants and clergy, bank clerks and supermarket supervisors are selected and trained as Samaritans varies from branch to branch, and while there is always a danger that a small yet busy branch, desperately trying to maintain double-manning round the clock with only sixty-five members, may be tempted to cut corners and accept volunteers they have doubts about (a potential drug-pusher once very nearly slipped through the net), the business of accepting suitable candidates and rejecting others is one the Samaritans take very seriously. With an almost constant need to recruit something like 7,000 volunteers every year merely to replace the thirty per cent of members who die, retire or resign, the movement wants a further 6,000 new members in order to improve existing services. 'A lot of people think we select just anyone,' a vice-chairman told a conference on selection held at Leeds University in 1986. 'In fact, our experience in my branch is that whenever we have accepted someone after training about whom we had our doubts, we have lived to regret it.' It has been estimated that about eighty per cent of those who make an initial inquiry about joining the Samaritans arrive for a first interview, twenty per cent having themselves decided not to go forward on realizing more fully what sort of work or commitment was involved, and only thirty per cent (some, again, having made their own decision not to proceed) are eventually accepted at the end of their period of training.

On receiving a telephone call from a potential recruit, some branches send out an initial application form, others invite a group of new volunteers to a social gathering prior to an initial interview. The first question usually asked is why the applicant applied, and behind the answer sometimes lies, in reality, a need not to become a Samaritan but to seek the help of the Samaritans. Two or three Samaritans in every branch have probably at some time in their life, quite often after joining the Samaritans, been a caller, and a number of potential callers seek contact with the Samaritans in the first place by seeming to apply as a volunteer. Providing an answer to the question 'Why do you want to be a Samaritan?' may prove the hardest test for applicants, seeming to make them sound smug ('I want to help other people.'), or unsure of their motives ('It just seemed like something I ought to do.'). There is a fear of acknowledging the very real possibility that altruism does not exist, that seeking to help other people makes one feel better when perhaps it should not. People often think it necessary to justify their motives, and they feel equally nervous about being judged by them, and then found in some way unworthy.

Having surmounted (or maybe stumbled over) this first hurdle, the applicant will probably be asked whether they hold religious or political attitudes which they feel could be *useful* (and on the form supplied to interviewers at one branch, the word 'useful' is underlined) as a Samaritan. Is this a trick question? Samaritans are strictly enjoined not to exhibit to callers any religious or political beliefs. They will also almost certainly be tested out on their feelings about abortion and homosexuality, and invited to discuss the things that shock them. They will be asked to throw their mind back to the biggest emotional crisis they have ever had to deal with, and to recall how they coped with it, and they will be asked if they have ever contacted the Samaritans before.

Questions about suicide loom large. '*Don't* be helpful if they're surprised by the question,' the interviewer is instructed on one questionnaire. The assumption that we all suffer from depression at some time is enshrined in a question on this subject, and the applicant is asked to talk about their friends, and to say how they think their friends would describe them. Information is prised out, too, about the applicant's home life, about whether they are married, single, divorced or living with someone to whom they are not married. Not every gay applicant would at this stage feel sufficiently at ease to disclose the fact, although others may make a point of doing so.

The procedure followed by a branch in London is to write, in the first place, to someone volunteering to be a Samaritan, inviting them to read a succinct but fairly detailed summary of Samaritan work and what is involved. It emphasizes, for example, that apart from helping a Samaritan to be available, the Samaritan's family will be positively excluded from that part of their life. 'You will not be able to discuss your work with them, for our clients' business is strictly confidential,' they are warned. They are told, too, that 'your own experience of distress will have enriched you and probably deepened your compassion and understanding. Equally, you may feel you have become too vulnerable to take on other people's troubles. If you are at present experiencing trouble or its immediate aftermath you may wish to be advised to postpone your application to a later date.' Only after the applicant has read and digested the fact sheet, and still expresses a desire to join, is an initial application form sent out. This starts with the daunting question, 'Why do you wish to become a Samaritan?' and invites information about physical disabilities, treatment for mental illness and previous contact with the Samaritans as a caller. Item 12 reads, 'Complete the following statements as spontaneously as possible: I feel encouraged when . . . It really bothers me when . . . I feel confident when . . .' And a referee is asked for.

Another branch, which sends out an application form straight away, asks new volunteers when they first heard about the Samaritans, and why they are volunteering now. 'I think this is actually quite a good question,' the director says. 'Why now rather than last week? Why now rather than six months ago? Has something happened to draw the Samaritans to their attention? And on the initial form we ask, "What makes you feel you are suitable for Samaritan work?" But I don't like that question. Some people feel they have to write an essay. I would much rather know the bare bones about somebody and develop the details at an interview. We are more articulate than we are literate, and it is easier for people to talk than to write.

'The application form is really just an indication of intent. It also includes an availability slip, and gives the person applying a chance to decide if they've really got the time to give to the kind of commitment we require. A lot of people are very vague about the Samaritans when they first offer their services. Some still think it's a religious organization. In our branch they are interviewed by just one person. Other branches have two people conducting the interview. Some branches even have a second person take over the interview half-way through. Everybody thinks theirs is the best method. Personally, I don't believe there is a best method. The matter of taking up references is also a contentious issue. In my branch we don't ask for them, because I think an applicant should be assessed on their own merits and not on what somebody else has to say about them. I don't know how many Samaritans would be recommended for Samaritan work by their employer or a friend, because these people don't know what it's like to be a Samaritan. It's not like recommending somebody for a job. At the interview and on the training course we have the means of assessing suitability better than anyone else.'

Debate about the best way to conduct selection interviews waxes strong. Those in favour of the technique of interviewing by panel maintain that a Samaritan needs to be able to relate to more than one person, and no opportunity to do this arises at a one-to-one interview. A clash of personalities is less likely, too, and while one member of the panel is questioning the interviewee, another is free to take notes. The overriding objection to three or four selectors meeting a new recruit, put forward by those who prefer the one-to-one approach, is that such a method is just too intimidating. 'People are being asked very personal questions,' an area representative points out, 'and if one selector is not competent to cover every area then I believe that two or three one-to-one interviews are preferable to the recruit having to face a panel. Many people who go for an interview do not realize before they get there how deeply their personality is going to be explored. Not many people are ever asked in the whole of their lives how they will be able to cope with behaviour and feelings. When a Samaritan is selecting candidates, he is not acting as a volunteer but as a selector, and he requires very special skills. He needs to be courteous but persistent, and sensitive but prepared to challenge views expressed by the candidate. Above all, he must be prepared to be tough, and for a Samaritan that isn't always easy. Whichever way you choose to conduct the selection process, we must always remember that selection is about creating an environment in which the candidate can do well.'

Skills required for rejecting candidates exercise the minds

of many Samaritans as much as those skills required for recommending they go forward for training. 'The application form should make it quite clear that you are only applying to be considered, and that for many reasons, not by any means detrimental to you, you may not get in,' a leader from the North East suggested at the conference in Leeds. 'We should be very careful not to raise people's hopes and expectations too high.' There seem to be as many ways of turning down a candidate as there are of conducting interviews and training classes. Some branches write a letter, some do the dreaded deed face to face, some on the telephone. Asked on a show of hands how they themselves would prefer to be rejected, a discussion group of some thirty Samaritans drawn from across the country seemed equally divided. One volunteer said he thought that whatever method was used it was important to put candidates out of their misery within twenty-four hours of an interview. Dismay was expressed at the disclosure that some branches funked the problem to the extent of sending out a cyclostyled letter, with even the director's signature stencilled. It was felt that not enough explanation was offered in the course of interviews to prepare the candidates for the possibility of rejection, so that because the Samaritans were in some positive way regarded as being run by 'good' people, those found unsuitable must feel morally tainted. Some branches apparently try to soften the blow by suggesting other areas of voluntary work where the candidate's particular aptitudes would fit in better, but as one selector emphatically put it, 'We never do this because it sounds as though you are offering a second prize.' Perhaps the most contentious issue regarding rejection is whether any reasons should be given. Many – perhaps most – branches offer no explanation at all. 'If any explanation is to be offered, be wary of putting it in writing,' is the advice of one director. 'People have a genius for misinterpreting letters. In any event, we are certainly under no obligation to justify ourselves, and if we are to offer reasons, one reason is sufficient. It should be some factor they will readily recognize in themselves, and not something they need feel badly about. It all comes down to making clear in the interview the whole range of reasons why certain perfectly admirable people are just not suitable for Samaritan work.'

If at the initial interview an applicant seems totally unsuitable, some branches take the bull by the horns and say so there and then. Others promise to communicate a decision within three weeks. Such factors as 'sensitivity', 'warmth', 'flexibility', 'ability to communicate', 'ability to listen' and 'ability to tolerate others' are assessed, and the interviewer is asked to consider whether they would be happy to work on a shift with the applicant, and whether they would feel happy confiding in them. If the impression is more favourable than otherwise, the applicant is accepted for training, on the understanding that at any stage they may be dropped, and likewise are free to leave. 'We should be very careful only to assess on observable facts,' one training officer strongly believes. 'It is almost impossible to assess such nebulous things as honesty and loyalty at an interview. One thing I'm certain of: we should do everything we can to eliminate unsuitable candidates before they go into a training class. This involves a commitment of sixteen hours over two months, and if you then reject them at the end of *that* they feel much more let down and unworthy to work for the Samaritans. They really feel they have failed. They are bound to. Obviously someone who has not measured up in training classes cannot be allowed to proceed, but it really is our responsibility to sort out our selection procedures so that these sort of disappointments are kept to a minimum.'

Like examinations, all interview situations are strictly unreliable, and many are looked back upon with laughter and incredulity. A Samaritan once interviewed by a fellow volunteer may, within half a dozen years, have become her interrogator's director. 'In an interview, everyone is on their best behaviour,' a leader who spends a fair amount of time selecting volunteers explains. 'And I think it is very revealing what people choose to tell you about themselves. I make it clear at the start that no one is going to be rejected because of anti-social behaviour, like attempting suicide. We have all sorts of people in the

Samaritans and we all have our own problems. I emphasize that the fact that you become a Samaritan doesn't guarantee immunity from stress. I always ask if they have ever contemplated suicide, because from knowledge of how a volunteer has coped with their own emotional problems you can make an assessment of their attitude to other people's. You get a gut feeling. I'm sorry, but I do get a gut feeling. I always ask applicants to give me an example of something they think they're not very good at, or an area in their own life where they think they haven't coped very well, and this is revealing in two ways. It tells you how they did actually cope, and what their attitude to it was.

'The things I look for as an interviewer are a responsiveness to others, an ability to establish a rapport with another person, and someone who has a fair amount of experience of life. But I make a distinction there, because we do have some quite young people coming forward. You can't expect a great experience of life from them, but everybody has potential, and if they haven't got experience then you look for the potential. Above all, we are looking for people who are honest – honest with you, honest about themselves and honest about their feelings.'

The question 'Why do you want to be a Samaritan?' is reserved until the end of the training programme in the case of a branch in the north-east region. 'The question about their motive is the question most people find most difficult to answer,' the director has found. 'I always ask it when I conduct the final interview, because by then they are much more relaxed, and we know them pretty well. At the initial interview, many people just don't know why they want to be a Samaritan. It isn't that they can't articulate it, they genuinely don't know.' Something into which he inquires very closely is the ability to make friends. 'Someone I can think of came along recently and didn't really know why he had come forward, and then told us his mother had thought it would be a good idea. Well, you think twice about that, don't you!'

'Interviews in my branch are quite intensive because we need to probe deeply to make sure that the applicant isn't going to be rocked by being a volunteer,' a member of the selection panel at a large branch in the Midlands explained. 'We take three weeks to inform applicants of the outcome because the report I make out is read by a group before a decision is made to accept someone for training. And although I use the word training, I don't actually believe you can train people to befriend. We develop skills, we're not trained. There are fewer misconceptions among applicants about the work we do than there used to be because we send them a packet of information, but they still don't realize how much they are supported when they come on duty. Samaritans are required to consult among themselves, and this comes as a revelation, too. If at the end of the three-week delay we turn someone down we never give a reason. There are some things you can't tell people.

'Basically, you've got to be stronger than the caller. If someone presenting themselves as a volunteer is going through an emotional crisis of their own, they are not ready to become a Samaritan. Which is not to say they won't be later on. Being a Samaritan is quite demanding, by any stretch of the imagination. In my branch, trainees take a phone call before the end of their training so they can discuss with the director how they felt they were supported. People get very anxious about their first call, and the sooner they take it the better. But what I always try to get over to new recruits is that taking a call as a Samaritan isn't all that different to having a friend ring you up in distress. We are not professionals. We are acting as friends. A professional is someone who has gone through a recognized training in a specific subject and come out with an accepted qualification at the end of it. I would most certainly accept the analogy that we are amateurs. Oh yes, absolutely. Absolutely. The word amateur comes from *amare*, love, and this is the basis of the caring we hope to give.'

The value of support for one another offered by volunteers in the branch was echoed by an experienced Samaritan, who said, 'Thank God we don't work at home, and thank God we always work in pairs. Very often, if you've had a really hairy call and you've been on the telephone for an hour and a half with someone who sounds pretty desperate, an hour and a half's concentrated listening, you need to blow off steam with somebody, and the great thing is, there's somebody else in the centre with whom you can nearly always discuss the call, and off-load it to some degree. This is especially necessary if you feel somehow you haven't been of any help. Sometimes you just feel so helpless, and that's when you most need support and reassurance from another volunteer.' And sometimes, of course, a caller can arouse in a volunteer strong feelings of resentment. One of the most able, and gentle, members of a training team told her class of recruits, 'Callers do sometimes make us very cross! And that is something you will need to recognize and come to terms with.'

Just as having experienced suicidal feelings in the past is no automatic bar to membership of the Samaritans, neither is physical disability, and a number of volunteers are confined to a wheelchair. The only handicap to their joining a branch may be ease of access to the centre, as some Samaritan premises, unfortunately, can only be reached by a flight of stairs. Many branches number among their members at least one blind Samaritan. This might at first seem like an insuperable disadvantage, when it comes to making notes after a call, or interviewing a caller face to face, for the loss of eye-to-eye contact undoubtedly invalidates a major dimension inherent in any personal meeting. But Ada, a cheerful widow in her mid-sixties, claims she overcomes most problems by her gift of a retentive memory. 'I had to develop that,' she says, 'when I went totally blind in my mid-twenties. When it comes to making a report, I dictate everything at the end of my shift. I've been a Samaritan now for ten years, with one break when I had a personal bereavement to cope with. You're no use to other people then. I act as a guide and mentor to recruits during our training sessions, and find blindness no disadvantage in my work at all.' Unlike many blind people, Ada smiles much of the time, and only feigns bad temper when reprimanding her dog.

A blind Samaritan in Manchester contributed some forthright comments on the selection of blind volunteers in an article he sent to the *Samaritan* in 1985. He urged the disabusement of certain myths about the blind; they are in no way especially wise, he wrote, with no special sixth sense or compensation. On the contrary, blindness brought its own 'crop of special hang-ups'. He said he would think very hard about accepting someone in the process of losing their sight. 'What such a person does not know is the extent to which he will have to reorganize his practical and psychological mode of life.' Some astringent advice included the following: 'Don't worry about your building. If a blind volunteer falls down your stairs it's his fault, just as it would be your fault if you fell down them. Once he knows where they are, it's up to him; they won't move.' He made the point that a blind volunteer must exercise the same responsibility as anyone else about getting to the centre on time, and should not look strange or 'off-putting in any way.' During thirteen years as a Samaritan, he wrote, 'visitors have talked to me very easily. A few have asked whether I have something wrong with my eyes, but once they know I can't see they forget about it. Most don't mention it at all, and I think some don't notice anything unusual, particularly when they are very distressed.'

The numbers of Samaritans married to a fellow Samaritan appear reasonably small, but the numbers who are married and whose spouse has in some measure to support the active Samaritan, and indirectly the work of the branch, is considerable. 'I think the Samaritans make very heavy demands on spouses,' a London-based volunteer considers, 'although when a Samaritan first joins we make sure that their husband, wife or partner understands they must turn up for duty. Sometimes at night, if you are a leader or a deputy director, as I am, you get phone calls at home, interrupting your home life. You may have to go off and do some fund-raising, and the pressures can be quite strong to help out with a variety of additional chores. Fortunately most spouses are very supportive, but you do get some who say enough is enough. And I think the strain on them can be quite considerable. This is the reason some volunteers drop out. Merely by supporting their partner in his or her work, a spouse is making a very real contribution, but they don't get the job satisfaction, and the more you can involve them in branch activities the better. They are never going to be told by a caller, "If it wasn't for you I wouldn't be alive."

'When I am on call to the centre at home, I deal with calls at night on an extension downstairs, but initially the phone rings by the bed, and inevitably it wakes up my husband. I think some people actually arrange to sleep in separate rooms so that the partner isn't disturbed. But a director can't do that or you'd be sleeping apart for three years. So before a director, or even a leader, takes on the job, I think they've got to sit down and have a good, hard, frank talk with their partner, and ask, "Are you prepared to put up with this, because if you're not, then we won't enter into it at all." But I honestly don't think directors know what is involved until they become a director. I think leaders do, because they know how often they've rung their own leader, but every leader in the branch can be ringing the director. So it's often much better to have a system of duty directors, where a duty director stands in for a week at a time and the director is only called as a last resort. It's very difficult to assess the disruption to family life until you're in the middle of it.'

Questioned about her religious attitudes when she first applied to join the Samaritans fifteen years ago, a mother of two sons has certainly found over the years that her personal attitudes have not just been useful but essential. She has a full-time job as a personnel officer in an industrial town on the Welsh coast, and as a Roman Catholic she attends Mass every Sunday. Her Church remains opposed to a whole range of activities to which Samaritans callers 'confess' every day of the week – abortion, homosexuality, masturbation, adultery and pre-marital sex – which many sections of society now regard as either natural or, in certain circumstances, excusable. How does she square her joint allegiance to the official teachings of the Catholic Church and to the non-judgemental approach of the Samaritans?

'I do square it,' she says, 'and I don't find a conflict. When I first joined the Samaritans I found I had to think this through very carefully, to see whether there was going to be any great conflict, but in fact there isn't, because for one thing we're not offering advice, we're not saying to people, "If I were you I would do that, or I would stop doing that," and in one sense we're not really concerned with their actions. We are concerned with callers as people, so that what they do and what they are are two different things. We all do things that we know are not really right, but we don't stop loving each other because of them, and I think you have got to say to yourself, "I am concerned with this person and how they feel, I'm offering them friendship and care, and I'm not passing any opinion on what they're doing, because it doesn't concern me." I'm not in the Samaritan centre to run their lives or to moralize.

'At the end of my probationary period I was interviewed by the director, and I mentioned to him that I was concerned about an abortion issue, which at that time was right at the centre of discussion. And he said, "Well, you know, you're not there to give advice." And that really opened it up for me. I realized I had in fact been thinking about it from quite the wrong angle. And once I began to look at it from that point of view I found it applied to all sorts of things that might have been problems had I not had that wise word at the time.

'I think I was motivated to become a Samaritan through my religious belief, in so far as I feel we all have a certain responsibility for each other, that we can't exist in a vacuum. No human being can really cut themself off from other people. And if your own life is pretty stable, at least for the moment, then you ought to be being of some use to somebody else. You don't know when the tables are going to be turned, and you're going to find you need support. But I think all Samaritans are aware of this, that for a time you are on one end of the phone, but within a matter of days or weeks you might need to be on the other end, as a caller. Because we're all very vulnerable. So yes, my religion did motivate me. It has also supported me in being a Samaritan, because from my point of view, speaking as a Catholic, it isn't possible to do this kind of work without prayer. And I think that any offering of yourself to other people has to be based on prayer if it's going to be valid. That doesn't mean to say I would ever go and tell anybody that I prayed regularly before I went on duty, but I do. Samaritans with no religious belief are often better Samaritans, but that is the way I find my support, and perhaps they have other ways of finding theirs. There are really super Samaritans who have no beliefs at all. But I don't know how they cope with it. The most difficult thing for me was coping with one caller who had a terminal illness, about twelve years ago, and I've never forgotten that girl. It was something that really got to me at the time, and I thought that once she had stopped contacting us, because she was too ill, the only use I could be to her was through prayer. So I used to remember her at Communion each Sunday. And in a way that comforted *me*. I felt I wasn't totally cut off from somebody whom I cared about very much. Becoming a Samaritan has totally changed my understanding of people and their problems. Totally.'

The former joint general secretary, Jean Burt, remembers a Catholic priest who was also a Samaritan. 'Girls used to come to him pregnant, and he used to say to them, "Look, as a priest I cannot advise you, but here's the number of the pregnancy advisory service." Which seemed to me very sound!'

Why *do* people become Samaritans? One answer out of thousands was supplied by a television producer in Hampstead, married with two children, whose husband is also a Samaritan. 'I've been a Samaritan for ten years. My husband joined first. At the time he joined, one of our neighbours, also a Samaritan, asked me, "What about you?" and I said, "No, no, I don't want to join the Samaritans, I've got far too many friends who burden me with their problems anyway, I'm not taking on other people's problems as well." So I didn't join, and it wasn't until about two years later, when Bill had been thoroughly involved in the branch in various ways, that I actually happened to go out one night on a flying squad with him. A flying squad is when a caller rings into a branch, and is obviously in such a suicidal state that you are fairly certain they have made, or are about to make, a suicide attempt, and you stay with the caller, or ring for an ambulance, or bring the caller back to the centre.

'Now, in our branch you don't have to be two Samaritans on a flying squad. A husband can take his wife, or vice versa, and on this occasion Bill was called out and I went with him.[1] We arrived at this lady's house. She was very distressed and had taken an overdose, and her husband had called the Samaritans. He had telephoned the police as well, and they arrived. He was frightened, basically. Bill asked to be allowed to talk to the wife, and eventually the police went away. I drove the lady to the centre, and Bill sat with her in the back. I'd never been there before, and Bill said to me, "Will you take her into the interview room and I'll make some coffee, then I'll come in." So while he was making the coffee she was talking to me, and by the time he came back with the coffee I had got most of the problem. And I'm afraid after that I thought, well, maybe I could do it. Maybe this *was* something I could do. I don't think I thought I *should*, but that I could if they would have me. I can actually live without it. I discovered that when I had three months off, about eighteen months ago.'

Every story behind every Samaritan is different, as it is with every caller. Three years ago Maureen, a charming and elegant woman who lives in a small, comfortable house by the Thames in Berkshire, decided the time had come to reshape her life. She was already doing voluntary driving for a local hospital, attending art classes twice a week and acting 'as an agony aunt to nieces and people who rang me up and bent my ear for an hour', but then she also decided to volunteer to be a Samaritan. 'I was looking for directions, really. I was looking for something to do in the useful line. I was too old to get employment, and I'd had a very rocky three or four years. I haven't any paper qualifications of any sort. However, I have been through quite a lot in my life, one way and another, and I thought, surely the experience that I've had can be of some use to somebody. I was nattering on

[1] Many branches would strongly disapprove of a non-Samaritan attending a flying squad call.

about this one day and a friend of mine said, "Why don't you try being a Samaritan?" She had been one. It was something I had thought of, actually, some years ago, before my home broke up, only I didn't realize, as so many people don't, that you don't do it at home, and I didn't really see my husband being prepared to be woken by calls in the middle of the night. So I didn't think about it any more, but later I thought, now I am free I could do it. So I went along, and took a training course, and decided, yes, I would like to do it.

'How I relate my own unhappy experiences to my work as a Samaritan I don't really know, except that there are certain things I know about – bereavement, for instance. Cruse[2] know much more because they've made a study of it, but I do know that when you've lost somebody, you want to talk about that person, and that you're mostly stopped from talking because it embarrasses everybody. People cross to the other side of the street because they don't know what to say to you. They don't like to talk about the person who's died, and if it's someone you've lived with for many, many years and has been part of your life, you desperately want to talk about them. I mean, they're part of your life, you can't write them out, and to have to put up a wall of silence between you and them is very painful.

'I've lost two children. I've been divorced. In the year I was divorced my brother died of cancer, and I was visiting him every day when his wife couldn't. And within a year, my mother died. And I moved three times. Life was kind of hectic. But I somehow came through. I sometimes think that when all these things happen at once it is a sort of blessing, because you are kept so busy and so occupied with everybody else you haven't got time to sit around and feel sorry for yourself. But I did come to realize people's need to talk about certain things, and when people go through a very difficult time they need to talk about it sometimes over and over and over again. I was very lucky. When we sold the house and my husband went off, an old friend

[2]The National Organisation for the Widowed and their Children, 126 Sheen Road, Richmond, Surrey.

of mine decided to share a house with me. So I wasn't immediately on my own, as a lot of people are. I did have someone to talk to.

'I lost the children a long time ago, one at ten months, in what they call a cot death, which I'd never heard of before it happened, and my second son was drowned when he was four. I have one married son left. I was married for twenty-four years, and then my husband fell in love with someone. I knew that he wasn't a philanderer in any sort of way, he was a one-woman man really, so I knew it must be serious. I hoped it might blow over, but it didn't. So eventually we sold the house and I got a divorce. It was three or four years before I decided to offer myself as a Samaritan. When I was interviewed, I was asked, would it worry me if I talked to people who had been divorced? Would it revive old hurts, and so forth? And I said no, I thought I'd got over that, the bitterness, which is inevitable. It's so sordid, working out finances. Other than that they didn't ask very much, so I didn't tell very much. I don't like telling people unless they ask. I thought I'd forgiven my husband a long time ago and I've really worked hard not to be bitter. In many ways it's been good for my soul, if you know what I mean. I just feel it was awful when it happened, but that it's been what you might call a growing experience. I've had to cope with life again independently.

'If you are a woman and you're divorced and you're not working, not only do you lose your emotional security and your financial security but you lose the structure of your life, you lose your job, the job of running a house, the whole thing you do. And you lose half your friends. You are literally thrown out as naked as the day you were born, to pick up the pieces and to start life all over again. I was lucky, because I had a house, and a roof over my head, but a friend who is staying with me, she was left with practically nothing to live on at all, and she had a total nervous breakdown. In fact, she tried to commit suicide. She was between life and death for three days. So I lived through that. She was with me when she did it. She was in hospital for six weeks.

'Funnily enough I've hardly had any experience as a Samaritan of callers suffering as a result of lost children. It's like losing a limb. It's like losing a whole part of yourself, like having an arm cut off. It's extremely painful.[3] Before I became a Samaritan I was never tempted to ring them. I was never suicidal. It sounds very stupid, but when I had small children I remember quite distinctly suddenly understanding there was a purpose to life. It was like being born again, and ever since then I've had a kind of faith. Very individual. I've never been a church-goer. When I had to go to church a lot of it was all mumbo-jumbo to me, and boring, just plain boring, but I now understand what they're trying to say. I also had the feeling that suicide is no escape, because there is a theory, believe it or not, that you can't escape; if you don't meet it this time you'll meet it next. It's reincarnation, basically. I tend to believe in reincarnation. There's no evidence, but it makes sense. How else do you explain the people who are much more evolved than others? How do you explain the Mozarts and the Leonardos? I think that I was either a ballet dancer in my last incarnation or I'm going to be one in my next. I'm a frustrated ballet dancer. I love dancing. The thing that gives me greatest pleasure is to move my body to music. For one year, I went to a very good ballet school, and I really got very keen, and then my mother took me away. But I've always liked to use my body.

'You can't sort out your own problems by being a Samaritan. It's nothing to do with that. What happened to you has no bearing, necessarily, on what happens to the other person. Everybody has to handle problems in their own way. That's the trouble. It's very difficult to give anybody any keys. The real thing is to try and throw back to the person what they're saying so that they can talk it out and sort it out themselves. It's a great skill. I don't think I'm very skilled at it, but I know that is what is really necessary.

'Since I've been a Samaritan I did call them myself, once. Not

[3] The Compassionate Friends, 6 Denmark Street, Bristol, specialize in befriending bereaved parents.

my own branch, though. I had been a volunteer about two years and I was frightfully upset about something to do with my family, and it was midnight and I thought, I've got to talk to somebody, but I can't phone anyone at midnight, and I suddenly thought, I'll phone the Samaritans. I'll phone another branch, which I did. And of course, when I started to try and explain what was bothering me I burst into tears. I wasn't making much sense to them because I was crying so. The business of trying to explain what was upsetting me helped me sort out my thoughts, what it was that caused me such distress. So from the point of view of being a Samaritan it was a very revealing process.'

Another volunteer who had occasion to become a caller reported his experience in the *Samaritan*. 'Whilst I was a caller,' he wrote, 'it made me aware of Samaritan techniques being applied by the volunteer. I realize now, with hindsight, that I took a tremendous risk in making the call. Had the volunteer offered only techniques I should have been rendered even more dispirited.' But it seems he was fortunate in encountering the ideal Samaritan approach towards which all training and theory aspires. 'She gave me her undivided attention,' the caller wrote. 'She was warm, but not patronizing; she was gentle, but not wet; she was strong, but not critical; she was in control, but was considerate. Her tone of voice said it all (literally and metaphorically) and I could sense her support during silent spells.'

It is sometimes assumed that if the Samaritans recruit a wide variety of volunteers, married, single, divorced, old, young, middle-aged, heterosexual, homosexual, they will inevitably arm themselves with a catholic cross-section of society and thus be equipped to cope with every variation in the human condition. First of all, they never will recruit one of every kind; by the very nature of the role Samaritans are expected to play (a non-directional, essentially acquiescent one) they are unlikely to attract intellectuals, only people of average intelligence, and those who are not particularly creative or ambitious – although like all small ponds, the Samaritans will inevitably attract minnows with aspirations to swim to the top against less fierce competition than they would ever encounter in ICI or politics. Samaritan volunteers will tend to be passive rather than active, decent rather than holy, sensible rather than brilliant. And of course people do not volunteer because they fit into a particular slot, nor are they chosen to fulfil a special role, to top-up the required quota of black one-legged bisexual single-parent volunteers. And therefore a homosexual caller wishing specifically to speak to another gay, for example, has no guarantee that a gay volunteer will be on duty, nor indeed any guarantee that his problem would be handled more effectively if one was. In the normal course of his or her duties, a Samaritan with specialized knowledge or experience, or unusual personal orientation, will in fact have relatively few opportunities to make specific use of them. A general awareness and sympathy are what are called for and expected. But an extra-curricular role certainly exists for someone like Leslie, a transvestite,[4] in the way of helping to educate fellow Samaritans through branch meetings, seminars and conferences. An alarmingly heavy smoker, he drives an almost silent Daimler and lives alone in a compact semi-detached house on a new suburban estate in Surrey, furnished with numerous typewriters and an ansafone.

'As far as my branch is concerned, I'm just an ordinary Samaritan. They know all about me, but whatever I may do for the Beaumont Trust[5] has no bearing on my work as a Samaritan. They are quite distinct. I have done two seminars on transvestism for the national conference at York, and I travel the country visiting various branches. But when I'm on duty as a Samaritan, if I get a call from my sort of people then I handle it just as any Samaritan would.

'The biggest problem for transvestites is that the vast bulk are terrified, guilty, secret people. They are frightened to death of

[4] Almost always a heterosexual man (and very often married) who experiences an overwhelming compulsion to dress as a woman.

[5] A counselling agency of the Beaumont Society, which exists to help transvestites to meet, and enjoy a social life. The address is BM Box 3084, London WC1N 3XX.

discovery, largely because of what they perceive the public's attitude to be, which is in fact often better than they think it will be. I spent forty-five years of my life dressing behind closed doors. I knew I was transvestite when I was nine. All real transvestites know by the age of puberty. I "came out" quite simply because I'd reached the end of the line. I finished up with ulcers, and I was verging on the suicidal. Now I live largely as Jean. I travel as Jean, I give lectures as Jean, I've appeared on television as Jean. It's no offence. And to the best of my knowledge, no one's ever realized who I was. You wouldn't know me as Jean. Well, you might from the photographs on the wall.

'When I applied to join the Samaritans I told them I was a transvestite because that is now my policy. I make no secret. They weren't really interested. I said, "Of course, you wouldn't meet me as my other self." They said, "Well, it's useful to have somebody who knows something about this subject, for helping callers." What I try to do is help Samaritans to recognize what a caller is, which he may not know himself, as between a transvestite and a transexual,[6] or a fetishist, who are more likely to be sex callers. Understanding about transvestism in Samaritan branches varies enormously, which is one of the reasons I'm trying to do so much. Some branches have virtually no knowledge of the subject. They are quite unable to distinguish between a transvestite and a transexual, a fetishist or anyone else. I think it's a weakness in the training programmes, because transvestism doesn't form part of the training as a subject in its own right. But there is a growing awareness of it. But then, it would be impossible to train Samaritans in depth in every single area. It's just not possible. And Samaritan training, of course, is on-going. I know of only one other Samaritan besides myself who is a transvestite. But statistically, there must be many more.'

If it is true that the many thousands of Samaritans who have

[6] A man who feels himself to be a woman trapped inside a man's body, and may ultimately wish to undergo surgery in order to regularize his gender.

pioneered and consolidated their movement over the past quarter of a century are in a fair degree typical of the era through which they have lived, it should come as no great shock to discover that despite the interviewing process and the training, designed at the very least to curb any exhibitions of irrational prejudice, those who would prefer not to fraternize with, never mind befriend, transvestites or homosexuals have sometimes slipped through the net. A decade after the Wolfenden proposals to legalize all homosexual conduct in private between consenting males over twenty-one had passed into law, a gay Samaritan who felt it necessary to remain anonymous wrote an account for the *Samaritan* of his experience at the annual conference.

He had, he said, left the conference with a feeling of profound and painful alienation, for one of the women delegates had, apparently, remarked that she thought homosexuals were disgusting and she would prefer not to talk to them. He pinpointed the problem as one of a lack of understanding, and suggested that in training classes, homosexuality should be presented as a condition, not a problem. 'Most heterosexuals,' he wrote, 'are unaware of the emotional anaesthesia to which homosexuals are subjected, and of the profound and intense sense of aloneness, alienation and needless guilt that is inflicted upon them by our culture. Verbal queer-bashing is alive and well and not unknown at annual conferences, or in our branches.' Unfortunately, Dr Doris Odlum herself had seen fit to refer to homosexuality as a 'problem' when writing a series of articles for the *Samaritan* called 'The Male Predicament', adding the astonishing assertion that the situation in which men are attracted only to other men was 'of course . . . extreme and comparatively rare.'

Samaritans were swift to reach for their pens with which to beat their breasts, and letters appeared in the following issue expressing dismay, and suggesting that the lady in question should examine her motives for being a Samaritan, and resign. A gay volunteer from Reading, however, thought his own homosexual orientation had seemed to his interviewers to offer advantages over the heterosexual applicants, but he failed to explain how.

Although at times we pride ourselves on living in an enlightened age, physical as well as verbal queer-bashing remains alive and well, and it must remain extremely probable that, whereas in many Samaritan branches gay volunteers are known to their friends as such and serve from time to time as branch directors, there will still lurk within the movement a number of volunteers, both male and female, infected, like society at large, with 2,000 years of Judaeo-Christian hate. Perhaps far more remarkable is the number of clergy and others who from the start have stood out against the prevailing culture and climate, so that today, distressing though the experience recounted not so very long ago must have been, it almost certainly represents a minority attitude within the Samaritans, whose members, while seeming to be so ordinary in their homes, undertake tasks when on duty which most of their friends and neighbours would never dare contemplate. The press officer of Gay Switchboard reports, 'We have a good working relationship with the Samaritans, and in general they handle calls from gay people in a sympathetic and supportive way. We have a number of callers referred to us from the Samaritans but we don't keep statistics; many Samaritan callers feel a stigma attached and wouldn't tell us they had come via the Samaritans, so that actual figures would be rather meaningless. The Samaritans send our annual report to every branch. In some provincial branches problems about accepting gays still exist, but in London especially the situation has been excellent for a number of years.'

The double-edged experience of Geoffrey illustrates in a most striking way the two sides of a single coin. 'A few years ago,' he says, 'I volunteered to be a Samaritan, and when I volunteered I told them that one of the reasons I was volunteering was that I had once called them, and that I had found it very useful in the circumstances, and one of the things that I thought was important was not to assume that everybody was part of a solution or part of a problem. I also told them that I was gay, and that really seemed to throw them. I had gone for an interview, and I was interviewed by two people, and when I told them I was gay you could see them sort of doing, "Of course, officially we know it's perfectly all right to be gay, but . . .". There seemed to be all kinds of alarm bells ringing. They rang me up and said they wanted me to have a second interview with a sort of higher-up person. So I went and had a second interview with a higher-up person, and what it basically came down to was whether I was going to start preaching gay lib down the telephone. There were lots of sort of odd questions about that. And they then said, "We'll accept you for training." But by that time I just felt wrong about the whole thing. I just felt that I was going to be patronized by them in some way, that I would have to conform to some idea they'd got of what a respectable gay person was, that there wasn't a genuine accepting of gay people, there was a particular category of gay person that was all right, which they presumably decided I didn't fit into. I just felt odd about it. So in fact I wrote to them and said I'd thought about it and I'd decided I didn't want to pursue this. And they wrote back and said, "If we can ever be of any help to you please let us know."

'There had been a gap of about nine months or a year between my being a caller and offering to join the Samaritans. I was teaching at the time. But it was during a year when I was back at university that I had this mad, passionate affair, with this boy. He was a boy of seventeen. I was twenty-six. It was lovely! *Absolutely* wonderful! I met him at Victoria Coach Station, and he asked me the time. And within a week he was living with me. He came from Macclesfield. After six months I went away for three weeks, and it was all tears and tragedy at his end, because I was going away and how would he be able to live without me. This was a holiday I had organized ages before, in India and Sri Lanka. So I went. And while I was away I was convinced I was attached to him, and when I got back he'd gone, with somebody else, just like that. And I was totally thrown. I've never been so thrown. It was a combination of jet lag and being just really upset, and a bit drunk, and I came home to the flat and I was just in a state. I was in *such* a bad state! And this is where I think the Samaritans are wonderful, the way they provide a kind of vehicle that nobody else does. Although I've got lots of friends I can talk to about being gay, I didn't want any of them to see me in such a state, because I really felt very ashamed of myself, being in such a state.

'And so I rang the Samaritans. I got this chap who was just so good. I talked to him for about half an hour, and then I put the phone down and had a few more drinks. Then I felt a bit better and I rang them again, but I got a woman. And I didn't want to talk to her. She wanted to talk to me, although I'd asked for John or whatever his name was, and she wanted to start all over again. I didn't want to go through it all over again, so I said, "No, I want to speak to John." Then I had a very kind of calm conversation with him. He was just extremely good. I'll tell you why. He managed to make me feel as though he had experienced similar things without ever suggesting for a minute that he had. I think that was really it. I also felt, talking to him, that in his mind there was no censoriousness about me saying I'd had a sexual relationship with a seventeen-year-old boy, quite apart from the fact that it's illegal. So far as he was concerned, it was just a relationship that had gone on the rocks. And he never said, which I knew was perfectly true, "That's what you get if you have relationships with seventeen-year-old boys."

'It took me months to get over it, partly because the boy went on living with me for two and a half months. I couldn't get him out of the flat, and he was having affairs with other people. So at this stage it was all just a great disaster. But the Samaritans provided at that crucial moment exactly the right kind of safety valve. I wasn't actually asked if I was feeling suicidal; I think I had said fairly early on I was not going to commit suicide, I just wanted to thrash it all out with a complete stranger. And I was weeping down the phone! Later, in fact, I did feel quite suicidal, on several occasions, but I never rang the Samaritans again. I don't know why. The time when I thought I felt most like it was about six months after the whole thing was officially over, and I really thought I had got over it, and I met this boy and his new boyfriend in a pub, and I just couldn't cope. And I was so cross with myself for not coping, and I walked to a bridge, and I was quite determined I was going to throw myself off this bridge. Anger is quite a good defence mechanism, and I know what it was – I stopped when I was crossing the road to avoid being knocked down by a car, and I suddenly started to laugh, and I thought, how can I be telling myself I'm about to commit suicide if on the way to do it I'm trying to avoid being knocked down by a car! Anyhow, I suddenly found it all very funny.

'So that was my experience of the Samaritans, which was that at the receiving end they were extremely good, but when I was a real person, not at the end of a telephone, I didn't like them so much. And what was so odd was that I encountered two such dissimilar experiences at the same branch.'

Rejecting a potential recruit is one thing; a job most directors find far more distasteful, and some will actually shrink from performing personally, is asking an established volunteer to leave. This is allowed to be done without any explanation being offered, and for the Samaritan concerned it is often a crippling experience because, for better or worse, the Samaritans often become a crucial part of someone's life. Judging from an account of a volunteer's experience of being sacked from the Medway branch in 1979, published in the *Samaritan*, her director handed responsibility for the deed to a leader, 'who was very good, very kind, [and] obviously found it a difficult task. He coped with my hurt, then my anger, then left. From then on, as far as the branch was concerned, I ceased to exist. My name was removed from the volunteers list. My card went from the availability book. It was as though I'd never been.' Unable to speak to former Samaritan friends for fear of seeming in search of sympathy, and unable to explain her sense of loss to non-Samaritans, she found she had no one to turn to. 'It would have been nice to have had occasional contact during that first week,' she wrote. 'There must be a better way.'

Her article provoked a flood of reminiscences. 'No reason was given for my dismissal, although I was given the dubious comfort of being told it had nothing to do with my work,' one former Samaritan wrote. 'A request for an interview with the director was refused. The sense of disillusionment is deep. I really believed in the goodness of the Samaritans, but an organization which can practise such double standards – one for callers and the complete opposite for its own members – can no longer be credible to me.'

'Where else in these days can a person be accused, found guilty and punished without knowing the crime and without being able to defend himself?' another wanted to know. 'I have never heard a convincing reason for this ruling, and suspect it is mainly designed to make things easier for directors. Unfortunately, an insecure or small-minded director can so easily convert the directorship into a petty dictatorship. If anyone disagrees with him he can just ask him to leave and no one can do anything about it.' It must also be a fact that as long as a director can fire volunteers at will, his power to do so may well staunch criticism of his conduct or of branch procedures for fear of the consequences. There are, however, according to a former director of the Norwich branch, Dr George Day, who has written a pamphlet called *What a Young Director Should Know*, 'certain offences [that] demand instant dismissal – e.g. breaches of confidentiality, being drunk on duty, unwelcome behaviour or sexual irregularities at the centre, and *wilful* disobedience of the Directives.' What might amount to 'unwelcome behaviour' he does not say, but he is quite specific about sexual irregularities. 'Bluntly put: volunteers must not sleep with their callers. Penalty: dismissal.'

Just as dramatically he goes on to explain that 'callers often become embarrassingly infatuated with their befrienders, and fantasize about them like mad. Volunteers must be sternly warned that when they suspect this is happening they must inform their leader, and discuss how to deal with the situation without harming the caller's self-respect or precipitating his parasuicide. All the more so should the volunteer inform the leader if he himself finds he is beginning to reciprocate the caller's feelings. His befriending that caller must cease. If he is hell-bent on consummating his passion, he must resign and cease to be a Samaritan.'

In an article two years later reviewing the whole procedure for dismissal, a volunteer from the Putney branch expressed the view that if 'dismissal is necessary it should be done with love and care and accompanied by follow-up from the individual's friends within the branch. This offer of continuing contact is essential. Whatever the circumstances,' he wrote, 'there can be no justification for dismissal, suspension or warning without a face-to-face interview.'

The problem of easing a Samaritan out of a branch highlights more than anything the importance of appointing suitable directors, and in order to supplement informal training of directors at regional meetings plans are being drawn up to extend training opportunities for new directors. One of the dangerous weaknesses at present within the movement is the reluctance, quite often, of the most able Samaritans to shoulder, even for three years, the very considerable responsibilities and time-consuming tasks that fall to a director, and the consequent danger that a second or even third choice, of a less than adequate member, deficient perhaps in the most basic management skills, who nevertheless regards themselves as the most experienced and competent Samaritan in the branch, will be called upon to fill the post by default. When this occurs, the chain reaction of lost morale, ending with callers being cared for by jittery volunteers who have lost confidence in the leadership within their branch, could prove catastrophic.

·4·
ROOTING

There can scarcely be a more important task for any branch than the selection of a team to undertake the training (or preparation, as some prefer to call it) of new volunteers. Yet overall there is a haphazard approach to the job of training that makes an assessment of its merits at a national level practically impossible. The reason for this stems, like so much in the movement, from the historical decision to allow as much autonomy as possible to the branches, and a direct result is the deliberate refusal to impose from on high any consistent and officially approved training programme. The Samaritans were thirty-one years old, with virtually all their branches already set up, before the council of management, in 1984, got around to appointing a National Training Co-ordinator, and then, for the first eighteen months, only on a part-time basis.

Norman Whiting, with twelve years' experience as a Samaritan and a career behind him in teacher training, was the man chosen for the diplomatic task of trying to filter a co-ordinated national training programme through the network of regional and branch training officers. At sixty-one he rather resembles a well-intentioned monk let loose at a public school mission, but he has swiftly acquired a reputation among area representatives for the quality of his teaching materials, and a quiet and unassuming modesty belies his abilities on the public platform. 'Training had grown up without very much co-ordination,' he explains. 'And it was eventually recognized that there was a need for greater communication between the council of management, the regions and the branches. But the movement might not willingly have accepted a full-time appointment to begin with. The council are very careful about what some people think of as professionalism, and there are areas of resistance to the appointment of salaried staff. I think when they chose my title they were being very cautious about the idea that 'training officer' might imply dashing around telling people what to do.

'I'm expected to be the professional adviser to the movement on training matters, and to develop training materials. But I have no formal authority to go to a branch and say you are doing this or that wrong.'

Mr Whiting depends primarily upon nothing more than goodwill and establishing a personal authority for getting across to thirteen regional and 180 branch training officers any ideas he may formulate for improving methods and materials – training officers whose own tasks in the past have been defined 180 different ways. Until recently it was even left to the regional representatives to decide whether their region should have a training officer.

'We are far less unified on training policy at national level than many other voluntary organizations,' says Mr Whiting. 'I suspect this is all to do with the way the Samaritans developed. It is partly a result of branches feeling very strongly about their autonomy. The acceptance of broad policy is one thing, but if we tried to lay down a national policy on training I'm sure there would be tremendous resistance. I don't think the council would accept, on behalf of the movement, any attempt to impose a standard preparation course. I'm sure it wouldn't be accepted. But while autonomy in the branches has the advantage of producing original ideas and freshness, it has the disadvantage, all too easily, of allowing very poor practices to be continued.'

One result of the lack of a standard preparation course is that because many branches frankly do not trust the training given elsewhere, it is common, although not universal, practice for branches to insist on retraining a volunteer who may move into their area, after giving many years of uncriticised service in another branch. Some directors allow an experienced Samaritan undergoing retraining to carry out a certain number of duties during the training course, but there is a strong argument that while the Samaritans claim to be desperately short of volunteers it is absurd to tie up volunteers in retraining just because they have moved house.

'If you lay down the law too much, people are going to resent it because they feel insecure,' says Jean Burt. 'My views on retraining are that every branch can do its own thing, but retraining, when we are so short of volunteers, does seem dotty.' Mr Whiting accepts that the case against almost automatic insistence on retraining seems to argue for greater standardization of training courses. 'But', he says, 'I think it is worth looking to see if we can answer this problem not so much by implementing a standard national preparation course – which I'm damn sure wouldn't be accepted anyway – but by doing everything we can to up-grade the quality of initial preparation where it is found to be manifestly inadequate. Changes are often brought about when a new director takes over. I had a long talk with a director recently, who said that the preparation course in his branch had been considered quite inadequate by a lot of people for a long time, but it was one of those inertia things, and there were some prestigious people involved, and no one quite liked to grasp the nettle. The last course had contained one or two pretty disastrous sessions, and he was now about to grasp the nettle himself.'

Allied to the argument about retraining volunteers when they move from one branch to another is the question of whether, after some length of time, all volunteers should undergo a refresher course, or even take a sabbatical. 'I think for everyone it's different,' says the assistant general secretary. 'It may be a good thing for someone to take a break when circumstances in their life alter, rather than because five years are up. It's all too easy to take for granted an involvement with the Samaritans and not take account of changed circumstances. There is an increasing trend in many branches towards retraining people after a certain length of time, the assumption being that it's not a bad thing anyway, and that people who have been in the movement for some time would benefit from having the opportunity to stand back and reflect on it. There's no reason to have a break for the sake of it, but perhaps we ought to look at the whole question of sabbaticals and retraining more than we do.'

To an outside observer, one of the most striking factors about involvement with Samaritan work is the sheer range and intricacy of personal problems with which callers are beset, and it must surely be a stark fact of life that soon to be added to these will be the distress, and almost certainly suicides, attributable to Aids. An inquest in Southwark was told in 1987 that a thirty-four-year-old London man had killed himself in the mistaken belief that he was a victim. After sixteen hours of training, how well-equipped with hard, incontrovertible knowledge regarding lesbianism, transvestism, drug abuse and so on were new Samaritan volunteers? 'Our training courses are a bit like training doctors,' Mr Whiting explained. 'Can the medical student, in training, meet every contingency? I don't think you can say that at the end of any initial preparation course you are going to be ready for every contingency, and if we were to try to cover everything before a volunteer went into Samaritan service we would need a vastly longer preparation course. There is an overseas branch which insists on four-hour training sessions once a week for six months. Are they x-number of times more effective than we as Samaritans? I doubt it. There is a sort of cut-off point, at which you say. "This person doesn't know it all but he knows enough to make a start." And after all, all Samaritan training is on-going, or it should be.'

Norman Whiting's responsibilities extend to the training of experienced Samaritans for particular – sometimes unglamorous – tasks within the branches. Writing in the *Samaritan* in 1986, a volunteer from Norwich complained that 'Some volunteers who do their duties at the centre with commendable regularity steadfastly refuse to play any part in the supporting activities of the branch, like publicity, fund-raising, talks, selection, training, the rota, the treasurer's work, the housekeeping, committee membership. They joined, they will tell you, to be Samaritans, not to do the chores.' And he went on: 'Largely to blame for this unfortunate attitude is our recruitment publicity and our selection and preparation of new volunteers, which all concentrate exclusively on listening and befriending, as if the other branch activities are the poor relations which you want to keep well in the background.'

Confronted with this criticism of training policy, Mr Whiting said, 'One can extend this to training people in local publicity. In this sort of field I am sometimes brought in to help plan, let's say, a residential school on publicity and fund-raising. I have a responsibility for anything that can be called training. I think we've got to help people to learn more about running a committee in a voluntary organization. There's an awful lot of time wasted. But diffusion of ideas is the principal problem. The training of leaders is vital, but even if we run two leader training schools a year, you can only attract to them a minute proportion of the leaders at work in branches all over the country. I'd like to get more money into the regions to start training leaders at regional level.'

Meanwhile, at a quarter to nine on a Saturday morning, a training team and a bunch of new volunteers are meeting for the first time. Everyone has arrived early, for what the branch calls an Acquaint Day; together with the training team there are other long-term Samaritans, chosen as 'mentors' to help steer the volunteers through an eight-week training programme. The centre, which is rented, is in a dreary street off a busy thoroughfare, on the first floor of a hideously ugly pebble-dash building, partly boarded up, with a crate of empty milk bottles on the steps. Closing the door to shut out the babble of voices (any inhibitions seem to have broken down within minutes) the training officer, recently appointed by the director and running his first course, explained there had been no need to advertise for recruits. 'This is a middle-class area,' he said, 'and let's face it, we're all middle-class.' This seemed like a *non sequitur*, but not to the training officer, who was a balding man of about forty wearing a thin blue vest. 'Some centres might get eight applications a year, but we run three training programmes every twelve months and usually have about sixty new volunteers. We have seventeen on this course. Some are former Samaritans who have been away for a time and are taking a refresher course.' He seemed unclear why five of the seventeen had not turned up, but very clear that the branch was proud of their traditions and training methods.

Before the session got under way, in a room furnished with a xerox machine, strip lighting and double glazing, there was a lot of kissing by Samaritans of one another, and a young man had his beard tweaked by the training officer. Everyone had taken note of the sign on the wall, 'Thank you for *not* smoking', or else, most unusually for Samaritans, they were all non-smokers, and in an atmosphere of quiet expectancy the branch director, a lay preacher and grandfather who had been a Samaritan for fifteen years, opened the proceedings. He was hot on statistics but not so up-to-date on terminology. The branch had been founded in 1970, he explained, because a policeman had been murdered in the area and a queer had been beaten up. No one blanched, and the connection between those two events and the founding of a Samaritan centre remained a mystery. The branch, he said, was staffed by 196 volunteers [if true, an exceptionally high number for the type of area], there were always two on duty, and last year they had taken 18,365 calls on the telephone from a catchment area of 400,000 people, not including 5,800 click calls (people who had rung in and then rung off). Of those who had contacted the branch 3,508 had been new callers, 1,479 or forty-two per cent of whom had had suicidal thoughts or impulses. Last year, 19,296 hours had been put in by volunteers on manning the centre – possibly nearer 20,000 hours when administrative tasks were taken into account. Only that night, the shift of two, who had come on at 11.20pm and stayed at their post without a break until 7.20 in the morning, had dealt with twenty-seven telephone calls.

He ran through some national facts and figures too. Although suicides per head in Britain were low compared to the rest of Europe [only two countries are lower, in fact], in 1984, 4,834 people had killed themselves. It had been guessed that 200,000 attempted suicides were made annually in Britain. [If the guess was correct, that would be an attempted suicide every two and a half minutes.] He ended by telling the volunteers he would require from them dedication and reliability, a minimum of one duty every ten days and four overnight duties every year. It was stressed that unsocial hours had to be covered, even Christmas Day. On-going training, administration, delivery of talks and attendance at conferences 'so that we don't become parochial' were additional activities that would take up their time. 'You will get the feeling how we understand, love and care for one another,' he told them.

The training officer referred to Samaritans as Sams. He wanted new volunteers and their mentors first of all to spend two minutes talking to one another to find out who they were, then they were to stand up and introduce their partner to everyone else. 'This,' he said, 'is all about listening, and understanding what we hear.' As everyone was talking at once, in a small room, it was a wonder anyone heard or understood anything. It later transpired that quite a few had not. After four minutes the training officer said, 'Right, we'll start with you beautiful people,' indicating an exceptionally ordinary looking couple. Harry introduced Joan. Joan, it transpired, had been a Samaritan for fifteen years; she was the wife of a doctor, and after suffering an accident she had come back to undertake a refresher course. 'She feels her only talent is to be able to provide a listening ear,' Harry said. Joan spoke about Harry in such an upper-crust voice that not one word was intelligible. Bill, dressed in brown corduroy trousers, a blue pullover and open-neck shirt, sported a monkish haircut, and steel-rimmed glasses that gave him an uncanny resemblance to Himmler. He turned out to be a Catholic priest, and he had previously served as a Samaritan in Rome. Mark, neatly dressed in a blue jacket, was a bachelor of thirty who was just about to lose his job, and had volunteered to be a Samaritan because he had been struck by the number of lonely people in London 'and would like to do something about it'.

Jenny's mentor introduced her as a divorcee with two sons, who lived 'very local' and would therefore have no excuse to be unpunctual. She loved concerts and books 'and all the things that make life worthwhile'. Mavis, Jenny's mentor, was blind, and had her guide dog with her. An 'insurance technician' called Pete, a stocky little man who was going bald but had a ginger moustache, mentioned to his mentor that he was 'ex-territorial army'. Jennifer, young and rather pretty with long straggly hair, apparently told *her* mentor that she was a 'seemingly intelligent person', which drew a laugh when it transpired that Jennifer was a spiritualist and healer. So was the next volunteer to be introduced, a secretary in the probation service and a 'practising Christian'. Christine (the new women volunteers outnumbered the men by two to one) was a solicitor, who thought she might be able to help over problems of bereavement because much of her practice was concerned with probate. A young looking man called Andrew had been married twice; he, too, had been a Samaritan before. The youngest volunteer was Linda, only nineteen, who worked in a local school as an audio-visual technician; she was comfortably plump, wore a blue skirt and green anorak, played badminton and helped with the Brownies. A middle-aged woman worked in the Foreign Office and liked walking and photography.

The 'Hello, I'm . . .' session closed with the training officer and two members of his team reading an extract from *The Wind in the Willows* in such flat, monotonous voices that they reduced one of the great works of twentieth-century literature to the level of a bus conductor singing out the stops in Oxford Street. Then coffee was served, in disposable containers. Still no one smoked. Next came a film called *Can I Help You?* intended to encourage discussion about Samaritan attitudes and the problems volunteers are called upon to face. A slight touch of unreality was provided by a young coloured actress in the role of a volunteer; they are so few on the ground as to be verging on the unique. A male caller asked to speak to a man. 'Well, you're over twenty-one, it is legal, you know . . . Have you discussed it with your wife?' The same chain-smoking Samaritan, who called everyone 'Love', interviewed a couple with a baby, with 'no money, no job, nowhere to live and not married – at least, not to one another.' The volunteers seemed to be running in circles a bit, with a backlog of callers waiting to be interviewed and looking suitably depressed. One woman who attempted to offer advice to a caller was ticked off at length by the leader while they both squatted on the landing. She seemed about to burst into tears, when the doorbell rang. 'Well, aren't you going to answer it?' said the leader. After the film show, the volunteers and mentors split into groups to discuss what they had seen, but no very definite views were formed, or at any rate expressed. Mark was somewhat surprised by 'the ton-up Granny,' as he described one of the volunteers in the film, who turned out to be a member of the branch he was hoping to join. 'One person's attitudes will suit some callers, someone else's another's' the lady from the Foreign Office felt.

'The purpose of all your training,' a member of the training team with a soft north-country accent explained, 'will be to help you come to a decision as to whether you want to do the work. My own view is that you've all been training all your lives. But we are rooting for you. We do need you. However, the decision-making process will largely be your own.' He explained that the mentor they had been given was someone who would hold their hand 'because we know it is stressful. We cannot do this work without support and we don't expect you to.' In private conversation, he later referred to those volunteers likely to be weeded out straight away as 'the real basket cases'. The training officer emphasized the commitment to time and told the volunteers to turn up punctually for their first training evening, three weeks hence. 'This,' he said, 'is a commitment I demand.' There was no hurry to disperse. The recruits seemed quite reluctant to drift away.

During the course of the next three weeks the volunteers were interviewed, and one 'basket case', Pete, the insurance technician, was politely shown the door; pressed again and again for a motive for wanting to be a Samaritan, he had declined to offer any reason at all. A well-fed young business man in his mid-thirties, dressed in a neat city suit and blue-and-white pin-striped shirt, who had failed to materialize on the Acquaint Day, rolled up five minutes late, and despite the training officer's admonitions about punctuality, he greeted Linda, who arrived twenty minutes late, with a kiss. The evening had got off to an even odder start. For the benefit of those who had not been present on the Acquaint Day, the director again unburdened himself of his list of statistics, and repeated word for word the ostensible reason the branch had come into existence; 'a queer' had been bashed up by a group of youngsters, he said. One would have thought that in the intervening three weeks at least one member of the team would have taken him on one side and brought his vocabulary up to date. He said he hoped the new volunteers would soon catch 'our sincerity and togetherness as a branch', an irony seemingly lost on everyone in the room. There was a good deal more in the traditional vein of a lay preacher, about everyone being human, about empathy, caring and the expenditure of time, and how his own life had been 'enriched and expanded' by meeting callers. 'I'd love,' he said, 'to go on talking all the time,' another remark that no one felt inclined to contradict. Then it was the turn of the volunteers and their mentors to talk to one another, for ten minutes, and this they did with gusto.

The director and the training officer took it in turns to run through the Samaritan principles, lacing each one with an appropriate home-spun anecdote. A member of the branch, for instance, had recently seen a girl on an underground platform (there were, the training officer said, three attempted suicides on the London Underground every week) who looked about to throw herself under a train, so the Samaritan had gone up to her and said, 'I'm Anne, can I help you?' and she and the girl had had a chat and then the Samaritan had gone on her way. That, said the training officer, was an example of being available at any hour of the day or night to befriend. 'Don't forget or break the principles and practices,' the director told the volunteers. 'If you do, I shall have no hesitation in asking you to resign.' He was himself due to retire as director in four weeks' time. No one seemed cowed, or queried a single item on the list of Dos and Don'ts.

Then the training officer said, smiling broadly, 'Now I'd like to introduce you to a very interesting person. I happen to share a house with him, so that I find it very interesting.' This very interesting, if very oddly worded, remark was likewise received in stony silence. The Very Interesting Person, a stocky Welshman with a lot of grey beard, wrote on a board, 'What Am I Doing?', and quickly demonstrated that depending on which word had the stress placed on it, the question could be posed four different ways. Moral: when eventually they lifted the telephone and said, 'The Samaritans, can I help you?' it was important how it sounded. He then divided the volunteers and their mentors into groups and gave them four tasks. They were asked to describe a person likely to commit suicide, to say how they would cope with a friend who revealed suicidal feelings, what they would do if they delivered Meals on Wheels to a formerly depressive old man who was now rather cheerful and talking of not seeing them again, and finally how they would react to a 'college room-mate' who had cut his wrists and had a poor relationship with his father, who thought him not manly enough. The Catholic priest talked of 'non-directionally pushing' the room-mate towards help. 'I wouldn't be shocked,' someone said of the friend who felt suicidal. 'I wouldn't belittle his problem,' someone else volunteered. 'I wouldn't give him a loaded gun,' emerged as another unexceptional solution. Physical contact, 'whether male or female', was what a young, bespectacled woman suggested was needed. 'Just give them a hug and make them know they are loved.' Rather ominously, the business man said of the suicidal friend, 'I wouldn't tell him to go to the Samaritans.' No one asked why. Linda, one of the brightest present, said she thought a person likely to commit suicide would seem 'edgy and uptight'. The Very Interesting Person reminded them all that bereavement could include the loss of a pet. Somehow the two-hour evening had seemed a bit disjointed and inconclusive, but perhaps it had been meant to.

A week later they were scheduled to learn about befriending, from a grey-haired man with a grey goatee beard. When taking a telephone call, he said, they should 'read between the lines' and 'give space to the caller'. This was what another member of the training team, helping out by role-playing, described as 'reflective listening'. Because different people use words in different ways, he said, the Samaritan should try to test what the caller was really trying to say. He read a hypothetical resumé of someone's telephone call, about a man who had difficulty keeping his food down, and had been given three months to decide his future at work. It all sounded very confusing. Then he asked for comments on the caller's general state of mind. The lady from the Foreign Office offered what sounded like a most intelligent appraisal, but received little encouragement from the team.

Then up popped the stereotyped lesbian, a caller who had said she found she was more attracted to women than to men and found it hard to face the day. 'Phoning you has made me realize I am not normal,' she had told the Samaritans. Sally, the member of the team posing the 'problem', suggested that a possible response was to say something like, 'You feel you have homosexual leanings and this makes you feel you are not normal?' But she got shot down by the cleric, who pointed out that the caller had never used the word 'homosexual', so neither would he. And then they were plunged into the 'suicide question'. Was it, the male role-player wanted to know, a good idea to ask a caller if they were feeling suicidal? Linda thought that by doing so you might sometimes put the idea of suicide into someone's head. 'Could you catch a headache?' the Samaritan inquired. The priest, who knew the right response, of course, from his previous experience in another branch, said that if someone had rung the Samaritans they were not going to be 'given a headache' by being asked the suicide question. The group were then firmly told that Samaritan policy was *always* to ask the suicide question, because by funking it a Samaritan might end up with a potentially suicidal caller ringing off without having been given the chance of discussing the most urgent reason that had prompted them to ring. The problem was deciding at what stage in the conversation to ask the question, and a number of tapes were played, offering possible variations on an exercise which, it was agreed by all the members of the team, was one which many Samaritans found particularly difficult to deal with.

How might the new volunteers pose the crucial question? Linda suggested asking the caller how they felt about their life, and was emphatically told that this was not the same thing as asking if they felt suicidal. Andrew quite seriously proposed, 'Have you thought about jacking it all in?' Would it be cheating to ask, 'Why did you ring us?' a rather earnest, middle-aged lady wanted to know. Her rhetorical question was greeted by a derisive chorus of 'Yes!' Other euphemisms suggested by the recruits included, 'Have you reached the point of no return?' One was beginning to realize just what they had taken on. How many people, before becoming a Samaritan, *have* ever asked anyone if they were feeling like killing themselves?

Finally, the class were told that one of the most difficult calls they would ever have to deal with was the silent call. 'You don't know whether the caller is a man, a woman, a hoaxer or someone about to commit suicide,' the man with the goatee explained. Then they listened, for what seemed like a very long time indeed, to a tape of a Samaritan trying to coax someone into speaking. It was an eerie experience. 'How do you actually know there is anyone there?' the secretary in the probation service wanted to know, but no one on the team picked up her question. 'Would you ever place a time limit on a silent call, before replacing the receiver?' she persisted, and again, in the general hubbub that had broken the tension of the silent call tape, her question was ignored. In conversation after the session had ended, the training officer said the longest silent call ever taken to his knowledge in his branch had lasted three hours, and had only then been terminated by the volunteer when he was as certain as he could be that there was no one on the other end. What no one asked, or was told, were the reasons for the silent call. One of the training team tried to interest the meeting in an adjournment to 'a local hostelry', but everyone remained glued to their chairs, chatting away like mad.

'It's lovely to see you all again, I think we're all here,' Basil, the trainer with the goatee beard, told the assembled volunteers eight days later. A bank holiday had intervened since their last session. In fact, two of the trainees who had been volunteers before were missing. In this branch, a certain flexibility is exercised in relation to re-training, and former Samaritans preparing to enter the branch are permitted to carry out shift work during the course of their preparation classes, so perhaps they were manning the switchboard. 'I hope you're all refreshed by that super weekend,' Basil went on. Most of it had been swept away by a howling gale.

On the subject of Communication, three versions of a call were played on a tape, after some technical difficulties and waste of time through a lack of proper rehearsal. A woman unable to sleep after taking several drinks and two mogadon tablets was ringing in at three o'clock in the morning. When the volunteers moved into groups to discuss the Samaritan's three different responses to the call they were talking in tones far more subdued that at the start of the course, as though they were now beginning to capture a sense of reality. But in questioning the groups about their response, the Welshman never really drew out any positive aspect of their conversations. Two prime weaknesses were beginning to show up. Individual volunteers were not being called upon, by name, specifically to speak out about their feelings and reactions to what was being taught, and the class, instead of being seated in a semi-circle, or even in a circle with the trainers in the middle, sat in rows with their backs to one another, so that visual and audio communication – the very subject under discussion – was minimal, and sometimes impossible. Even the director sat at the back of the room, and whenever he interjected a remark, necks had to be craned to hear what he had to say.

In order to demonstrate a Samaritan's need for consolation after taking a call, one of the team pretended to take a call while finding it hard to sympathize with the caller. Some may have felt she had earned a pep talk rather than the hug she got. Avoid questions that can be answered by Yes or No, the trainees were told. Open-ended questions that might lead on to a further exploration of someone's problems tended to start with the letter 'w'; why, when, who, what.

The Welshman ended by emphasizing that the Samaritans were not a religious organization, but then got Basil to read the parable of the Good Samaritan. Laughing heartily, he then explained the relevance of the parable to the Samaritans; the Samaritan had not asked if the man battered by thieves had been worthy of help.

Before the next session began, the training officer explained how his team worked behind the scenes. 'Assessment is a continuous process. After each session we get together and we fully debrief the evening. And an essential part of it is to discuss any problems we might have seen or felt from some of the volunteers. Last week, for instance, two of them showed a lot of reticence in speaking about death. "Have you thought about jacking it all in" was a throw-away line, really. We felt sure that it must be a throw-away line, but it's being watched. It does show an attitude that might be slightly less than what we want. I've tried to make it not too obvious that they are being assessed. Our previous training officer was much harder, and the last lot of volunteers were far less responsive. They never entered fully into discussion. You had to drag everything out. It was like standing in front of a sea of porridge. They know they're being assessed, but I've kept it very low key so as not to inhibit them and influence what they do say.

'There is no one I'm seriously concerned about at this stage, but there are four we're looking at specially, with doubts. Two of them because they have told me already they are not going to be able to complete the course, and we feel it is essential that they miss not more than one evening at the very most. I know it's difficult but we have to cram a lot in. And the two who expressed this problem last week with death. It's fairly basic in a suicide situation. It was when they started to talk about death in their groups that two of the girls said, "I don't know that I could cope with talking about death." This was picked up by the mentors. At some stage or other when you're on line you are going to join a person in a situation where maybe they are dying. So the prospect of death must be something with which you can cope. We've had nobody self-select out, but then we're still in the relatively easy part of the course, and I would say that with doubts hovering over four heads out of sixteen we're in an average situation. They're a good bunch, and we'll probably get some good Samaritans from them. Certainly, I should imagine, between twelve and fifteen on the rota.'

Jennifer's comments at this stage were as follows: 'When I was first interviewed, they said to me, "How are you going to cope with all this? It's going to be outside your experience." And I said, "I don't know," and I still don't. I don't think any training in the world will do anything for you, and I think the people training us actually get that feeling too. It's almost as if there's not a lot they can do to prepare us for it. There is, however, a family feeling developing, so that you feel you can depend on other people, and I think that's the most important thing. I'm not very good with people who are really nice to me, who are immediately nice; I rather step back! The important thing they've said is, "You can't actually expect to change anybody." I really do feel that. I'm enjoying the sessions, though sometimes I'd like to go into discussions a bit more deeply. Maybe there is an element of morbid curiosity behind my motives.'

The secretary from the probation service: 'I think it's a very good course. I'm getting a lot out of it. I think it's extremely good. The reservation I've got, if I have one at all, is that I feel a little bit as if I'm in a goldfish bowl, and I'm being assessed by all these mentors, and I feel they're all looking at me, and I have a nasty feeling that at the end they're going to say, "Sorry, you haven't quite made it." It's a bit as if they're all looking at me and waiting for me to say something stupid. Which I could, easily. That's inhibiting. So I daren't always say exactly what I feel in case I get chucked out, and I'd be very sad about that, I really would, because I really want to be a Samaritan. I think the Samaritan policy is fine, I'm very happy with it. I just wonder if I can do it. I wonder if I'm good enough, you see, that's part of my anxiety about being watched by so many people who obviously wonder if I can do it, too. Certainly last week, when they were doing the role-play, I felt very stirred up; the second one, when the woman just put down the phone at the end and said, "I'm going to take my tablets now, thank you for listening," I was very much with it. I was very much being the volunteer and thinking, "I would never know what to say." I'm not sure at the end of the day whether I'm going to be suitable. I can't come to the last two sessions and I wonder if at the end of six I'm going to be able to tell if I'm ready.'[1]

James, the business man: 'I had very few expectations, actually. I find it quite exhausting. I feel pretty nackered at the end of the sessions, obviously one's concentrating pretty hard. And that will no doubt increase as we get more intense. And it's an indication of what one will be feeling when one is doing duties. So it's a good training in that respect. I'm conscious that we're being watched but I don't find that disturbing. I say what I feel. Nothing has arisen yet that I couldn't cope with but obviously I'm apprehensive. But there hasn't been one particular thing yet that I've thought, "Oh God, I wouldn't cope with that!" But I can imagine with the silent call, if I was in that situation I wouldn't know what the hell to do. So that struck me as something I thought would be very difficult. I know people who have committed suicide, acquaintances rather than friends.'

A session on Anger was opened by the training officer and another Samaritan pretending to be having a blazing row,

[1] In the event, she did attend the final session.

which most of the class described afterwards as 'embarrassing' or 'frightening'. Rosemary, a calm and self-assured Samaritan who clearly knew what she was doing, addressed each volunteer by name and drew them out individually. Outside the centre she could have been a very efficient and successful schoolmistress. She asked the volunteers to note down the things that made them angry. The room, for once, became almost entirely silent. Someone said that what got her going was seeing a baby seal being bashed on the head. 'I get very angry if a good friend gets hurt,' a smart housewife volunteered. 'I like to get my own way and I feel quite cross when I don't,' said the probation secretary. 'Men who wee in the street,' turned out to be Jennifer's *bête noire*. A second member of the training team, a rather elegant lady who looked like a retired Russian ballet dancer, said *she* could be driven demented by someone continually sniffing. James said he thought a caller with racial prejudice might make *him* feel angry.

'How would you feel if someone rang and said he had raped a child?' the class was asked. 'Very angry,' said the smart housewife. And how would they feel if another Samaritan had felt so angry that he had reported the matter to the police? 'Angry' was what they were told they should feel, because he would have broken his promise of confidentiality.

The evening became really lively when for the first time three trainees volunteered to take a call from one of the trainers. The first role-play concerned a widow who said that her husband had died young of a heart attack. She was angry with the hospital staff. The volunteer on the receiving end of her wrath was the over-confident joker who had suggested the euphemism about 'jacking it in'. He seemed to flounder horribly, but after his ordeal was over Rosemary reassured him. Everyone said how well all the volunteers had taken their calls, but everyone who had not volunteered felt they had had a lucky let-out. At last the course seemed to be beginning to understand just how incredibly difficult it was to take a call from a complete stranger who felt angry, often at the expense of the Samaritan, who in turn was forbidden to offer advice. To soothe any ruffled feathers, Rosemary ended the evening by playing some music not entirely dissociated with a television commercial for wool.

A week later, outside the centre five ten-year-old boys were bending over the pavement, intent and probing, and then they moved away with exclamations of disgust. In the gutter, on her back, lay a pregnant squirrel, hit by a car, gasping and dying. Inside, the trainees were gathering to discuss Pain. The training officer was on holiday, and three of his recruits turned up late. One was the priest, who smartly bagged someone else's chair which the occupier had vacated for an instant, and refused to give it up.

Nicholas, rather a willowy young man who twisted and turned as he spoke, but spoke well, said, 'We are not trying to be super people. Calls are a nerve-wracking experience on both sides. Samaritans are only ordinary people who expose themselves to a whole area of feelings which are unpleasant.' They moved into groups to discuss any painful experiences they may have had in the past. Several could be heard discussing bereavement. 'If you haven't had a painful experience, try to imagine what it would be like,' Nicholas told them. The priest gave a guffaw.

The articulate lady from the Foreign Office reported back that her group thought pain a very isolating experience, that the person experiencing pain probably felt in a unique position and better able to speak to a stranger. A large Samaritan in a white linen track suit warned against offering false optimism. 'I know how you feel', was also offered by the doctor's wife as a recipe for disaster, and this elicited a lively exchange of views; some thought it was perfectly possible to know how other people felt. How else was language to be used? 'If I had not experienced loneliness I would not be a Samaritan,' the cleric, who had a lot to say for himself on this occasion, informed the class.

Nicholas said that one of the most difficult aspects of taking a call was when the caller's pain seemed to be getting worse and the call was getting nowhere. 'Then words do begin to seem fairly pointless.' He said he usually suggested they had got as far as they could, and it might be better to leave the matter for a while. Another volunteer suggested inviting the caller round to the centre. 'Yes,' said the lady in the track suit, 'let them come in, and hold them while they cry.'

The mentors were taking a very verbal role during this session. One young man assured the trainees that the Samaritans were at their best at a point of crisis, and the words would come, he said, 'Believe me.' A young volunteer said she had taken a call the previous day from a woman who said she was going to die, and felt she had failed because the caller rang off. 'It's all right, she rang back,' a colleague reassured her. 'We are blotting paper, to absorb the pain of other people,' Nicholas ended by saying. 'Always remember, they called the Samaritans, not some other organization. We must be prepared to be hurt. Never bottle up the experience. You won't survive if you do.' Outside, when they left, the squirrel was dead.

On a sweltering evening when, for the first time, sunburnt shoulders were in evidence, the trainees were handed an application form for membership, although none of them had yet been accepted as a volunteer. 'I promise implicit obedience to instructions whilst carrying out the work of the organization,' it read. It also committed them to the possibility of having their membership terminated by the director at any time without reasons being given, and released the Samaritans from 'any legal responsibility for injury or loss . . . in carrying out my duties with clients.' It was strange that the word client, privately frowned upon by the director, had, even in 1986, crept back into an official document.

After scrutiny of the legal clause it seemed appropriate that the class should be asked to consider the subject of Loss Adjustment. 'This,' explained the young north-country volunteer, togged out in a yellow track suit, 'is one of the biggest background areas we work in.' The trainees were invited to compile a list of likely lost causes, starting with death itself. The lady from the probation service suggested the inability to walk. Loss of self-respect, and childen leaving home, came from others, and then the probation secretary added, 'If I lost my car for any reason.' Helen, another member of the training team, said that many psychiatrists now believed reactions to loss from any cause were no different to those experienced through bereavement. The attachment of the caller to the lost object, whether their parrot or their purse, was what counted.

One of the mentors, who had never had drama classes in her life, left the room to act the part, on the telephone, of a woman whose eighteen-year-old son had been killed on his motorbike. The blind Samaritan took the call. The class became very subdued as the 'caller' wept copiously down the phone, and the Samaritan gently but firmly questioned her about her feelings. The role-play in fact became almost too painful to listen to; one felt like an intruder on private grief. Afterwards the trainees were clearly impressed, and many expressed serious reservations about their own ability to take such a call and to deal with it effectively. A rallying cry went up from the Samaritans. 'You will, you will, the words will come, your own pauses are valuable, the day I arrive for duty without a gut feeling I shall give up and go home . . .'

'But what would happen if I did it wrong?' asked the young man out of work.

'What is wrong?' came the reply.

Then the class went into pairs, each trainee taking a call from a mentor. The lady from the Foreign Office felt very diffident about her performance, but her mentor assured her she had displayed a kind and sympathetic voice, 'and that's often all you want to hear, someone being nice for a change.' Someone again expressed concern about asking if a caller felt suicidal in case it might encourage suicidal feelings. 'Talking about suicide often has a salutary effect,' he was told. By the end of the evening there was a distinct feeling that the class was suddenly beginning to mature.

The training officer, back from holiday and looking sun-tanned, spent a session on Loneliness and Isolation elsewhere than in the training room, so the training team were sharply called to order by the blind mentor and began eight minutes late. Snippets were played on a tape. A man's voice said, 'It's easier to be a transvestite if you're married.' A woman commented, 'I think loneliness is a state of mind.' 'I daren't tell anyone I'm gay,' someone whined. The trainees were asked to discuss their reactions to what they had heard, but no one made sure they knew what a transvestite was, or, indeed, a 'gay'.

'If you didn't know about loneliness, you wouldn't have come along here to offer to be Samaritans,' a young man called Henry informed the volunteers. He had only been assigned to the course at the last minute and seemed very badly prepared. 'Everyone is going to be in some way lonely,' he limped on. A lot more time was wasted while fact sheets were handed out that could have been distributed on arrival, and then the trainees went into huddles to simulate a call from someone so lonely he wanted to know their name so that he could form a relationship and always ask for the same person when he rang the centre. Really getting into his stride, Henry told the class he was not at all sure the Samaritans offered friendship, though some might contradict him which, he said, they were very welcome to do. The relationship between a Samaritan and a caller was one-way, he said by way of explanation, 'so it wasn't friendship.'

'Now,' said Maureen, a member of the training team who was trying hard not to sound as though she had been postponing the inevitable hour for ever, 'I'm afraid to say we do get some calls from men who ring to make obscene calls, or to masturbate, or generally abuse the person on the other end. But it's better that a person like a Samaritan who is prepared for such a call should take it than an unprepared housewife at home.' Once Henry had managed to disentangle the tape recorder from the xerox machine, a voice boomed across the room, 'Can I wank on your tits?' You could have heard a pin drop, were it not for the whirring of the copier. 'When that happens, you are all at liberty to put the phone down,' Maureen assured her perfectly placid trainees. 'Harder to identify is the person who isn't so overt. It is vital not to encourage the man who just wants to masturbate and not to put off the man who has a real hidden problem, and is seeking help.'

Now Henry and a female Samaritan prepared to enact a variety of sex calls, but at this point the telephone would not work at all. The most sensitive and potentially embarrassing session was rapidly turning into farce. Afterwards, a lively and not always totally coherent young recruit called Jane, who had missed the last two sessions, said she now knew heaps about the Samaritans she had not known before. 'I had a very naïve view, when I think about it. I was actually thinking, "Crumbs, what is the substance of the course going to be like? Is it going to be sort of psychological? Or could it be a test of ourselves drawing on our own experience and our own energies?" That's what it's been, in fact. It's been like a mirror reflection. It's been an opening-out for me. It's made me evaluate myself and think, "Could I be good enough?"

'But the more they go on about it the more I keep thinking, "Crumbs, I don't know if I could hold that sort of level of not letting my own personality botch it up." There is a sort of ideal. There is a thread. I'd never really thought about sex calls before, but when I came for my interview, the lady who was there started talking about it and asked, "How would you handle a telephone masturbator?" and I thought, "Well, there must be some policy Samaritans have about that." When the chap phoned up and said, "I'd like to wank over your tits," my immediate reaction was to laugh. I was shocked in a way, but not threatened. I think we all have to accept that none of us in this entire world is pure. All of us are subject to masturbating and having weird thoughts so we all have something in common with each other.'

A middle-aged spinster now had this to say: 'My views, or attitudes, I hope have changed during the course. I envisaged that Samaritan work would obviously be listening, I knew that was important, but also being able to be practical, and perhaps suggest things they might do, things they might move on to, but I now realize that's not the way this branch works, anyway. It's not a disappointment. The intensity of what is being asked is greater than that. It's much more difficult for me. I would still like to be accepted, but I've no idea if I will be. It's quite an awe-inspiring – quite a frightening – thing, always with the anxiety of thinking, "Shall I say the right thing?" The course has been very valuable, very valuable. One looks forward to coming. I was prepared for this evening, unexpectedly, in a way. Like most women, occasionally I've had that sort of call at home. I have, once or twice, although I'm not down as female in the telephone book. But I feel if it happens in the centre I shall be able to cope much better than if I hadn't had that session tonight.'

The smart housewife: 'I don't think I had great thoughts about what the course was going to be like. I don't think I stopped to think about it very much. I think it's been immensely valuable, it's been an interesting and stimulating mixture between just talking and discussing various ideas and then actually interleafing it with role-plays and telephone calls, and it's beginning to give one a feel of what it might actually be like. As to whether one is better prepared, it's impossible to tell until you actually start on the thing for real. In some ways one is not necessarily reassured because you are now more aware of what some of the difficulties might be. I suppose I was aware there could be obscene calls and there could be sex calls and that sort of thing, and I suppose it was helpful to have some idea how you might lead into it and how you might be involved. I certainly wasn't unaware that such things occurred. But it was certainly useful to discuss how far one should let it go and how one could reasonably end it. Now the course is almost over I'm more keen than before to be a Samaritan. Whether I shall be accepted I can't tell at all. One hopes one will be.'

It was again a sweltering evening, and for the last night of the course the chairs had been rearranged in a semi-circle. The Catholic priest was sporting a green T-shirt with 'J.D's Hamburgers' on the back. Members of the training team presented a resumé of the topics that had been covered in the course, one of whom came up with the *bon mot*: 'Try to hear what the caller means as well as what he says.' The branch chairman, a nice young man who had swopped spectacles for contact lenses in the fifth week and looked even younger than before, explained about fund-raising and other essential activities, and the rota secretary said that although the branch was up to 170 members [the director had said 196], a hard core of thirty were always stepping in to do extra duties, and really a minimum of three duties a month and twelve overnight duties a year would be essential. [Seven overnight duties a year is regarded in most branches as a reasonable commitment.] The new volunteers, he said, should try to vary the times of their shifts, to avoid being telephoned by the same persistent callers and to gain experience of working with a variety of other Samaritans.

Then came the set piece, a demonstration of how an operations room might function on a night when the flying squad had to be called out. There was only one telephone – which whistled and shrieked – and one of the two Samaritans on duty had to go 'ring-ring, ring-ring', like a benevolent uncle playing games at a children's party. A chap called Mike, alias the training officer, rang in. He had taken a bottle of whisky and twenty codeine, and was getting drowsy. The Samaritan on the make-believe telephone rang the poisons unit to seek advice while his female colleague, in soft and rather soapy tones, tried to keep Mike on the phone and *compos mentis*. Hastily scribbled notes flew across the table, and eventually the duty director was contacted at home, who said a flying squad should be sent out. And then the muddle really got under way. A Samaritan was telephoned who had no car, then another was contacted who seemed less than sure of his way around the area, or where anyone lived, and while time for Mike seemed to be slipping away a persistent caller arrived at the door, and was cheerfully supplied with coffee and biscuits. However, all ended happily and in a welter of self-congratulations, the flying squad arrived in time, the duty director quite needlessly left her post and turned up at the centre, and when the performance was over there was a good deal of statutory hugging and kissing, well-earned on this occasion by the training officer: to pretend to be dying from an overdose for half an hour is quite a taxing task.

All that was left was to make sure that every trainee had booked in for an interview in a week's time. 'Arrive ten minutes early,' they were told. They would be interviewed by a deputy director, who might not have been a member of the training team, but who would have a report to go on. If they were rejected, they would be told on the spot; if accepted, they would undergo a preliminary observer duty, a second observer duty during which they would take their first call, and then an overnight duty, when they would be accompanied by only one other Samaritan, and be expected to take fifty per cent of the calls. If all was still well, they would be placed on probation for a three-month period or for a series of ten duties, best taken, they were told, at regular weekly intervals. Then everyone held hands and had a singsong. And then they all went home.

It transpired that one volunteer had dropped out half-way through the course. All but one of the others passed their final selection interviews, but as soon as Jennifer had begun to take up her observation duties she learned that she had been offered a job overseas. For some weeks a question mark hung over the lady from the Foreign Office. The team felt strongly that she needed the Samaritans in order to fill emotional gaps in her own life, and they doubted her ability to cope with demands the work would make on her. But she complained that she had been put off by her mentor, and in order that she should be seen to have received 'the best possible deal from us' her case was referred to the new director. The director confirmed the view of the team, and rejected her. 'She did not seem to have much contact with other people and there was not much warmth there,' the training officer explained. 'In a nutshell, we felt she wanted to be a Samaritan for the wrong reasons.' Out of seventeen potential volunteers, thirteen had joined the rota.

·5·

LONG-TERM BEFRIENDING

Always assuming the lines are not engaged, when a caller telephones a Samaritan centre he or she will hear the phone ring at least twice; this is to avoid the impression that someone has been sitting by it all day ready to spring into action. And the first words they will hear are, 'The Samaritans, can I help you?' The Samaritan, before he or she has picked up the receiver, and no matter how much of an open mind he or she has been taught to try to exercise, will have, stored somewhere in the recesses of their memory, a set of criteria for guidance in any number of possible situations. The lynchpin of those criteria was spelled out by Basil Higginson in the *Samaritan* in 1975, when he wrote, 'The Samaritans are an *emergency service* for the suicidal and despairing – not a long-term support service,' and he went on to quote a dictum of the founder: 'We do not permit our service to those whom we can help to be impeded by those who cannot benefit from it.' The New Testament itself provides a respectable pedigree for hard sayings such as these. Who can always judge, especially on the telephone, whether a caller is likely to benefit from talking to a Samaritan? And how do you terminate the conversation if you decide that a caller who cannot benefit is possibly preventing a suicidal caller from ringing in? There have been occasional surveys of calls that have received the engaged signal, and the numbers are high. Part of a Samaritan's task is trying tactfully to weed out those who cannot be helped by Samaritan methods from those who can in such a way as to leave the lines open while leaving the Samaritan ethos of a caring and compassionate organization intact.

Neither does anyone know how many callers, in desperate need of help, have failed to have their expectations matched by the Samaritans, and have even been propelled into a disastrous course of action as a result. In 1967, shortly before he murdered the playwright Joe Orton and then committed suicide, Kenneth Halliwell went to see the Samaritans. 'He started telling me how ill he was,' the actress Sheila Ballantine reported to Orton's biographer, John Lahr, 'how he was going to have a nervous breakdown. And how awful he felt. He was a bit strange. He'd rung the Samaritans and gone there. He said that was no good, they just make cups of tea.'[1]

Borderlines between feeling desperate or in despair, of contemplating suicide and attempting or committing suicide, of feeling lonely or just fed-up, overlap and are often wafer thin. Endemic loneliness may have little to do with being alone but a great deal to do with an inability to enjoy or even tolerate your own company; depression may represent a passing sense of sadness or a disabling and permanent incapacity to get out of bed; suicidal impulses can range from a wish to make someone feel sorry for you to an overwhelming desire to blank out for ever the pain of existence. The spectrum of what most Samaritans would regard as a genuine Samaritan caller is wide, but leads to little debate. Where Samaritans do often disagree among themselves is in the more nebulous context of persistent callers, particularly of those who treat the Samaritans as an extension of the National Health Service, as part of a welfare state that never shuts up shop and never sends out bills, and whose centres may even be regarded as surrogate massage parlours, albeit of the most rudimentary and voyeuristic kind.

So that while you are certainly not automatically expected to be feeling suicidal to ring the Samaritans, during the course of

[1] *The Orton Diaries* (Methuen, 1986). When Halliwell was eleven his mother choked to death in front of him; when he was twenty-three he found his father dead with his head in the gas oven.

any conversation with a caller the volunteer is expected to ask what is known in the movement as the 'suicide question'. 'The way in which it is asked and the point in the conversation at which it is best introduced should – and will – depend very much on how the contact has developed and what the needs of the caller are,' Simon Armson explains. 'There is no stock phrase. I think the sort of phrase, "Do you ever find life is getting to the point where you can't carry on any longer?" is one used quite frequently, rather than, "Are you contemplating committing suicide?" which is pretty harsh and narrow and rather cold and uncaring.' Why a caller feels suicidal – if they do – is far less important than whether he or she is in imminent danger of taking their life, and the criteria used by the Samaritans for determining a caller's state of mind are radically at variance with popular conceptions on the subject of suicide. People often say that someone genuinely intent on suicide would never talk about it, but the Samaritans estimate that at least four out of five people who kill themselves will have given quite definite warning of their intentions. Few dinner parties at which the subject comes up lack, too, the knowledgeable guest who avows that if someone is seriously intent on committing suicide, they will do so whatever happens. The truth is that many people who succeed in killing themselves never make a clear-cut decision; they seem more to gamble with death by playing a kind of Russian roulette, leaving it to others to save them. Almost the most pertinent fact about suicide, in relation to the work of the Samaritans, is that while suicidal feelings are far from permanent, most suicides occur within about three months of the onset of a period of 'improvement', for this is precisely the time when the potential victim is able to summon up enough energy to channel morbid thoughts into physical action. Another source of comfort to society has traditionally been the myth that everyone who commits suicide is mentally ill. A psychotic person – a paranoid schizophrenic, for instance – may be very seriously at risk, but the vast majority of successful suicides are carried out by people temporarily incapable of coping with unhappiness. They constitute a large proportion of the callers prompted to contact the Samaritans in their desperate search for a lifeline.

Depression, in its most virulent form an illness, commonly leads to suicide and masks a large number of calls to the Samaritans. For many people who suffer from depression fail to recognize the symptoms; they do not even know what illness they are suffering from. Guide-lines on the subject produced by one branch aptly describe a truly depressed person as living in a kind of fog or mist, where everything and everyone seems dull and hopeless, and adds the stark warning, 'We can regard depression as a killer.' No amount of love, money or privilege seems to protect a victim of depression; it strikes at royalty, artists and fathers-in-God. Prince Henrik of Denmark is frequently incapacitated through depressive illness; Elgar was almost certainly a paranoid schizophrenic; some years ago a suffragan bishop committed suicide in a London hotel. One reason a depressive may call the Samaritans is because his illness has alienated him from his family; he may have been told to pull himself together, and failed, and he can sense an irritation at his withdrawn condition growing in those he loves, who seem quite unable to help him. Depression is socially unacceptable because many of those who suffer most severely are highly intelligent people who hold responsible or demanding jobs, feel guilty about their 'failings', have been conditioned to put on a stiff upper lip and to set an example to others, and experience great difficulty in admitting to a form of mental rather than physical illness. They suffer from an acute emotional pain in the mind, without apparent cause and with no easily accessible cure. While dispirin will take away a headache, depression remains impervious to drink, sympathy or self-discipline. 'You cannot take the depression away,' the Samaritans tell their volunteers, 'but you can gently explain that this is an illness and the feelings described are the classical symptoms of the illness.' These symptoms often involve an inability to make decisions, and, if the depression is really bad, an almost total incapacity to act. Insomnia, loss of interest in work, a general lack of concentration and a liability to burst into tears at the slightest provocation are all pointers to depression, but not necessarily factors the caller will mention without some gentle probing.

Most people who suffer from depression find it a condition almost impossible to describe. A Samaritan who has experienced severe depression has said you might as well try to tell a man what childbirth is like; you cannot. A caller who is well aware that she suffers from depression, and of her sense of inadequacy that seems to trigger it off, is Kay, twenty-one, highly educated but somehow tangled up in a web of words. 'I rang the Samaritans because of severe depression,' she explains. 'I was having a very bad time on the personal and professional level. I think I've always found it difficult dealing with people. There's usually been one individual in each job I've had a violent personality clash with. I think it's my lack of assertiveness that's been the cause of it, and this lack of assertiveness and lack of ability to just knuckle under and cope with crises of a professional nature has led to this severe depression. I feel I've failed, you see. And this sense of failure has led me to become almost hopeless, to feel hopeless, to feel that there's no future, to feel that I'm just no good in the eyes of society.

'I talk of my problems to certain friends, but there are times when I feel I can't burden them any more. In the past few years they must have come in for quite a bit of earache. They've got problems of their own. What's really going on in my mind, I feel it's impossible to express it. I feel that the patience of friends is limited. They will listen, but the ones who are my best friends tend to be wrapped up in their own problems. There are times when I feel trapped. That's why I went to the Samaritans. The worst spell of depression I've ever had, which I would describe as true depression, was in 1982. The worst time is when you wake up in the morning and you've got to get up and face the day, and there just seems to be a blank wall ahead of you.'

Kay later had the misfortune to set up for herself a situation which was almost bound to end in disappointment; she offered to join the Samaritans. And although her personal unsuitability may have been an extreme example of the sort of potential volunteer who has to be turned down, her sense of rejection, even though it was born of so much unreality, was probably fairly typical.

'I felt that I'd been through the pits, and I just wanted to help other people, because I knew I could overcome it, and I thought, Gosh, if I can overcome what I went through four years ago then I'd like other people to get over their crises. You know, just sort of talk them through it. I think there are some people who can benefit more from going to the Samaritans than others. So I phoned them up. There was an advertising campaign at the time. I filled in a form and then later I went for an interview. When I filled in the form I thought I did it quite well, really, and I got one or two friends to go through it with me. So I went for my interview, and a lot of the interview was going over the things I had written on the form, and a lot about my background, how I coped with depression, how I'd react in certain circumstances. It was a very in-depth interview, actually. And also my attitude towards suicide. That was very important. I was interviewed by a woman, in her late thirties or early forties. I thought it was slightly unnecessary to go over the same ground as was on the form. She was calm and precise. I thought I was on quite an even keel. But looking back, I think I looked an absolute wreck. I think I may have looked like a depressive, for a start. And I think she might have questioned my motivation. She might have seen things I couldn't even dream were visible, you know, such as seeing into somebody's mental state. At the end, I thought it was not too bad. It lasted about an hour, maybe a little less.

'A few weeks later things were going badly for me again. I was very depressed, actually. I'd had a very, very unhappy time with this man over the last six years. There was a bit of a bad scene in April 1985, about two weeks after my interview with the Samaritans. There was a bad scene with the man, and there was also a crisis in my job. Again, a personality-based sort of crisis. So I was feeling very low because of work, and I had a scene with the man, which set me off feeling pretty depressed, and I got home feeling in a very bad state to see I'd got this rejection letter from the Samaritans. Now, there was no reason given. And I found that a bit upsetting. I'd have liked to have known. A possible reason could have been my attitude towards suicide. Because that was one of the main topics of conversation in the interview. I said that I thought suicide was justifiable in some circumstances and I thought it was quite understandable, and the woman said, "Well, what do you mean, why would it be justifiable, under what circumstances?" and I said, "If a person, for example, is terminally ill, or they've got some very severe disability, or if they're old, their friends have died, they've got no family, they've got nothing to live for, they're on the decline, they don't feel like carrying on. I think that's perfectly justifiable," I said. I wouldn't encourage them, but she may have thought from what I said that I might encourage them. But I'll never know, because they never told me why I was rejected. I found that more hurtful than being rejected. I thought of various unflattering reasons to myself. She might have just guessed that I was potentially a depressive person, in the future as well as in the past, because you have to admit whether you've ever been to the Samaritans as a caller. You fill in the form and you have to state that. But that doesn't prejudice your application. I admitted it, of course.'

A major cause of depression, and a reason high on the list of personal disasters that prompts callers to ring the Samaritans, is one form or another of bereavement. The death of an animal can cause similar symptoms to the death of a person; so can the loss of a job or a home. Although as common as the birth rate, death has become a taboo subject in our time, partly because with astonishing advances in medicine our expectations of a long life – perhaps of living for ever – have been increased out of all proportion to our inherent vulnerability to illness and accident, thus exacerbating our disappointment when the Great Reaper does in fact appear, and partly through a universal loss of religious conviction, and thus at least some sort of rationale for pain and suffering. Few people any longer believe in life after death. Old age, too, holds far greater material terrors than in the past, with the prospect of a prolonged and senile decay locked away in a geriatic hospital, abandoned by family and friends.

Society has come to despise old people rather than respect them, to regard them as a drain on national resources, and by some young men, equally the victims of a sense of alienation, as a source of hatred so violent as to lead to rape. Death is no longer celebrated. Few people have watched at a deathbed,[2] or paid their respects to a bereaved family, and few hearses leave these days for the church from the dead person's house; most sneak off from the impersonal side door of a uniform firm of undertakers. No wonder that with death swept under the carpet, expressions of bereavement have become an almost intolerable burden to those who would once have been only too pleased to join in the process. When a recently widowed neighbour comes into view there is a hasty retreat to the other side of the street.

Many of those who call the Samaritans are in a way preparing themselves for bereavement; they may have a husband or wife suffering from a terminal illness, and be wishing that death would interpose, relieving them of the chore of nursing, along with the anguish of watching someone die. Such feelings give rise to anger, guilt and shame. 'To prompt them to talk about their anger,' volunteers are reminded, 'can obviate the ensuing guilt. Perhaps to be assured by another human being that they are not wicked, cruel, callous and thoughtless is the most healing way of all.' Many relationships founder through an inability on the part of the partners to talk in depth, yet many relationships survive non-communication sometimes for fifty years, and much that was never verbalized in life will haunt the surviving partner. Yet those who mourn seldom have anyone to mourn with or to moan at; after the funeral, life is meant to go on as before, and callers often complain that their friends think they should have 'got over it.' The widow is a potent symbol of ill-luck; what has happened to her could so easily happen to you, and the sooner she bucks up and pulls herself together the sooner we shall all be able to ignore reality once more. And of course, coping with bereavement is one of the hardest tasks a Samaritan may be faced with because, as a branch who have

[2] Four out of five of those who still die in bed do so in hospital.

supplied an *aide memoire* on the subject to its members very sensibly points out, 'Most of us have suffered some form of bereavement at some time, and we should be aware of our own vulnerability and not gloss over parts that we found particularly painful, as we will then be defending ourselves and not helping our clients.'

The Samaritans recognize the vital importance of giving people time to mourn: 'We must be careful not to "cheer them up",' they say. They are also aware that callers may in some way be asking permission to stop mourning, for to some extent we still cling to the Victorian idea that ever to cease fixing one's thoughts upon the dear departed is unthinkable, and remarriage obscene. A form of first marriage still obscene in the eyes of many people is a permanent homosexual partnership, and if society is bad at dealing with heterosexual bereavement it can hardly be expected to take seriously the destruction by death of a loving relationship it refused to accept when it existed. So in bereavement, homosexuals frequently turn to the Samaritans for support, for they often have nowhere else to go. The family may not have known of the most important person in their life, and the homosexual subculture is notoriously inept at dealing with death, preferring to concentrate on the illusory 'gaiety' of the passing scene. 'Bereaved homosexuals can be the most difficult to help,' one branch informs its volunteers. 'Their isolation can often become so acute that their thoughts turn to suicide. We must help them to mourn, to accept their grief.'

It should come as no surprise that a large number of callers will actually be clinically neurotic or psychotic, nor come as any surprise that as a consequence, a common misconception about the Samaritans has grown up to the effect that they are ill-equipped do-gooders dabbling in amateur psychiatry. In no circumstances does an individual Samaritan comment on a caller's psychological state of mind or offer psychiatric advice, but in deciding how best to steer a conversation, and whether to regard a caller as temporarily distressed or in need of expert medical help (which might be made available if a caller were invited to visit the centre for further befriending), it is thought advisable for Samaritans to be provided with some outline understanding of the most commonly defined psychological problems. In preparing guide-lines for the members of the country's busiest branch, central London, the director, John Eldrid, makes a very general distinction between people who can be said to be in touch with reality and those who are not. What is most noticeable about callers out of touch with reality, he says, is that the volunteer will find it very difficult to recognize some of their feelings and ideas. 'The caller who speaks in detail about being followed by the police, and sexual attacks through the use of radar, does seem to be, at the least, a bit unusual. Those who have these experiences seem quite unaware of any personal identity or sense of disintegration.'

Mr Eldrid specifically draws his members' attention to characteristics of the manic depressive – mood changes that swing from very excessive excitement to utter and complete feelings of despair – and schizophrenics, who 'are most likely to be very withdrawn and to be living in a world of their own.' He is careful to warn of similarities between those who are depressive and those who are schizophrenic, but cites as examples of schizophrenic behaviour callers who speak of voices giving them special directions, 'which may involve them in wanting to take special responsibilities in political or religious activities, or suicide. Sometimes the voices may be very condemning and threatening, and accuse them of all kinds of strange sexual behaviour.' Evelyn Waugh's *The Ordeal of Gilbert Pinfold*[3] is an autobiographical account of just such an experience. Mr Eldrid has gone on to warn Samaritans of the dangers a psychotic caller may present. 'It is not always easy,' he says, 'to recognize how very disturbed they really are. Many people who feel persecuted and paranoid can be very convincing indeed, and it is always important to recognize that those who are out of touch with reality seem very quick to pick up your weak points, and sometimes you may feel very threatened by their attitudes.'

In trying to encourage a caller with a severe psychological

[3] Chapman & Hall, 1957.

problem to accept on-going befriending John Eldrid says it is important to recognize that although we can say mentally ill people have no apparent insight into their state of unreality, there does seem to be, more often than not, some hidden awareness that they may need support and psychiatric help. 'It is possible that when the caller feels more secure and has trust in the Samaritans he or she will accept some professional help. This is especially true of those suffering from depression. Befriending will help to combat the awful feeling of isolation and loneliness of the depressed. I would suggest that it is essential for befriending contacts to be maintained on a daily and nightly basis together with the making of every effort to arrange psychiatric medical help. As always, a lot of care, patience and tact is required.'

A branch in the North East has a deputy director responsible for 'on-going befriending', a service they have extended on a permanent basis to a local psychiatric hospital. 'We have two or three volunteers who go to the hospital regularly,' she explains. They speak to all the patients who want to speak to them, and we play exactly the same role there as we do in the centre. The nurses are very short of time, and time is the essential thing we are able to offer. Some of our callers are regular inmates of the hospital, in and out, in and out, and they like to see the volunteers every week. There are no special gifts involved, just the ability to listen. Our volunteers involved in the scheme are of course approved by the hospital. Every time we speak to a caller we're really befriending them, but those we officially 'befriend' are people who need that little bit more, who may be going through a particular crisis when we offer them extra support. But it doesn't mean we automatically agree to befriend someone. Some people think we are a branch of Age Concern. We don't just go out to sit with people who need a visitor. We like to use our befrienders for people who are going through a crisis. They may have been accused of shoplifting, and be very distressed.[4] If a volunteer feels that a caller may possibly benefit

[4] Isabel Barnett, the television entertainer, who was also a magistrate, committed suicide when accused of shoplifting.

from befriending they will discuss it with their day leader, and if the leader agrees, they come to me and we discuss it. We try to match the caller to a suitable volunteer. No volunteer should ever promise off their own bat that a befriender will be sent out in an emergency. If we couldn't find someone that would leave the caller in a dreadful mess.'

Not every caller who ends up being befriended is mentally ill, and as the general secretary says, 'Branches define the operation differently. One branch will say they are currently befriending 100 people and another six, and when you poke around they're both befriending perhaps twenty or twenty-five. Befriending is usually undertaken if the branch thinks a caller is at continuing risk of suicide and would be helped by an on-going relationship with one or a pair of Samaritans. The volunteer would then give this person quite a lot of time outside the centre. To avoid the danger of dependence, the volunteer is supported by a leader.'

A personal experience of befriending, not entirely successful, is recalled by a leader in Scotland. 'I did it once, for a woman, and it was very difficult. She was a very clingy lady, and at the end of the time I felt that she actually didn't need the befriending but it was quite hard to get rid of her. She lived alone, and she had had a dreadful upbringing, but she had managed to get a degree, and to bring up two boys, and she had a secretarial training, but she couldn't get a job. And she found this completely demoralizing. Also, she couldn't make relationships, and this, I think, was basically the problem. She had married the first man she thought would marry her. And I think she felt she had found a kindred spirit in me, which was probably true, she had. She was very keen on dancing, and music, and all the things that I enjoy, and so it could have developed into a friendship, but she was very clinging, so in the end I had to sort of distance myself. I could see that the longer it went on the more difficult it was going to be to get out of. She would never phone unless I was on duty, and I said, "There are other people to talk to," but I have a feeling in a way that we didn't do her much good because she wanted more than we could actually offer. I mean, she actually wanted a long, on-going friendship.

'Not all branches will refer people to other organizations equipped to give long-term assistance. But a lot of branches will. If, for instance, a caller is alcoholic we will refer them, if we feel they are in need of help that we cannot give, to Alcoholics Anonymous, gays to Gay Switchboard and transvestites to the Beaumont Society. And of course for people who are afraid they have got Aids, there is the Terrence Higgins Trust.[5] We are very aware of all the other agencies we can turn to to help the caller.'

Other reasons for seeing a caller outside the centre were given by a leader whose special responsibility is to make such decisions. 'A caller might not have a telephone at home, and in order to ring the centre she is crammed into a phonebox, with her children outside in the street.' Some long-term befriending is conducted by means of a weekly visit by the volunteer to the caller's home; but if a caller wishes to preserve the anonymity of their own home, the meeting place may be a café. No Samaritan reveals their surname, address or telephone number to the caller without their director's permission, for no befriender can guarantee to be available at home twenty-four hours a day, and the person being befriended needs to be reminded that in an emergency, help will always be available at the centre. One of the tasks of a befriender is to try to steer the caller away from feeling he or she is just a person with problems, to try and encourage them to see themselves as part of the community. There are no hard and fast rules about the length of time befriending may last, but something like three months seems to be a generally accepted maximum. 'Make it a happy ending, not a rejection,' volunteers are advised. 'Discuss ending the befriending with a caller; don't let it peter out. Summarize what has happened in the course of the befriending.' Above all, they are told to remind the caller that the Samaritans are always there.

[5] BM A.I.D.S., London WCIN 3XX.

From the earliest days, long-term befriending has been seen as essential for certain callers. Basil Higginson warned that 'One of the great weaknesses – indeed, dangers – of our work is that depressed people are often allowed to telephone once, or make one visit to the centre, and then go out and kill themselves,' and in 1975 he was drawing attention to the vital necessity for every client's form and continuation sheet to be assessed as soon as possible by a director or leader, 'one with considerable experience as a Samaritan . . . to see if necessary further interviews and perhaps referral (with the client's consent) has been offered – especially if the enquiries on the report form about suicide and consent to follow up have not been filled in by the volunteer.' And with disarming honesty he went on to point out that 'this lack of competent assessment has been justly criticized by responsible friends of the Samaritans.' He quoted some tragic examples of deaths that had followed negligent assessment of callers' problems at a basic level: the case, for example, of a thirty-five-year-old widow who called at a centre, where the volunteer failed to ask how her husband had died, or encourage her to express her anger at his death and her loss, but assured her instead that time would heal her feelings. Six weeks later, she took an overdose. And of a man of forty-five suffering from depression: 'He was worried about his declining business. The Samaritan talked about business today and reminded him that many others were in the same boat. John perked up and said he would "get by". The Samaritan said, "I'm sure you will." John went home and shot himself at the bottom of his garden within an hour.'

One form of befriending which gives rise to controversy among Samaritans themselves concerns the degree of attention and length of time that should be lavished on persistent callers; younger, more impatient volunteers particularly seem to wish that the Samaritans would stay at the grass roots level of being available in a crisis. 'This is what we're good at,' a social worker in his thirties, contemplating resignation after five years, firmly believes. 'Far too much time is wasted, in my opinion, dishing out tea and sympathy to casual callers who don't really need us or benefit from an emergency service.' Nevertheless the Samaritans do put themselves out for a hefty proportion of callers who are so lonely or inadequate they feel the need to telephone their local centre at regular intervals, or call in, perhaps only for a cup of coffee and a chat. There is a universal awareness that the befriending of such people must never interfere with emergency work, yet a persistent caller has only to be on the telephone for a couple of minutes to block an emergency line. Once a caller has been marked down as a regular, he or she is often allocated a specific length of call, or stay. Such decisions are necessarily taken on their merits. One particularly busy branch has as a regular visitor a young man who is schizophrenic, who wanders in, leaves his money lying around, makes a cup of tea, talks to anyone who may be available, usually on topics of no relevance to his mental or physical state (like many schizophrenics, he is intelligent, totally unemployable and often sleeps rough), and then drifts off again. The centre at least provides one point of reference in his otherwise tragically dislocated life.

The regular or persistent caller comes in a variety of guises. A deputy director at one of the London branches, where regular callers are inevitably more numerous than in small country branches, said, 'I would say a regular caller is someone who has been calling maybe half a dozen times. I think a lot of them are just lonely. A lot need some sort of reassurance. Some of them become like alcoholics – telephonics, if you like – and they can't stop ringing. There are others who have the need to make a phone call quite literally to wind up the person on the other end, the so-called fantasy or hysterical caller. They ring us because they know we will never put the phone down. If you get a caller with a very bizarre but nevertheless believable problem it is very easy to get caught up in the whole presentation. I know, because it's happened to me. And you think, "I must go on listening. If it's true, it's horrendous." We are always trained to go for feelings rather than what the "presenting problem" is. But with hysterical or fantasy callers, they can wind you up to such a point that you totally forget about feelings and start trying to resolve the problem, whatever it is, although we are not there to give advice. And they know they are doing this.

'So far as some of the persistent callers are concerned, there simply are people who don't develop at all. They will talk through a problem with one volunteer, and then do exactly the same with another. Because we don't offer advice or solutions, people sometimes get quite angry. If they get really angry and frustrated, they will put the phone down. If you have a call where you have been talking through the problem and trying to discuss how they feel there comes a point, sometimes, when the caller himself will say, "Thank you very much, I think we've talked enough, I've got a lot to think about but I will ring you again, thank you and goodbye." At other times you have to make the first move to end the call. You can say to them, after you've been talking for an hour, say, and sometimes they go on much longer than that, "I think possibly we're beginning to go over the same ground again. Wouldn't it be a good idea now just to have a break and for you to think about what we've said and then, if you want to ring us again, do so?" That's one way. There are a lot of other ways of doing it. The thing is, you mustn't make the caller feel you are rejecting them. But there is a point where you actually don't do any good by going on talking for hours and hours and hours.

'I can think of perhaps four or five people I've spoken to in the last year who didn't ring again. But one never knows if one has actually helped them, or whether you haven't helped them and they think it just wasn't worth ringing again, or if they ring another branch. You would know if they had rung your branch again but spoken to a different volunteer because we have a system of recording calls. But the real problem is when you have a caller who gives different volunteers a different name. It's generally the callers who are afraid that if they keep ringing under the same name they're going to be turned away or rejected in some way. After every call you fill in the log book with the time, and their suicidal factor, from 3 to x. Three is absolutely suicidal at that moment, 2 and 1 are lesser degrees of that. Nought is not suicidal and x means you have failed to ascertain. You generally make notes on a piece of paper while you're talking, and if you're so busy you haven't time to log it there and then you do so as soon as you are free. Then we have a card system on which we write down the essential points of the story; how suicidal they were and what were the factors that were making them suicidal – bereavement, isolation, depression, whether they live alone, whether they're employed or sick and things like that. And they're given a number. In my branch it's the year and then a number after that. They don't know this, though I'm sure some callers suspect we do. The card is really to help the leaders to ensure continuity.'

The question of maintaining and eventually destroying caller records is a sensitive one. Definitive advice was approved by the executive committee in 1985 in the following terms: 'Records must contain the minimum of information which might indicate the identity of a caller. They should be kept for the minimum length of time compatible with our care for the caller.' Simon Armson explains: 'If there hasn't been a contact for six months then the record is destroyed, and it's up to branches to work through their records and to destroy on that basis. If this had not been done properly it is something the Visitors would pick up. Of course, it may cause problems over the compiling of statistics, because if someone contacts a branch in the month, let us say, after their records have been destroyed, they will go into the statistics for individual callers twice that year, but that's a small price to pay for ensuring that we're doing all we can to protect the confidential information that is kept.'

'Not all regular callers are manipulative or unable to be helped,' one branch reminds its volunteers in a set of standing orders. 'The branch has frequently helped callers over a period of time by applying a consistent policy.' When carrying out instructions drawn up for dealing with persistent callers, it reminds Samaritans to be 'as gentle as possible, and only as firm as necessary', to be alert to a deterioration in a regular caller's situation, and always to ask about suicide.

An amusing anecdote about a persistent caller was recounted by a volunteer in a seaside town. 'We have one woman who is only allowed to call once a day, but she uses fifty different names. Fortunately she has quite a strong German accent. She got the director the other day, and she'd already rung twice, so he was very firm. This caller is agoraphobic, lives on the ninth floor of a block of flats, and she is always telling us she wants to put an end to it all and throw herself off. Some days she is worse than others, and she has long tales of woe, about people next door playing their radios and so on. She nearly always rings at midday, and she would talk for an hour if you let her. Well, she rang me up one day and said, "He's going to kill me, he's going to kill me!" So I asked who was going to kill her and she said, "My husband. He's just paid one phone bill and now another one's come in!' So I told her, "If you call after one o'clock it's a lot cheaper!" Now she tends only to be on the phone for about half an hour.'

The relationship between a Samaritan volunteer and a caller is unique in one specific way if in no other, as cinema-goers who recall Rita Tushingham rushing up a garden path and shouting at the lady of the house, 'Rape!' will readily realize. 'No, not today, thank you,' came the response. Few of us listen to a word that anyone says, either because what is said falls outside our expectations or comprehension, or because we are quite simply waiting for a pause in the 'conversation' to express our own beliefs, ignorance, prejudice or witticism. Learning to listen is perhaps the hardest task the Samaritan faces, and not solely on account of the persistent urge we have to talk. Most of us think about four times as fast as an average person speaks, so that a person listening has three-quarters of a minute of spare thinking time for each listening minute. It is like being left with a kind of blank space we feel we need to fill, and usually we do it by thinking about our own concerns. Once you do that you have ceased to listen, and once you begin to comprehend the social attitudes to silence you begin to realize how unnaturally listening comes to most of us. 'Have you nothing to say for yourself?' we petulantly enquire of the silent child, and monks and nuns who enter silent orders we look upon as the most extraordinary eccentrics. In fact, what the Samaritans list as 'barriers to good listening' are almost endless. They warn their volunteers against taking up a defensive attitude if they hear mention such emotive words as 'should', 'must', 'police' or 'unions', and they remind them that often we jump to the conclusion that either the subject or the speaker is going to be boring and make no sense. 'When we listen to ideas that are too complex and complicated there is a danger we will shut off,' they are told. And again, 'Sometimes we concentrate on the problem and not the person. Detail and fact about an incident become more important than what people are saying about themselves.'

If at the best of times listening takes practice and a determined effort of the will, how much harder is it for a Samaritan to cope with a call from someone who for whatever reason refuses or declines to speak? The silent call is every volunteer's nightmare. In a piece of unconscious humour, the members of one branch are reminded not to assume that every silent call is a sex call: 'On the contrary, heavy breathing may denote considerable distress and not sexual desire.' There seems, not surprisingly, to be little solid research into the genesis of the silent caller, but just as there are people who find it hard to stop talking so there are people who find it almost impossible to articulate their thoughts and feelings, more than ever when under stress. They may be content merely to hear a sympathetic voice on the other end of the line. Volunteers are encouraged to join in the atmosphere of silence by not talking continuously themselves, and by reassuring the caller that no matter how long they wish to remain on the line, the Samaritan will not replace the receiver. Giving the caller the volunteer's name and asking for theirs is a personal touch which sometimes elicits a response, but above all, the volunteer is enjoined not to hurry, to make it plain that they have all the time in the world, and to allow variable amounts of time between their own remarks. Anything between ten and thirty-five seconds is regarded as reasonable, and it is not until you time the second hand of your watch slowly ticking away that you realize just how long thirty-five seconds can seem.

Even though every silent call is not a sex call, the fact remains that people with sexual problems constitute a very large proportion of callers to the Samaritans; their problems may be something physical, albeit with psychological origins, like premature ejaculation or impotence, or something emotional, like an inability to come to terms with being homosexual. Whatever the 'presenting problem' may appear to be, Samaritans are told not to exhibit any attitude of shock or disapproval, although certain forms of sexual behaviour, taboo in our society, such as bestiality, incest or sexual relations with a child, may be difficult for the average Samaritan, being an average sort of person, to sympathize with. For some people, even such sexual activities as fellatio, sado-masochism, lesbianism and heterosexual buggery (still illegal in the United Kingdom but commonly adopted in Roman Catholic countries as a form of contraception) are difficult to comprehend. 'Callers coming to the Samaritans with sexual difficulties will in the majority feel very guilty about them,' John Eldrid has explained to his volunteers in central London. 'So it is essential for us to be accepting and not in any way condemning or shockable.' And he has gone on to warn that, 'Even if you do not express your shock or condemnation verbally, your negative feelings will be communicated to the caller, so one of the best preparations for Samaritan befriending is to come to terms with our own psychosexual make-up. Most of us are going to have hang-ups of one kind or another, but it makes all the difference if you are aware of them and have insight into your reactions.'

As a priest, Eldrid is in a useful position to admit that it is not easy for Samaritans neither to condemn nor condone a caller's actions, 'because we are all contaminated with perverted moral and theological ideas about sex. At the same time,' he says, 'we have to realize that some guilt feelings are healthy, and in fact, if you are not capable of feeling guilt, you are sick.' He also sees clear similarities in the sexual field – as in so many others ('There but for the grace of God go I') – between the volunteer and the caller: 'The majority of us, whether Samaritans or callers, can afford to improve our emotional and sexual relations,' he says. He might have added that some volunteers need to give attention to their vocabulary; one noted in the log-book, 'Could have been a sex caller but he did not expand.'

For all the absurd pretence that we live in some sort of permanent permissive orgy, agony columns in newspapers and phone-in programmes on the radio are daily flooded with letters and calls from people unable to express or talk about their sexual difficulties at home or with friends, difficulties and desires that often seem to stem from an inner loneliness and anxiety, fed by outrageous demands by the advertising industry for women to be glamorous and for men to be masculine, and by prejudiced and ignorant educationalists intent on forcing children from infancy to enact polarized gender roles to the exclusion of a development of their full human potential. 'Sex is really about relationships,' John Eldrid is at pains to point out, and this is why he believes it is a great help to create, within the Samaritans, the kind of atmosphere where a caller feels they can speak about their sexual difficulties. 'The majority of callers will agree that just to speak about them is a tremendous relief. I think it is essential for Samaritans to recognize that what we are offering are not solutions to problems – although we can arrange counselling and other professional help as required – but the presence of another human being. This is a positive step towards making life more worth living.'

However easy (or difficult) a Samaritan may find it to be confronted with another person's sexual hang-up, most well-selected and well-trained Samaritans will recognize that no matter how bizarre or unpalatable someone's 'sexual difficulty' may seem to them, for the caller it could well constitute such a source of anxiety as to present a serious threat of suicide. Yet there is a division of opinion as to how to deal with one category of caller presenting a sexual problem, the man known throughout the Samaritan movement as the telephone masturbator, whose calls are variously labelled M-calls or TM-calls. Unless the frequency of such calls were often made light of, many female volunteers would find it even more difficult than they do to absorb into their work as Samaritans the kind of experience that can send an innocent housewife, chosen at random from the telephone directory, flying beneath the kitchen table for cover, or even to the police for protection.

One reason given by some volunteers for the frequency of obscene telephone calls to the Samaritans is because the caller knows, in theory at any rate, that a Samaritan, unlike a random victim, will not slam down the telephone; also, a Samaritan centre is manned twenty-four hours a day, and by a large proportion of women. In point of fact, once a volunteer is satisfied that a caller is intent only on trying to sustain a conversation with a woman long enough to masturbate and then to ring off she is nowadays at liberty to terminate the call after explaining that she is not there to be used in that way, yet leaving the door open for the caller to ring back or visit the centre if he really wishes to discuss his situation.

One director in the Eastern Region says: 'It is mostly the women who have to cope, but male volunteers have taken M-calls. I've taken many, both homosexual and heterosexual. I've got a fairly light voice, and there have been occasions when I've been mistaken for a woman. And sometimes when I say, "Do you realize that I'm a man?" the caller has rung off. But on one occasion he said, "Well, it doesn't matter." We've occasionally had women ringing up wanting to masturbate. Why not? I haven't spoken to any, but I have spoken to quite a few men.'

There is a standing joke that whenever a newly trained female volunteer takes her first call, it is always an M-call. An attractive volunteer of thirty-four, now with seven years' experience, recalls her first call, and it was a sex call 'that went on for an hour and a half. It was very explicit, and most of it was certainly an eye-opener to me!' Many of what are known as click-calls, when the emergency line is answered and someone just rings off, are potential M-callers waiting until the phone is answered by a woman. A Samaritan in Surrey remembers that at her branch, 'We had a wonderful girl, a very pretty girl from Australia, who's left us, unfortunately, and gone back to Australia. When I was being trained she gave a demonstration in the class, and she just said outright to the other Samaritan in the role-play,

"Are you masturbating?" I'm reasonably unshockable and I must say I now find it much easier to use plain language to people, but it was the kind of thing I would have found very difficult to say at that time. Now, thank goodness, we are permitted to say, "This is an emergency service and I'm afraid I can't help you but if you have a real problem you are welcome to come in and discuss it with the director," and then to ring off. If you give way to them all the time the phones are just blocked with these calls. And all they want is for you to talk until they've got what they want. Then they hang up. I think it should not be encouraged. They obviously have a problem but we're not equipped to deal with it, really. We're not experts in sexual problems and inadequate people, but you have to be frightfully careful that somebody hasn't got a real problem.

'I had a chap who rang me three times. He would take twenty minutes to get talking, and his story was that he was having incest with his mother, and it was usually pretty much the same story; his mother had come back from the pub, and it had always started that day or the day before, and then I discovered he'd been calling quite three months before, and then he started describing what was happening and he was thoroughly enjoying himself. And I suddenly realized he was having himself a fine old time. It was basically a sex call. Some of them are very clever, they've worked out their story. I haven't had nearly so many of these calls lately, but when I first joined there seemed to be an awful lot of them, and I found that you started being cautious. Instead of listening really sympathetically you were making judgements all the time and you were being careful. You don't want to be made a fool of, although you're supposed to be prepared to be made a fool of, but you do have to acquire a kind of sixth sense, and it therefore means that if you've had two or three of these manipulative calls, when somebody serious calls you tend to be careful and cautious, which is very bad for the real caller.

'But you have to take every call as potentially serious. After a while, of course, you get to know certain voices – although one man kept changing his voice. We've had him for years. He's aggressive and there's nothing we can do for him. It's always difficult to assess if you've helped someone. Just occasionally somebody says "Thank you for listening, I feel better now," or you feel that they've let off a lot of steam, or they've cried, and you always leave the door open for them to call you back. To have someone ring who is clearly suicidal, and you don't know, when they ring off, if they are going to kill themselves, that's very distressing. That's why it's good to have somebody else there, to have a back-up, someone to talk to. My morning bath is my great time for thinking. I suddenly think in the bath, I didn't handle that one right. You can't get it right all the time, anyway.'

The difficulty in sorting out the manipulative callers unable or unwilling to achieve sexual stimulation in proximity to a real person, but intent on using a Samaritan as a voyeuristic vehicle, from the genuine caller too nervous, perhaps, to articulate at first the matter he really wants to talk about, lies at the core of 'TM Procedure'. A branch in Wales has been told that 'some indicators to help you to do this' include whether the caller expresses strong interest in the Samaritan's personality, in the colour of her eyes or her underwear, whether he speaks of his sexual problems in graphic detail, and in particular whether he tries to explore the Samaritan's own sexuality. Talk of fetishes, like spanking, and fantasies (about 'the woman upstairs') are all regarded as clear indications that the caller will soon lose interest if an offer of real help is extended; he has no desire to shed his voyeuristic impulses, and the volunteers are warned that 'by providing him with a telephone prostitute (i.e. you) you are doing nothing for his isolation. We merely satisfy temporarily a symptom of the problem, while at the same time reinforcing the need for inadequate relief.' But in terminating a call with such a person, the branch members are reminded never to be angry, sarcastic, clever or indulgent: 'These are totally inappropriate responses to any Samaritan call.'

In 1973, an experiment was launched, at the central London branch, and taken up for a time in a number of other branches, to see if in fact positive assistance could usefully be offered to men initially wanting to masturbate on the telephone. In order to carry it out, female volunteers were required to engage in prolonged conversation with M-callers. The result of this was a composite Samaritan called Brenda, in reality a group of ladies all using one pseudonym, to whom certain M-callers (those believed capable of benefiting from befriending) were transferred. Not surprisingly, although less widely applied in the movement today, Brenda's role became a controversial one, both inside the Samaritans and outside. As one of their number wrote in justification in the *Samaritan* when reporting on the scheme in 1978, by which time some 5,000 'Brenda calls' had been dealt with (an average of twenty a week), 'They are willing to help some clients masturbate *as part of a real befriending relationship*.' (The italics were the volunteer's own.) It was as a result of this experiment that in 1976 Chad Varah wrote his booklet, *Telephone Masturbators And How to Befriend Them*. Opposition to dealing with Brenda calls in other branches came not entirely from hang-ups or over anxiety, Dr Varah wrote, but mostly from imagining that all Brenda callers were tarred with the same brush, 'that they are people who haven't a real problem at all but are just doing it for kicks.'

Until recently, although the numbers have since declined, half a dozen branches ran a Brenda scheme, all based on principles originally laid down by the central London branch, although in Birmingham, for instance, the lady is known as Sandra. A very attractive, single Samaritan in her thirties, with four years' experience as a Brenda volunteer, explains how the system operates in her branch, and how she copes, as a Samaritan, with calls from men on whom she would slam down the telephone if they rang her at home:

'Originally it was really a way of identifying sex calls, when the branch was getting about 250 to 300 a week, and they were tying up the emergency lines. And it was found they weren't in fact 300 individual callers, just a few who were ringing in with different names, some of them several times a day.

'The Brenda system has changed quite dramatically since it

was started. Nowadays we befriend one type of caller, and one type of caller only, or one type of problem , if you want to put it that way – addictive telephone masturbators. And addictive is the operative word. The caller we befriend is not someone who might make obscene phone calls a few times, over perhaps a few months, because he got some sort of pleasure out of it. They are men who are actually addicted; it is their only form of sexual gratification. And a person selected for befriending must actually perceive this addiction as a problem, and want to do something about stopping it. In other words, he is chosen because he will respond to befriending. Somebody who rings up and asks direct questions, about the colour of your knickers, or something of that sort, and will not move on from that topic, hangs up if he's not getting what he wants, because obviously we don't respond to questions like that.

'It's not only the Samaritans who get calls from men wanting sexual gratification with a woman they've never even seen. If you ask anybody who runs a telephone service of any sort, they will tell you they get their fair share of obscene telephone calls. Telephone operators get them all the time, apparently. Very often there is a difficulty in relating to women, and therefore it is less threatening to relate to an unknown voice than to a physical presence standing next to you. The caller suitable for befriending by Brenda will actually move away from the topic of knickers and start talking about his feelings. He may begin to talk about the fact that he hasn't got a girlfriend, that he's very lonely, that he lives alone and feels depressed about this. By talking about these sorts of feelings you are not denying him the opportunity to talk about his feelings about sexuality at all, but he will be a candidate for befriending because he is able to respond to what the Samaritans have to offer. It may take him some time to reach this stage. He may ask what colour your knickers are and hang up and ring up and ring up, and it might be six months later that he begins to respond to befriending. The volunteer would then say something like, "I can see that this is worrying you. We have a volunteer called Brenda, who understands this problem, who may be able to offer more support. Would you like to contact her?" You then explain when she is on duty.

'In my branch one of the Brenda team is on duty four to six hours a week. At present we have eight Brendas, doing a two-hour duty once a fortnight. This is a commitment in addition to their normal duties. A leader may recognize in a volunteer that they are particularly helpful with telephone masturbators and suggest they might consider joining the Brenda scheme. We work very closely together and hold regular meetings. We are befriending approximately thirty to forty men at present, but they're not all ringing currently. Probably a dozen ring on a regular basis. If we decide that a caller is befriendable by Brenda we will give him a telephone number, tell him when we're here, and explain that there is more than one Brenda but that we all work together in a team. So every time he rings he doesn't have to start a fresh conversation. He starts from where he left off, so it's on-going befriending. We keep notes, and he knows that.

'On the whole, a Brenda caller is in his twenties and single. Very many have never had a successful sexual relationship, and certainly at the time of befriending are unable to have a sexual relationship. Success is difficult to measure. As with the majority of Samaritan callers, usually they stop ringing, and one hopes that when a regular caller stops ringing it's because the situation in their life has changed for the better and they don't need us any more. Very, very occasionally someone will actually say, "Thanks, I feel better. Goodbye." But very occasionally. Some tail off in a way, remaining in contact, but although they stop ringing Brenda they go into face-to-face befriending in the centre on a regular basis. The aim with Brenda is quite tough. It is to get the men to stop making obscene telephone calls to anyone. The first stage is actually to contain the addiction, which means that we may allow them to masturbate. Not necessarily. But we may. It's for a limited time, and with conditions. But it's not just a case of sitting there, listening to someone masturbating. It's a very controlled and structured on-going befriending situation, with definite aims and periods set, and if those goals aren't reached, the contract, if you like, begins to change. The idea, I suppose, is that if it is an addiction then it's like alcoholism, you can't make anybody stop. That person has got to reach the point of controlling the addiction themselves. Some go cold turkey, and some wean themselves off it. We work on the assumption that they want to be weaned off the addiction. If after a period of time it appeared there was no change, the situation would be reassessed. It's always a two-way thing. We never make decisions without involving the caller. And after six months they *must* come and visit the centre, and have a face-to-face interview with a leader. People get emotive over the whole issue because I suspect – in fact, I know – that a lot of people are not aware of the structure of it. Because the majority of volunteers get "what colour are your knickers?" calls they think we actually sit and respond to that. And we don't. If the caller needs to masturbate on the telephone, what we are doing is saying, "If you can't stop it, fine, but you do it with our knowledge, so you will not be deceiving us. You're not actually lying. If you are unable not to, it must be on our terms." The aim, if somebody does masturbate on the telephone, is to restrain their fantasy within a loving relationship. We would not listen to a lot of obscenity. We would not allow that. They are addicted to telephone masturbating because they cannot form relationships, and not only with women. With men as well. They tend to be quite lacking in the skills of relationships. The aim, within the fantasy, is for them to relate to a woman as a human being with feelings. We ask him to set a scene, and it has to be normal; no whips. And we ask, "What does she look like?" that sort of thing. And the only help we would give, if help is the right word, is simply to interject with things like, "How does she feel? Does she like you?" As a real person, we are aiding a fantasy within a loving relationship. Our aim is to help them to see women as whole human beings with feelings, not as objects to relieve your feelings on but as someone whose feelings and thoughts have to be accommodated.

'Very often these men had unhappiness in their childhood. Often their parents were divorced during their adolescence.

They lack what they perceive as love from their mother. They have feelings of rejection. Very many are suicidal, and many have attempted suicide. Most, if not all, suffer from depression, whether they are suicidal or not. Many are unemployed as well, which makes their isolation even stronger. They have very few friends. Maybe they've had a bad sexual experience. Many haven't had a sexual experience at all. Some simply cannot masturbate alone, so that their addiction to telephone masturbating is actually their only form of sexual release.[6] Sometimes part of what we do, in fact, is to help them find their imagination, to learn to fantasize. In the beginning they are unable to create images in their own head. We would never ever take on as a Brenda caller someone who was in a successful sexual relationship, because telephone masturbating for them would be an extra.

'Some of our Brenda volunteers are married, and their husbands know what they are doing, and accept it. I know of one Brenda volunteer who was a virgin, and actually had had no sexual experience herself. But that doesn't preclude befriending telephone masturbators because you may not have been bereaved yourself but that doesn't mean you can't befriend someone who has. I think if there was difficulty in a relationship, the volunteer wouldn't volunteer. Apart from the usual qualities any Samaritan requires, in a Brenda there needs to be a certain amount of toughness, and a certain amount of directness, because one way in which Brenda befriending is different from normal Samaritan befriending is that we are directive. We do actually make boundaries and set goals, and we try to keep within them with the caller. An ability to stick to the contract with the caller is very important because, like all people who are desperate, Brenda callers can be very persuasive in their desperation. It's important not to give into that persuasiveness. You couldn't do the job unless you had an empathy for the predicament of the man. But it's funny, if I get an

[6] For a sympathetic exposition of masturbation as a component of human sexual experience the reader is referred to chapter four of *The Psychology of Sex* by Oswald Schwarz (Penguin, 1949).

obscene phone call at home, my reaction is as me and I put the phone down, but in the centre I have my Samaritan hat on, and in a way I'm role-playing. A Brenda volunteer couldn't do it unless she recognized the distress created by the problem.

'I'm sure every woman in the country has had an obscene phone call. If men were honest, and you took a survey, you'd find that almost every man at some point in their life has done it once, even if it was just to see what it was like. Very few men get addicted. It's the addiction which is the peg to hang the coat on. There are always other problems. It's never only a sexual problem. Conversations that we have are very rarely sexual conversations. It's very much about their feelings of despair, distress, suicide, loneliness and fear. It's no different, in a way, from the befriending we normally do except that the caller may at some point need to masturbate during the telephone call. We know all about it before they do it. They don't masturbate without actually saying that that's what they're going to do. That's part of the contract. We expect honesty, and in return we're honest with them. If we have doubts we will express them. That's what I mean when I say we are very much more directive, and we may actually say, "I don't think you're being honest, and therefore I don't think this befriending is at all helpful." And if they wanted to masturbate on their own terms – perhaps, say, by having fantasies about bondage or something – we would just say, "I'm not prepared to be here while that goes on, I find it offensive and unpleasant." It would not be within the context of a loving relationship, because although some successful relations depend on bondage, in this case there would be no actual woman in front of them. They would not be relating to another human being, just a bit of anatomy, and they would just be talking about leather or rubber or whatever. All we would be doing, I feel, is perpetuating something that is not going to help them to form a relationship.

'You can't join the Samaritans and two months later become a Brenda. You need to have been a Samaritan at least a year. But the length of training is extremely flexible. A new volunteer will be on duty with an experienced Brenda for just as long as she feels she needs support. Our Brendas range in age from their sixties downwards. They are simply women able to empathize with the problem. It has nothing to do with age or type or whether you're married or single. We have had at least one caller who got married. But not to a Brenda! It is certainly a controversial issue. Some professional sex therapists believe it's unhelpful actually to allow somebody to masturbate. Others believe that in a controlled, weaning-off process it is actually helpful. So the professionals are divided about it, and about the handling of sex calls in general. It is such an emotive subject. The Samaritans put themselves on the line over the two most controversial issues that we have in life, death and sex, and we all have our own hang-ups and concerns about both subjects. Then we actually fling ourselves up front, which means we're bound to have our differences. Death and sex create the most hang-ups in the most people, so by definition they are very emotive subjects. Quite frankly, I don't know how positive the results are, how beneficial it all is, but in a way I think that's quite healthy, because it means at least I have no axe to grind.'

There is another type of caller other than the 'sex caller' who for many years has been a source of contention within the movement – the third-party caller, someone who telephones the Samaritans to say, perhaps, that they are worried because a neighbour seems very depressed, or has been talking of committing suicide. The problem about acting on a third-party call is the possibility that the caller is only trying to make trouble, or is a natural busybody. In 1974, the Lincoln branch received a telephone call from a hotel manager about a guest he was worried about; a volunteer went round, found the guest had taken barbiturates, and arranged for him to be admitted to hospital, where he recovered, and there now seems to be a fairly standard procedure that is followed in most branches. The caller is asked for their name and telephone number, and for that of the person they are telephoning about, and where there definitely seems to be a risk of suicide, the volunteer will contact the person at risk provided the caller allows their name to be used by way of introduction. The caller is also asked to advise his neighbour that the Samaritans will be ringing, so that a call from the centre does not come as a complete surprise. 'The rules are a bit hazy,' one leader confessed. 'The other day a woman telephoned to say she was very concerned about her neighbour, whose wife had died about three months previously. She said she had tried to befriend him in her own way but that he was becoming more and more introverted, and she had been in to see him that evening and had found him with a bottle of aspirin and a bottle of whisky. She had talked to him, but she didn't really know where to go from there, and so she rang the Samaritans to see if we could do anything.

'An important point to remember is that the woman who rang us needed support while we were making up our minds what to do about her neighbour. In any situation like that, the leader is always contacted. And we always say to the caller, "I don't know if we can take action, we'll see, but we will come back to you and let you know whether we are doing anything or not. And we always ask if we can use their name. Obviously we prefer to, because it's not very nice to arrive at somebody's front door and say, "Somebody tells us that . . ." If they won't let us use their name, we might just say, "A neighbour is worried about you." What we never do is pass on messages.'

There is one potential category of caller who has always been less than enthusiastic about contacting the Samaritans – always assuming they have any need to do so; the non-European immigrant and their British descendants. An article in the *Samaritan* in 1977 asked why this is so. It is still being asked, and no certain answers have been supplied, even by branches in towns where the non-European ethnic communities have expanded rapidly, in some cases overtaking in numbers the indigenous British. Asians, Africans and West Indians are in fact unlikely to respond to the sort of publicity currently emanating from the Samaritans, if indeed they ever encounter it; and they are unlikely, for historical reasons, to entertain any perception of white English people as altruistic helpers. As immigration policies of successive governments have consistently failed to make provision for any kind of cultural assimilation, it seems inevitable that for emotional support in times of stress, members of immigrant populations will continue to turn not to the Samaritans but to one another.

·6·
BEFRIENDING IN THE OPEN

A cynic searching for a common denominator among Samaritan centres might conclude, such is the degree of independence and diversity they display, that their need to be self-financing is all they share. They exist in as many different environmental situations as can be found throughout the length and breadth of the British Isles, and the key to their effectiveness lies in their ability to blend in with the background of local people likely to call in person. Very few seem remotely ostentatious; many give an almost claustrophobic impression of cramped and slightly chaotic conditions. Some seem constructed entirely of staircases. Volunteers with initiative furnish the waiting rooms with cheerful posters and *Country Life*; those without create a funeral parlour atmosphere with plastic flowers. The majority of Samaritan centres are to be found in former private houses, which usually convert quite easily, for the basic ingredients of any centre are a minimum of two interview rooms, an operations room where volunteers man the telephones, an office and a kitchen. The operations room should, but does not always, contain a library, funded by the branch itself. Very unusually, Weybridge boasts a custom-built centre, originally opened in 1969 on land loaned free of charge and then repossessed, so that twelve years later the branch had to start hunting for a suitable site for premises all over again. Eventually a new centre was erected at a cost of £26,000, consisting of two small interview rooms, a small operations room, a large office and a kitchen.

The volunteers regard the place as 'comfortable, warm, and tastefully furnished and decorated.' Modest and appropriate, the building may look a bit like a scout hut, but there can have been few suitable existing buildings available at the time for the price, and clearly it was functional from the start.

Another method of acquiring rather grander premises than the average two-storey terrace house is for a centre, where such facilities exist, to apply for a grant from the Urban Programme, intended 'to relieve the stress of Inner Urban Deprivation'.[1] Today, the Sunderland branch enjoys a beautifully renovated and elegant early nineteenth century house because they took the plunge, and a considerable risk, in applying for a grant, and the result is a centre that would leave volunteers from central London, used to knocking on broom cupboard doors to find a square inch of privacy, gasping with amazement. Sunderland began 'with £1,000 to our name' and received a grant of £80,000. But as the director at the time humorously points out, 'You must be prepared to gamble. It is much more likely that help will appear if you are in debt than if you are timorously considering your project. A bank must be persuaded to offer a loan to launch the scheme while you are juggling with your Urban Aid application. As we all know, banks don't want to lend you money unless you can prove that you don't need it, and the only security you will have is the building, which you must be prepared to sell if your plans go awry. If you can find a donor to pay your bank interest for a year you will have a breathing space. This was our position in early 1983.'

Under the scheme, capital grants are allocated for purchase, repair and equipment, and revenue grants exist to meet increased running costs, which may include telephones. On top of their £80,000 capital grant, Sunderland received a revenue grant of £5,000 for four years. Sunderland did well, and the results are a reception area callers can walk straight into without having to hang around outside the door, and a ray that detects

[1] At the time of writing, some thirty authorities were operating an Urban Programme.

their presence and rings a bell upstairs. Here the rooms are strikingly cool and welcoming, with plenty of space for training new volunteers and holding branch meetings. But as their former director explains, 'It is essential to present a very good case which reflects the Urban Programme's aims of relieving stress within the deprived area. It's quite clear we relieve social services of a great deal of work. People who come to us may also need their help, but for others it is quite sufficient to come to us. And if we didn't operate the service that we do, social services couldn't possibly cope. We also applied to the metropolitan council for a grant for a chair-lift, so that disabled volunteers could get to the first floor for duties and to the basement for training. In a town with an urban scheme there is usually an official at the civic centre whose job it is to advise you how to put forward your case.'

The size of accommodation needed (but not always obtained), the numbers of volunteers milling about and the general ambience of a centre will to a large extent reflect the size and nature of the area it is designed to serve. When the Shetland branch opened in 1985, it did so with just twenty-six volunteers; the branch covers seventeen islands and a population of 22,500, traditionally employed in crofting, fishing and knitting. One of the Shetlands' claims to fame is a profusion of no less than 750 species of wild flowers. 'It might be difficult to imagine that a place like this would need the services of Samaritans,' said one of the first volunteers. 'But behind this beauty lie problems of all descriptions, some brought about by the isolation of the islands. Many problems came with the oil boom at Sullom Voe Oil Terminal, the largest in Europe, and the very fact that it is a close-knit community can in itself create its own special problems. The main problems seem to be alcoholism, depression and loneliness.'

At the other end of the social spectrum from the Shetlands lies the first branch ever founded, now known as central London, where, with 380 volunteers, a rota secretary has to be employed full-time to ensure that, if necessary, ten telephones could be manned day and night and enough volunteers still remain available to interview an erratic stream of callers. The branch estimates that thirty-seven per cent of all callers are suicidal. They depend to a large extent on volunteers who are nurses and actors, and therefore liable to have free time during the day, always the most difficult period to cover in any branch. Because of the itinerant nature of London's population, its central branch attracts between 150 and 200 callers every year with nowhere to sleep at night except on Samaritan premises. Like all centres, London receives its share of regular callers; it also takes two calls every hour from people who have never contacted them before, a total of 13,000 new callers a year out of an annual tally of 80,000 incidents. Obviously not every telephone is ringing all the time; during the day six calls could be in progress simultaneously, and at night perhaps eight or nine. London may well be the most hectic centre but there are others not far behind; Birmingham, for instance, takes care of around 11,000 new callers every year out of a total of 40,000 calls, and Manchester deals with approximately 17,500 first-time calls out of a total of over 43,000.

The constant flux in London's population affects not just the incessant through-flow of callers but the stable rota of volunteers, many of whom move away because of a change of job, and almost all of whom leave London on retirement. The current director in Bournemouth was once a volunteer in London. Between 400 and 500 potential new Samaritans volunteer in London every year, and about 100 are taken on. On a day-to-day basis, the centre is run by a team of twenty-four leaders, who inevitably carry a larger than average load of responsibility for administration; the full-time director, who believes that because of the ceaseless change-over of personnel in the centre there is a great advantage in having at least one permanent figure around, undertakes no administration at all but keeps a watching brief on every aspect of training and befriending. In recent years, London has become a far more violent city than it used to be, and inevitably some of this violence has overflowed into the Samaritan premises, although in fact any Samaritan centre has always been vulnerable to violence, for people with dependency needs which the Samaritans are unable to meet are always liable to turn their aggression on to people they see as failed benefactors. Two men started smashing up St Stephen Walbrook not long after it had first opened its doors to Samaritan callers, and the staff on duty felt obliged to act against their principles and call in the police for protection. There is no recorded case of a suicide actually being committed on Samaritan premises, but distressed callers seeking attention, sympathy or help may well overdose and then pass out in a centre, an occasion that calls for considerable discretion; the last thing the Samaritans want are wailing police or ambulance sirens outside their door. John Eldrid says he has been attacked about five times in thirty years. 'There is a problem,' he says, 'because the Samaritans don't want to keep ringing the police, so we are pretty strict about admitting callers we regard as manipulative and difficult. Volunteers are told that if someone has been barred, then they are barred, and if they let that person in or don't obey instructions they are probably out as well. We bar someone if we feel they are not befriendable.' The central London branch has a long history of befriending, for resources in the capital in terms of psychiatric consultants, clinical psychologists and psychotherapists to whom callers can readily be referred exist in greater profusion than elsewhere. At least 300 callers are being befriended by central London at any time.

The central London branch covers Camden, the City of London, Hackney, Islington, Kensington & Chelsea, Tower Hamlets and Westminster, encompassing a population of about 990,000. But it is practically impossible to arrive at any 'success rate' to be deduced from an apparent recent reduction in the suicide rate in London in relation to an enormous expenditure of time, energy and money, partly because the statistics relating to the capital's population are so confused. In the decade between 1971 and 1981, the overall population of London decreased by 234,900 and the numbers of people living in the City of London, Kensington & Chelsea and Westminster have continued to fall, whereas some recent growth in population in the boroughs of Camden, Hackney, Islington and Tower

Hamlets has been recorded. It has to be remembered too that non-residential workers who enter the area by day and leave by night help to make population statistics for London socially meaningless; non-residential workers may well spend a third of their life in the area without qualifying as residents. But for what it is worth, there were 146 suicides recorded in central London in 1980 and 124 in 1983.

As you enter the railway station an advertisment on a hoarding tells you the town offers a warm welcome to industry, and there follows an invitation to telephone for information. The hoarding is attached to a derelict building without a single window intact. The Samaritan centre looked after 10,982 callers last year, and in one month their numbers of volunteers have risen from ninety-six to 120, but they say they could do with 150. These are figures the director, a Samaritan for seventeen years, who has lived for nearly as long with another man, reels off without a pause for thought. His welcome is warm and friendly. The reason they need yet more volunteers? 'Our callers are up 2,200 on last year. The economic climate has something to do with it, but sex problems are on the increase. Women are now more aggressive, and men can't cope so well.' The branch was founded nineteen years ago. 'It's become a sausage machine,' the director says. 'This is a very transient town. Sixty per cent of our volunteers are not even locals. And you have to live here a long time to be accepted.'

A blind piano tuner, who has been a Samaritan for eleven years, arrives to meet a young man he is befriending, a bisexual fantasist with an identity crisis, so lonely and desperate for affection that he has even tried to have an affair with his blind befriender. 'The situation got completely out of hand!' says the volunteer, who takes his caller upstairs to the attic, the only unoccupied space available, weaving his way with confidence through an obstacle course of tables and chairs. In the operations room, it is Evelyn's first day on duty. She is a shop manager with Finefare, married to a professional footballer, with two young children. They came to the town because her husband got a transfer, liked it and decided to stay. 'I wasn't frightened when I came in this morning,' she says, 'but I *was* rather apprehensive.' She had spent the first half of her first shift familiarizing herself with paperwork, and listening in while another volunteer dealt with a phone call. Suddenly the phone rang again, and the volunteer told her to answer it. Sure enough, at 11.30 in the morning she had a sex caller on the line. She said afterwards, 'I ignored his request to talk about sex and tried to turn the problem back on to the caller. He got a bit fed up and put the phone down.' The director said he thought Evelyn had dealt with the call beautifully. 'She sounded very warm and calm.'

In a university city, with its statutory Dunn & Co, its Pizzaland, empty icecream cornets blowing down the street and its dingy pubs run by disinterested young bartenders and dispossessed Irish landladies, the Samaritan centre lies closer to the bus and railway stations than the city centre, in a poky house off a one-way system, where all is muddle, and even the volunteer who opened the door had forgotten that her regional representative was calling. The branch costs £10,000 a year to run, £1 for every caller, one-tenth of whom last year put through a silent call. Family problems led the field in the list of reasons prompting calls, with depression running second and unemployment at the bottom of the list, although unemployment in the area is high. The regional representative had said he thought this was rather an inward-looking branch, not much involved with matters outside their own region. 'This is partly because they are short of volunteers,' he explained, 'and they are very much concerned with manning their rota, so they never get around to offering a paper at a conference, or putting on a workshop somewhere. I also think some branches just tend to imagine that if they're doing what they can for their own callers, they don't really need to get involved with the movement in a wider sense, and it's a great pity if they think that. You can learn so much by becoming involved at an inter-regional level. If a branch does cut itself off and become inward-looking it impoverishes the region as well as the branch. You've got to be aware of how each unit fits into the whole.'

In the operations room, furnished with a battered sofa and looking pretty grubby, one of the volunteers on duty, a middle-aged lady with unkempt hair and slacks she might have been better advised not to wear, was sorting through a stack of record cards. Suddenly she clasped her hand to her mouth to half-stifle a scream. 'Oh, my God, he *did* die!' Later, after she had put her arm round her colleague to comfort her, a much younger volunteer, of twenty-two, explained what had happened. 'It was someone she had been out to visit on an emergency. She'd talked to him a couple of times afterwards, and she thought he was OK, she thought she'd pulled him through. But he's died. We're not sure whether he had a heart attack or committed suicide. So she's sort of half blaming herself. It was an unfortunate way for her to find out. But this does tend to happen. I suppose ideally a leader or someone should have telephoned her at home and told her the man had died, rather than let her come on duty and find out like that. We try to keep in touch with each other and keep tabs on cases, but you can't know every single thing that happens immediately, we haven't got that close a communication.'

Fifty-nine calls a day are being taken at a branch in the North-West, by a membership of 120. A volunteer is on the telephone, in a cubicle; the second telephone is off the hook, because the only other volunteer on duty is interviewing someone. There is provision for a third line, but no purpose in installing it when even two telephones cannot always be covered. Downstairs, a preparation class is in progress. An experienced volunteer is telling a trainee, apprehensive about violence, that she once went to the aid of a woman being assaulted by her husband, and was told by the woman to mind her own business. Back in the duty room, the telephone rings again. A mountainous lady, her face half hidden by enormous glasses, heaves herself out of a chair to answer it. Quickly she replaces the receiver and sits down at a table to write her report.

'He just said something rude, and rang off,' she explains. 'It won't surprise me if he rings back.' Without support from their local borough and a couple of trust funds, who contributed, between them, £6,500, the branch would have been hard pressed last year to raise enough money to keep going. A Catholic Women's League coffee morning produced a sprightly £105.40, and a rotary club a surprising £100, but a local Business and Professional Women's Club only managed to spare £3.

At the other end of England, the Samaritans function in a tiny compact house tucked away in a neat street near the station, the bus routes and the shopping centre. Trains rattle past the windows, and in summer they bring day trippers longing for a sight of the sea. The branch paid off their mortage five years ago, on premises that look as if they might once have belonged to a veterinary surgeon, or perhaps a boot mender. The town itself sprawls along the coast, a combination of imposing Victorian villas and dull, peeling boarding-houses painted canary-yellow, which merge into a modern glass and concrete shopping jungle and a seafront given over to amusement arcades, children's empty playgrounds, listless pubs and a fish restaurant charging exorbitant prices. When the tide goes out the sea becomes a memory on the horizon. One grandiloquent hotel clings to the edge of a cliff, and old-age pensioners knit in the shelters while they wait to comment on new faces as the season gets under way. Plenty of people live here, but as so often in ugly overspill towns, one wonders why. There is nothing to go down to the Esplanade for except to get away from the shopping centre.

The Samaritan centre itself is spotlessly clean if sparsely furnished. In the kitchen at the back volunteers congregate with coffee mugs. In the operations room, a thin young married woman, with a job in the mornings so that she is free for afternoon shifts, waits nervously for the phone to ring. On the wall hangs a map of the town, with the homes of all the volunteers marked with pins and categorized by gender. The volunteer is still on probation. Her first call had been from a woman with a rubber fetish. 'It's not at all what I thought it would be like,' she says. 'Better, really.' How had she coped with the rubber lady? 'Terrible!' The branch is in the process of changing over directors. The director-designate, a quietly spoken, serious woman of fifty, smokes heavily. She has only been a Samaritan five years, and became a leader after only one. 'It's daunting, isn't it?' she keeps reminding herself. She and the volunteer who first interviewed her swap reminiscences. 'She was lovely', the new director recalls. 'I was terribly nervous and she really put me at my ease.' The out-going director recalls his interview. He was twenty-five at the time, and he says the interview lasted five minutes. 'Not very good,' he comments. 'My interviews last at least an hour.' There seems to be little activity, but days are recalled when visitors have been sitting on the stairs. The branch has 106 volunteers and last year they dealt with 12,000 calls. They are finding it increasingly difficult to cover afternoon shifts, despite so many people being out of work – not that people out of work are necessarily best qualified to be Samaritans. 'I suppose,' says the director, 'the unemployed are just too dispirited. And don't forget, there are so many more voluntary agencies now than there were fifteen years ago, all competing for unpaid help, and we require a very full commitment.'

The idea that all Samaritan activity, apart from controlled befriending, is confined to the centres is rapidly becoming an old-fashioned one. Tentative experiments with broadcasting have been carried out in one branch, invited by their local radio station to supply a volunteer to join a clergyman and a doctor on a Sunday evening phone-in. 'I have mixed feelings about the programme,' one of the leaders confessed, 'but our director is terrific. The problem is, you are more or less forced to give some sort of advice or comment, but Bill is very good at making comments which are not actually constructive advice. He will throw the question or problem back to the person who rings in, offering food for thought, and leaves the solid advice to the other people on the panel. But you have to say something quickly on the air, you can't play for time. The programme does act as free publicity for us, and we know that people who have rung into the programme have become callers, so in that way it works very well.' At a national level, in 1984 the Samaritans were invited to take part in Christmas Line, a co-operative venture run by Capital Radio, London Weekend Television and Thames Television with a view to filling the gap in emergency services caused by a general closing down of facilities over the Christmas period. The Samaritans provided three volunteers for each shift.

But co-operation in agony radio shows is small fry by comparison with the rapidly accelerating scale of what is now known as 'befriending in the open', a major departure which began as a public relations exercise carried out on market squares and has spread to hospitals and prisons. Many Samaritans, impatient with what they regard as the excessive stress laid upon anonymity when befriending on the telephone, see this new development in technique as a blueprint for the future. 'I love our centre', a volunteer from King's Lynn wrote in the *Samaritan* in 1985. 'It's warm, inviting, situated in just the right part of town. We have about 10,000 contacts a year. The population we serve is around 222,000. The branch has a marvellous group of friends. We need £10,000 a year. The suicide rate here has been falling. It sounds all right – well, comfortable, anyway. I had this feeling, though, niggling away; should we not be reaching out and working where it's actually happening?' In co-operation with the area social services officer, the branch, with twenty-six per cent of its callers aged under twenty, is now involved in a project called the Samaritan Youth Counselling Support Group.

The branch involved with their local radio station is also 'working where it's actually happening', both in prison and in hospital. 'For many years we've been giving talks in the local women's prison,' a deputy director explained. 'We used to meet the pre-release group in the youth detention centre, and then we suggested to the governor the possibility of befriending on a one-to-one basis, because the girls couldn't really talk when they were in a group. We always had to have a prison warder with us, and it was very difficult. A year ago the governor agreed, so we selected some pretty experienced volunteers, and I had to send details of their names and addresses and where they were born. If a girl feels that she wants to talk to a Samaritan she has to apply to the probation service, and I think at first this put the girls off, because they felt it might affect their parole. But once the first girl had actually done it and applied and realized it was totally confidential her befriending went on for several months, and she felt so much better afterwards that she spread the word, and I think that so far we've had about half a dozen. It's a slow trickle, but the ones we've had very much needed to talk. We were quite impressed because we were given a room to ourselves. The only problem came when the prison was having a blitz on drugs. We have to be very careful. We're not allowed to take anything out. We're not allowed to post letters or anything like that. Sometimes volunteers want to send a card, which is all right, but we have to be very careful that we stick to prison rules.

'Problems in prison are very much the same as outside. Depression is the most obvious problem, and the girls can be suicidal. They suffer from isolation and loneliness and the feeling there is no one they can talk to. And of course they have family problems. A lot of girls have left children behind. The youngest we have befriended was a fifteen-year-old, in for robbery with violence. Some of them, at fourteen and fifteen, have been living rough for a couple of years. They've no stable background at all. It helps them to be able to talk about the whole experience of the crime. I think they've become more honest as the befriending's gone on. They start off being very guarded, and quite quickly realize it doesn't matter to a Samaritan, you can say what you like, so you might just as well tell the truth. But you have to gain their trust first. You can't actually condone what sometimes they are telling you they've done: that would be dishonest on our part. You just try to take a very objective approach. We concentrate on their feelings more than on the actual crime they've committed.'

The major pioneering work of befriending in prison has been carried out in a former market town, now an ever-expanding multi-racial industrial zone, which contains, almost exactly opposite the Samaritan centre, the grim redbrick county gaol. A volunteer who works in local government, joined the Samaritans at the age of twenty and became director of his branch when he was twenty-four, explains the philosophy behind his activities on the other side of the wall.

'Although fifteen suicides a year are reported in prisons, we believe there are many more that are not reported.[2] We hear from other prisoners, "Oh, did you know, so-and-so topped himself last night?" And nothing appears in the press or in any reports. It's often put down to an accident or an accidental overdose.

'I was director when we first made contact with the prison. Part of my duties, I thought, was to make more contact with the community. We were still very much an enclosed sort of branch, waiting for people to come to us, and I thought it was time to start getting into the community and getting known. So I made a direct approach to the governor, and that's how it started. I've personally been inside the prison about a dozen times. It is reportedly the most overcrowded prison in the country, with three men to every cell, and about one hour's exercise a day – and not even that if there's a prison dispute on, which seems to be a fairly regular occurrence, with some sort of work-to-rule or industrial action, or there's a security clamp-down. There's always a problem of some sort.

'We don't get much feedback from the staff. The educational department, who are slightly separate, are more open in their feelings than the warders, and they feel frustrated at having their activities curtailed. Prisoners complain about the short amount of recreational time. Conditions are bad. They don't

[2] According to a Home Office working group on suicide prevention which reported in 1986, the risk of suicide in prison was four times greater than the rate outside.

have much opportunity to talk problems over with people. Even though there are people around, there is no privacy. Ours is a transit prison, and holds prisoners on short sentences. The longest they are there is from nine to twelve months. They have a remand centre as well. So whenever we go in we see a new set of faces.

'The governor was very enthusiastic, but he said everything would really depend on his education officer. We prefer working under the education department to the probation service. The probation service wanted us to liaise with them over individuals, which we were not happy to do. We have to make do with a classroom, so if we get a dozen prisoners, which is all we can manage at one time, then we see them as a group, identify those who need individual attention, and then sort of pluck them out somehow or other so that the next week when we go in we have already allocated a volunteer to a prisoner. The group of volunteers comes to about twelve as well. We always have to wait to be called, but we chase up the invitations. Linked to the education department we're also linked to school terms, and we have to finish at a certain time, and so we try to see individual prisoners on visiting orders, and also correspond with them. That way we continue the contact without actually going in on a formal basis. We go in as a visitor, basically.

'We are on our third governor in three years. The present one is more accessible in the sense that he encourages officials to come to the centre to hear what our role is, so they are not suspicious of our motives. And since this new governor took over they have been more ready to come out and talk to us. The education department, prison visitors, the probation service and the chaplains have all come to the centre to discuss various ways we can improve liaison. But last year we were promised better facilities and nothing has materialized.

'The problems we deal with range from finance and housing to personal relationships, with wife, girlfriend or boyfriend. Relationships often deteriorate while men are in prison and they can't get out to deal with them. Most of those we talk to have a drug addiction problem, and they worry about getting back on to drugs when they leave prison. There's not much concern about going back to crime because they all say they won't. What worries them more are the chances of getting a job when they have a record.'

Eight days after the Samaritan gave this interview, a thirty-seven-year-old burglar, given a seven-year sentence at the Crown Court, was discovered hanged at the prison. He had been found with jewellery valued at £1,000 and had asked for 164 offences to be considered. As his death was reported in *The Times*, presumably it will constitute part of the official statistics on suicides in prison in 1986.

Perhaps the most impressive experiment in befriending in the open has been carried out at Addenbrookes Hospital, Cambridge, where the consultant in the accident and emergency unit conducted a discussion about its origins and effects with the director of the Cambridge Samaritans, who says her membership is currently down to 99 – 'lower than it's ever been since I've been here, and that's nine years'. They really need 160 members. A team of eight volunteers visit the accident and emergency unit, visiting in pairs for three hours once a week.

Director: It's a very token appearance. We had gained some previous experience of befriending in the open from a caravan in town centres, and at fairs. There is a danger, in open befriending, of a loss of anonymity, but that's something you have to accept. If you were paranoid about anonymity there wouldn't be any befriending in the open at all. When we visit the hospital we wear a badge with our Christian name and 'Samaritan' on it. Last night, for example, I came on duty with one other Samaritan at half past seven. It was very busy. We usually wander around first and see what's happening. There had been a traffic accident. Two people had been involved, and they were in different areas of the department. There were a lot of children around, several with eye injuries. Most of the children had come in with parents. If you bring one child you have to bring the rest of the family, very often. I think I spoke first to a girl who was on her own. You have to be sensitive to family groups and to what is happening within that group. They may be befriending each other, they may not need you.

People who have been in a traffic accident may have given a statement to the police, and explained to the medical people where they hurt, but they haven't been able to talk about the accident. They need to do this, and we have the time, the doctors haven't. One gentleman went over his accident several times, repeating, 'I don't know why it happened . . .'

Consultant: One of the problems about psychological shock is that it's very similar to grief. Sometimes there is a feeling of guilt, and they don't see it as a medical problem. They are preoccupied with insurance claims. You go through the stunned phase, where you don't accept what's happened, then there is the anger phase, then there is the sorrow or depressed phase, then there is the recovery. Days two and three after an accident are much worse than day one, both physically and mentally. So for someone who may be on an emotional high, having survived an accident, to meet up with a Samaritan here may prove very valuable in the days ahead, when he or she is feeling depressed and suffering severe reaction.

Director: People need to talk after a visit to a hospital for all sorts of reasons. Last week we had a child brought in, who had fallen from a window. The whole family came in. They were all obviously very upset. The child came in still just about alive, and a nurse asked one of the Samaritans on duty to take tea in to the family, and she stayed with them most of the evening. The child died, and the family have stayed in touch with us, and put a thank-you in the paper, thanking the hospital staff and the Samaritans for all they did, which was very touching.

We've had several opportunities of talking with people who have attempted suicide, because not all are suffering from a drug overdose. Some have cut their arms. And we make sure they know where to come if they want to contact us again in the future. Sometimes someone is here with a minor injury, and you get to talk to them and find they have much larger emotional problems. A man who had left home and been walking the streets turned up at the unit with blisters on his feet. He was also suicidal. He had left home on the Sunday evening and he arrived here mid-evening the next Friday. He'd been walking the streets and living rough. One of his sons had been killed in a road accident last year. He had had heart by-pass surgery last November.

I had an aversion to hospitals, and when we started this experiment I thought, Crumbs, I'll never cope with it, but there isn't the pressure on you once you're here. When the sight of blood and the smell of hospitals is not connected with your own family, and when you're not expected to do anything medical, you can just be a Samaritan and do exactly what you're trained to do. The gory sights haven't affected me. I was hooked from the first night I came.

Consultant: The most impressive comment picked up by the nurses when the Samaritans first suggested coming here was when one of them said, 'We can sit and listen for two hours.' That actually had a few jaws dropping, because at times we are literally with a patient for a matter of seconds. Accident departments are geared to the management of physical injury, but the emotional after-effects of a road accident may take months to heal. I think developments over the next decade will be in dealing with psychological injury, and counselling won't be done by doctors. We are trained scientists who carry out highly sophisticated procedures to exclude serious disease, but the caring element, at present, is someone else's problem.

I am sure the Samaritans would not want to get into psychiatric assessment, but there is plenty of scope for people who will treat the psyche by being charitable, kind and caring. I see the Samaritans having a role simply because I now understand how they operate. A voluntary first-aider can be a professional by having a high standard of expertise, and the Samaritan system allows checks and controls. Until we became involved with the Samaritans we thought they were a rather nebulous group who answered telephones, and that was their own public image, because they were rather secretive about what they did. I would like to see the scheme extended. The Americans are more advanced. They now realize that you need to counsel rescue workers who work under stress. I go to about 170 traffic accidents a year, and I have never come to terms with pronouncing a child dead. I don't think in the health service we take enough note of stress. I'm very worried about the rescue services in Bradford. There is an immense psychological stress still on the police and firemen who were there.[3]

A vivid and revolting example of the type of trauma our rescue services are faced with, and so seldom helped to come to terms with, was presented by a report in *The Times* on 24 July 1986 following a crash on the M4 motorway in which a grossly overcrowded van crossed the central crash barrier, killing a total of thirteen people, four of them members of one family travelling in the opposite direction. 'Those who arrived at the scene of the crash were sickened by the sight,' two *Times* staff writers reported, and a fire officer was quoted as saying, 'The carnage was absolutely staggering. When I returned home I could not sleep and could only hear the screams of a woman who was dying by the side of the decimated van.' He said that he and his men were sickened and left numb by their experience of the accident. Of 400 police officers who attended the Bradford

[3] On 11 May 1985, fifty-six people died in a fire at the Valley Football Ground in Bradford. The Bradford branch publicized their services in a local newspaper, and one of the nurses who attended the fire telephoned to say she could not get the sound of the screams out of her head and was unable to sleep. A young policewoman, similarly affected, was immediately befriended. When the Townsend Thoresen ferry *The Herald of Free Enterprise* capsized outside Zeebrugge harbour on 6 March 1987, the Folkestone and Canterbury branches jointly set up a temporary caravan centre in Dover to befriend in the open relatives and friends of the dead and missing passengers. They were assured of the availability of continued support if this was wanted and many were given the address and telephone number of their local Samaritan branch.

football stadium fire, all were offered counselling, fifty were thought to be in need of such help, and thirty-four took up the offer; they were counselled by an occupational psychologist in Leeds. Feelings of guilt for having failed to save more lives, and for themselves surviving, appear to have been the salient feature of their continuing waking nightmare. One problem about police officers traditionally putting on a brave, macho image of indifference to suffering, and in the past declining to unburden themselves of their own true feelings, has been for them to acquire a very real hardened crust of indifference to the sufferings and anguish of other people. Another result is that 1.5 million police working days are lost on average each year through illness – in a service necessarily staffed by men and women who enjoy outstanding physical fitness.

Another branch who have taken up the challenge of befriending in their local hospital's accident centre has found both male and female volunteers equally in demand. A deputy director recalls: 'A male volunteer of sixty, on his first night in casualty, had to feed a baby and change its nappy. He was suddenly pushed into this role, so he did it, and I was relating this story to one of our female volunteers, who said, "I would give it up tomorrow if I thought I had to do that, I hate babies." On the other hand, when someone comes in who has been raped, then obviously a woman volunteer is needed.

'We are there to comfort relatives, and also just to talk to people who are waiting, and have got nothing better to do. There's nothing more boring than waiting in an accident centre. It's an excellent way of giving out information. It's very good propaganda. It gives us an opportunity to say, "Here we are, we're not just shut away in our centre, we actually come out sometimes." People with minor injuries sometimes have a long wait and they don't see emergency cases coming in by ambulance, and we can help staff by explaining to the patients why they've got to wait, and sometimes by going into the treatment rooms and then reassuring relatives who have been waiting a long time for news. It took the nursing staff a few weeks to realize how they could use the Samaritans, and now nursing staff actually say, "Thank God you're here, we're waiting for you, somebody's been raped, or somebody's overdosed," and they can't spend two hours listening to someone talk. I used to be a nurse myself, and I remember patients who were being prepared for major surgery, who knew they might not come out of it, and I knew they really wanted someone to sit with them and put everything right the night before. There was no time, as a nurse, to do any of that.

'We don't very often get an opportunity to see people who have overdosed when they are coming round. Mostly we are there when they come in. They don't do so many stomach wash-outs now. It's not medically necessary. It was felt it was often done as a punitive gesture. Very often, now, they're left to sleep it off. In quiet moments we talk to the staff, and I think that's one of the most valuable bits of our work. When I was a student nurse and worked in casualty I constantly heard it said, when a repeated overdoser was brought in, "Oh, for God's sake, why can't they do it properly?" I don't think for one moment they actually meant it, I think it was just sheer pressure of work. They were always overloaded with work, as they are now. But I must say, since we've been befriending in casualty they are much more enlightened. I think they realize there is a need for greater care for these people, but they just can't provide it.'

·7·

EMOTIONAL TIME AND SPACE

Every other year, when Samaritan Week gets under way, provincial journalists, no doubt primed by someone in the local Samaritan centre, and certainly grateful for a peg on which to hang a 'human interest story', trot out with faithful regularity heart-stopping features about the Samaritans suddenly being inundated with ten-year-old callers, and tales about primary school children contemplating suicide are invariably passed off as international scoops. The truth is, children have been calling the Samaritans for a very long time indeed. In 1973 a vice-chairman was writing in the *Samaritan*, 'An increasing number of young people under the age of eighteen and down to the tender age of eight are telephoning the branches and this has caused some concern, particularly about the way in which they should be befriended.' He went on to say there were a few golden rules which must be observed, and the first was that every child should be treated in the same way as an adult. What these 'golden rules' could therefore lead to is a traumatic testing of the basic criteria of Samaritan conduct, a situation in which a child turns up at a centre at night, is taken in and befriended by the volunteers on duty, and possibly given a bed, while the child's parents are going frantic with worry, the police are out searching for him and no one at the Samaritans is prepared to contact anyone even to say the child is safe unless the child gives permission.

This is only one reason why some volunteers find the

befriending of child callers a confusing, even on occasions distasteful, part of their duties. In the first place, not every adult finds it easy to establish a rapport with children. Many of us actively dislike children, feeling envious of their freedom and lack of responsibility and of what we see as their sexual licence, threatened by their contempt for, or at least their challenge of, authority, and irritated by what we regard as their lack of a logical perception of grown-up values and judgements. The desire to give advice and instructions to children is almost overwhelming, and the concept of consulting with children is alien to our entire educational and parental system. If you cannot persuade a child to obey you by verbal threats or coercion, then a beating should do the trick: this has been the philosophy for moulding one generation into the footsteps of another for centuries. These habits and attitudes are hard to break, even assuming we wish to break them. Many Samaritans are themselves parents, have sometimes felt tempted to throttle their own children when nerves have become frayed, and yet have fought hard to fend off the worst fears a parent can imagine, of their child being run over or kidnapped. There is no situation ever likely to confront a Samaritan in which the movement's practices and principles are more likely to clash with their own emotional reactions than when confronted with a caller who also happens to be a child.

Even back in 1973, no fewer than one caller in four was under the age of twenty – the majority of them fortunately teenagers rather than children. Basil Higginson listed their reasons for contacting the Samaritans as depression, loneliness, 'boy or girlfriend', pregnancy, drugs and examinations, but the real cause of distress, he said, 'is nearly always family or other personal relationships'. Of the child callers, categorized by him as aged between eight and twelve, he said they sometimes spoke immediately and directly of tensions and quarrels at home, and he did not believe that the increase of child and teenage calls indicated a dramatic breakdown of family life in Britain. 'Rather, it suggests that "The Samaritans" is now a household word . . . and that people – especially the young who have grown up with the telephone – are more accustomed to dialling for help.' Samaritans who are themselves all too acutely aware of their own short-comings as parents, of the quarrels and tensions in their own family life, may easily feel an instinctive impulse to advise a child to return home rather than admit that any home – and by extension, their own – might be an undesirable place to which to return.

Strange as it may seem, just as there is no statutory law against trespassing, and squatters cannot automatically be evicted by the police when you return from holiday and find they have taken over your house, there is no legal obligation to return a child to its parents or legal custodians, even if the police have been notified of its absence, and no Samaritan could be prosecuted for kidnapping a child unless the child was held in a centre against its will. 'It is very easy to think that the first thing a child should do is to go and discuss his problem with parents or schoolteachers,' the vice-chairman, who was also a solicitor, wrote in 1973, 'but very rarely is this the case when he has a deep-rooted anxiety about home, school or sexual difficulty. The last person he wishes to discuss this with is a parent, schoolteacher or family doctor.' Young clients, he went on, must be offered complete and utter confidentiality, 'and it is about this point I believe that there is most anxiety. All volunteers must remember when listening to a child, either on the telephone or face to face, that their own anxiety at the thought of a child having run away from school, home, children's hostel or some other establishment must never be shown. Their instinctive reaction to tell him to go back and that everything will then be "quite all right" is about the worst thing that could be done.'

Of course, not every child caller has run away from home or a hostel. Some merely telephone out of devilment, perhaps to say something shocking to find out how the Samaritans will react, and a good deal of giggling in the background may indicate a crowded phone booth. But just as no one writes graffiti on a lavatory wall without wishing to have it read – and to get it off their chest – so no one telephones the Samaritans without a serious reason of some sort, even if part of the reason is not immediately apparent to the caller or acknowledged by them. It takes time and trouble to discover a Samaritan phone number. It costs money to make a phone call. The expenditure of any effort and cash is never made without good cause. Yet the inherent seriousness of child callers (we take children less than seriously in almost every aspect of their lives) has, by their own admission, been difficult for a good many Samaritans to accept. In 1976, by which time some 3,000 new callers annually were aged under fifteen, a member of the Leicester branch, who was also a schoolteacher, sent a questionnaire on the subject of young callers to every branch in the country. From one director he elicited this response: 'Far too much fuss is made about young clients. I propose in this branch to do nothing special about young callers.' In Hampshire every secondary school had agreed to display a Samaritan poster, whereas a group of Norwich headmasters retorted that, 'Children shouldn't need Samaritans while at school.' At this time, three boys and girls under sixteen were committing suicide in England and Wales every month. The director of the Norwich branch, however, replying to the questionnaire, wrote, 'Some volunteers immediately think, "Oh, here is some poor child," and so are apt to talk down to them in a patronizing sort of way.' From Wigan it was learned, 'We feel that a lot of adults do not really listen to children without imposing their own mores.' The Liverpool branch reported, 'There is always the tendency to forget how deeply sensitive the young are; and perhaps we tend to have an underlying belief that the teenager is "sure to grow out of it", whatever "it" may be.'

In a pamphlet titled *Young Callers and the Samaritans*, John Eldrid lists a selection of case histories illustrating the reasons a number of teenagers between the ages of twelve and sixteen contacted the Samaritans. A boy of fifteen was fed up with being nagged all day by his parents over the clothes he wore. A girl of fifteen with a newly acquired stepmother no longer felt wanted at home. Another girl of fifteen had been in love with a man in his twenties. She killed herself. Because, he said, no one spoke to him at home, a boy of fifteen was pretending to be seventeen in order to join the army. An academically brilliant sixteen-year-old public-school boy was developing alarming symptoms of schizophrenia. A girl of twelve, bored at school, hating her older sister and aware that her mother was having a lesbian affair, was reluctant to return home at night. A girl of fifteen had broken off with her boyfriend; she killed herself with an overdose of sleeping pills.

Eldrid writes, 'It is a great mistake to think that the adolescent may not be as seriously ill or depressed as a much older person, or to disregard the importance of a suicide attempt.' But, he writes, 'Few teenagers want to die in the suicide attempts. This is much more an expression of anger born out of feelings of emotional frustration; a protest, if you like, against the environment in which they find themselves enclosed, an expression of the emotional hopelessness of their situation. There may be a feeling that they can stand no more emotional pain; a natural emotional weariness makes sleep a most attractive answer.' In offering advice on first encountering a young caller, he reminds the Samaritans that they need to recognize that the typical young caller has little or no experience of being accepted by older people. If they had, he says, they might not have needed to contact the Samaritans in the first place. 'So this will be one of the barriers which prevent the young caller opening up to the volunteer. Like all of us, the young caller wants to be taken seriously, yet it is all too easy for us to dismiss early teenage worries too lightly.' Like most of us in a crisis, 'the young caller will forget what they intended to present and end up with rather a confused presentation. This is very likely to involve a certain amount of laughing, giggling and general lack of seriousness, so beware of dismissing such encounters as hoaxes.'

Currently, says Eldrid, about 500 fifteen to sixteen-year-olds are in touch with the central London branch, 'and we are not going to give information about them to the police or anyone else unless we have their permission. If these kids run away and they know there's confidentiality, that is a great attraction, I think. And it's more than likely that if they stay with us and talk with us they will open up negotiations with the home they've run away from. If an eight-year-old turned up on the doorstep one would have to talk round the situation. We have no right to inform on callers. I have met eight-year-olds who were very much on the ball. And for an eight-year-old to go to the Samaritans requires a certain amount of sophistication.'

'Try not to get over-anxious about police enquiries,' the Samaritans are told. 'If the police telephone or call about a particular caller and ask directly if you are in touch, the answer is NO.' And if a young caller asks to telephone his parents, volunteers are particularly warned – whether a Samaritan or the caller telephones the parents – not to mention the Samaritans. 'If you mention Samaritans then it is very likely that the parents will tell the police and you will be visited.' Again, 'As we do keep summary forms, it is probably best if we omit or disguise references to actual criminal offences,' Samaritans are advised. They are further cautioned that in point of fact 'The only circumstances in which we are legally bound to contact the police is when we are present at the scene of a crime and see a body.' On the whole parents do not appear to make the first contact, 'and some do not wish to contact their child at all.' And social workers, one learns from John Eldrid's pamphlet, 'seldom seem to contact the Samaritans about runaways.' Accept their enquiries as you do from the police, volunteers are told. 'Children under care orders are not of immediate interest to social workers.' He makes the point that it is natural for parents to feel guilty if their child turns to the Samaritans for help. 'The parents will often show their feelings of guilt, failure and sadness in rigid, angry reaction.' He goes on: 'The befriending and supporting of the parents is never likely to be easy and for the most part few parents will allow us to get close to them, but we should always try and keep the lines of communication open for them. On many occasions we will need considerable patience, because many parents will have little or no insight into how they are causing problems for their child. This kind of reaction is not so surprising since concern for children as individuals is still in the early stages of development in our society.'

Speaking about the befriending of children, a leader in the Midlands confirmed from her own experience all the general principles upheld by the movement as a whole. 'I think the youngest caller I've encountered personally was about fourteen,' she said. 'They're becoming more frequent partly because we're getting better known, and, for a child, confidentiality is really important. I think the youngest we've actually had in the branch was eight. There aren't that many organizations that deal specifically with young people, are there? For a young person to talk to anybody is quite a difficult thing to do. It can be very hard, especially if we get the parents of a young caller ringing in. Then we might try to get permission from the young person to tell his parents he was safe. We are under no moral obligation to return a runaway child to its home. Any caller who contacts us, no matter what their age, is assured of complete confidentiality. Even if we knew the parents were worried stiff, if the child refused permission to disclose his whereabouts we would respect his wishes. If children come to us knowing we are an agency that deals with suicide and related problems, then it's got to be pretty serious before they actually pluck up the courage to get in touch with us. And when they do, all our practices and principles apply to them as they would to anyone else.

'Yet although we treat child callers in the same way as everybody else, one is a bit taken aback. It's important to remember that young people don't always have the words – adults don't either – to explain how they are feeling. We still ask the suicide question, but it's how you ask it that is quite a different matter. Young people don't understand what death is. They don't have an idea of the permanence of death. They think of it as going to sleep. They've heard about grandfather "passing away". They ring up about various things, exams, not knowing how their bodies work, feeling they might be gay. Of course, we don't know if they're gay, we can't give them a test. But I think it depends on their age. If, say, they are ten or eleven and they've got a best friend and they're worried about that, that's a different matter to being seventeen or eighteen.'

The youthful age of callers is only one of the cultural shocks the Samaritans have in store. Equally surprising, at first encounter, is the lower age limit for volunteers, nationally a mere seventeen, although individual branches are free to decide on a higher minimum age if they wish. At one time Cambridge, reputed to be run entirely by the wives of dons, refused to recruit anybody under the age of thirty. Someone with radical and firmly held beliefs both on young callers and youthful volunteers is Nick Ellerby, appointed honorary youth officer in 1985 at the age of twenty-six, and a year later director of the branch he joined when he was only seventeen. He has an almost passionate obsession with trying to eliminate concepts of age in relation to ability. At Hull University he read psychology, with a special option on child and adolescent suicide, and he has worked for or among young people ever since, in schools and with young offenders.

'At seventeen I had a lot of doubts about joining the Samaritans,' he recalls, 'but things were different in those days. The branch at that time was taking quite a risk. I don't think they'd had any volunteers under the age of twenty-four. They had to put up with a lot, really, things like my impatience with other volunteers! But the average age now is much lower than it was ten years ago. I know in my own branch that's the case.

'Last year, when we had a very strong drive for new volunteers, there was a tremendous response from seventeen and eighteen-year-olds – some younger. This may be the beginning of a different response to unemployment, as quite a number of young volunteers are unemployed. Also perhaps there is a change in attitude towards doing voluntary work; it's no longer seen as something you're going to waste your time at. By class, too, the Samaritans are a more representative cross-section of society than they were. More working-class people join.

'When I first became a Samaritan one of my biggest fears was my age. I felt very inadequate. I thought, what happens if I get a call from a lady of thirty-eight with two kids? Here am I, seventeen. Some people do ask how old you are. What I used to say was, "I'm seventeen, is that of concern to you?" If they found it was important, either we worked through it or perhaps we found another volunteer. On the one hand, I do see that older people have an experience of life, and can use it. But on the other hand, you are, at seventeen, to a certain extent more open.

'Twenty-five per cent of our callers are under the age of twenty-five. Last year, between 8,000 and 9,000 were under sixteen. But statistics are dodgy. Many branches don't include testing calls, and some branches only log a call statistically if it goes on longer than fifteen minutes. A testing call is one the Samaritans find difficult to deal with. They think the person is not being serious. But a testing call is not a hoax, it's somebody who has heard about the Samaritans and quite understandably doesn't believe what they've heard. You talk to schools, and you say, "Here's an organization made up of people who are non-judgemental, non-parental and totally accepting of you as a person. They won't judge what you do, they will just accept you, and whatever you've done or thought, or want to do, that is completely confidential." And they don't believe it. I wouldn't have believed it. I would have wanted to find out, even if I didn't have a problem, and what better way to find out than to ring up and actually test them. Invent a story. Sometimes, when you do a role-play in school they pick that up and feed it back to the branch. Some young callers touch on the thing they really want to talk about but see how the Samaritans are going to react first. Others will pick up the phone and dial and when you say, "The Samaritans, can I help you?" they'll shout, "Fuck off," and put the phone down. Or call you a stupid bag, or something. Sometimes you see volunteers getting upset at this, frustrated, but we need to remember back to how it was when we were younger, how we found it very difficult to put into words how someone could help us. Young people often find it difficult to communicate on a feelings level. And so I suppose part of my job as youth officer is to say to the Samaritans, This is difficult to cope with, but if you look at why it's happening it's a very natural thing for young people to ring and not say anything, because the fact that we are there is the important thing.

'I think for Samaritans there is a big difficulty about respect for young people. Maybe we weren't respected, or we didn't feel we were when we were young. But when we join the Samaritans we try to move away from the general view of society that a youngster is unable to make his own decisions: "I'm older so I know better". In a way it's easy to look after children because we think they're more vulnerable and therefore we don't need to give them much time to make their own decisions. If anything, with a young person a Samaritan has got to give so much more time. Training for dealing with children varies tremendously from branch to branch. In workshops, we say, "If anything, you need more discipline as a person, because it's not the problem that's affecting you, it's the age of the person. And you can justify it by saying things like, "A nine-year-old can't make his own decisions." But a nine-year-old has already made some decisions if he gets in contact with you. I suppose part of my role is just reminding Samaritans all the time that age should not change the quality of care. That for young callers the quality of care should be increased, because a young caller has less power than any other group. There are fewer people willing to believe you. There are fewer people around you feel you can trust. And that's going to get worse.

'I think this generation is going to find it more difficult to find people to trust and to share with, and there are going to be more secrets. And I suppose I see the Samaritans as providing something that no one else provides; nowhere else can you go where you are promised a safe place and to be given emotional time and space. That is just so incredibly important. I think the difference between a Samaritan and someone else is time. Because you can get people to advise you and do things for you in every other walk of life.

'As far as young volunteers are concerned, they may not have experience but they have care and acceptance. The problem is one of getting hung up on age. I know personally fourteen-year-olds who I would feel comfortable talking with, who would give me time and would care. And there are a lot of fourteen-year-olds I wouldn't want to talk to in any way whatsoever. But there are a lot of sixty-year-olds I wouldn't want to talk to either. And there are sixty-year-olds who would give me time and space. So I think it's wrong for the Samaritans, of all organizations, whose principles and practices are there regardless of age, to get hung up with age. If the person has the right attitudes, despite their age, then we should count that as being something very positive. Whether young volunteers stay depends on how much they're used. I was used fairly quickly. I'm sure that where antagonism exists between old and young volunteers, it is both ways. You get young people who are not tolerant of older volunteers, and you get some older volunteers who aren't tolerant of young ones. The Samaritans is an organization in which everything takes time. Evolution rather than revolution. And I think we've got a long way to go. There are still young volunteers who look at still younger volunteers in an odd light. It's the age thing again. They think, "I'm thirty-two and the seventeen-year-old seems to be doing quite a good job, and that upsets me a bit."'

A volunteer of fifty-two in one of the London branches, who interviews a lot of potential new recruits, said the youngest she had interviewed personally was twenty. 'My basic attitude to all volunteers is that they have something special to offer. Young people have their freshness, their spontaneity, their natural friendliness. They are closer to the up and down feelings of teenagers. I have no experience of the pressures of young people today. In my own personal life it was totally different when I was a young girl. Young people today have so much more choice and therefore so many more pressures put upon them. I've seen my own nieces and nephews be of tremendous value to older people in their community. They can be very sensitive. Just because they're young I don't think it matters that they haven't experienced all of life. They have a much more open, accepting way than we had. And I think life is tougher for them, actually.'

Her comments were echoed by another middle-aged volunteer, from Surrey. 'We've had one or two young people in our branch who have been absolutely wonderful. I couldn't have done it at their age, not in a million years. They are so patient, and they are so wonderfully compassionate. I was much too taken up with my own concerns at that age. I could never have done it. I'm fascinated. I certainly had a very protected childhood and upbringing, and I didn't know how the rest of the world lived at all. We've got a couple of nineteen and twenty-year-olds in my branch, men and women. I'm thinking particularly of a couple of young men we've had. One is still doing his "A" levels. We had one young man for three or four years who was particularly good with the young callers. As you know, the main thing is listening – and getting people to talk. Some people ring up and don't draw breath for an hour! Our young volunteers are much more patient with these gasbags than I am!'

By 1972, the particular needs of certain young callers and the understanding aptitudes of certain young volunteers were drawn together by the formation of the Festival branch, formally recognized two years later, an *ad hoc* selection of volunteers, about half of whom are drawn from centres throughout the country, 'with a sympathetic attitude towards the pop music world and the type of people who attend pop festivals.' The Festival branch got their first real taste of the work that lay ahead when they attended the Reading Pop Festival in 1973. Since then they have appeared, among many other places, at Wembley, Knebworth, Stonehenge, Glastonbury, Alexandra Palace and Trafalgar Square. It is a form of befriending in the open with a vengeance, a very public and visible presence, with a large tent proclaiming 'The Samaritans', from which are distributed leaflets that read, 'It's not always fun for everybody; if that's the way it is with you, look out for THE SAMARITANS.' And there are volunteers wandering around, not actually going up to people and offering their services but making contact in a very definite way. A volunteer normally based in London reported on the branch's baptism, and nothing, in essence, has changed very much since then: 'Though we were equipped for Samaritan work of the most general nature,' he wrote, 'the type of client we encountered, being predictably younger than average, that's to say, exclusively in the fourteen to thirty years age group, gave the emphasis of the problems presented a distinct "slant". Given that young people in any case have problems associated with their age – those which for lack of a better phrase we term "the problems of adolescence" – we found that the specific circumstances of the festival, the carnival atmosphere, the excitement of the music, camping out, and the like, coupled with the ready availability of drugs and alcohol, led to us caring mainly for people who were drug users of one category or another. Naturally enough we also encountered crises provoked by other factors, disillusionment with the festival, anxiety about brief, personal and intimate relationships, depression, no money and so on. A high percentage of our clients were, however, "stoned", and not particularly enjoying the experience.'

He went on to say that the 'state of chaos which reigns at events like Reading puts a special strain on the Samaritans on duty. The very nature of the event produces relatively large numbers of potentially disturbed clients who may have very serious problems indeed. All the familiar background details of being on duty are also absent and the fact that nearly every client is a new client who is asking for immediate attention can make a turn of duty a very wearing affair.' Despite the 'state of chaos' he concluded by saying the Reading Festival was by far the best organized of the regular festivals, but two major concerns cropped up. 'Unfortunately the promised financial assistance never materialized from the promoters. The other depressing aspect of the event was the large quantity of alcohol consumed, especially by young people not old enough to be out of a schoolroom.'

At a pop festival lasting three days, the Festival branch, manned by perhaps twenty-five volunteers, may befriend some ninety young people, usually far more young men and boys than young women and girls. Problems relating to drugs, including alcohol, and emotional situations of one sort or another will account for about sixty per cent of the reasons for Samaritans being consulted. General enquiries about Samaritan services will account for perhaps fifteen per cent of contacts, and then there is a rapid falling off to some five per cent who might be complaining of loneliness, and three or four per cent with medical or legal problems.

A member of the Festival branch attached at other times to a centre in a university city, which is also an area of high unemployment, works in the local supplementary benefits office, and therefore sees something of the practical difficulties facing potential Samaritan callers in the course of her everyday life. She was accepted as a Samaritan three years ago, when she was twenty-two. She looks alarmingly vulnerable but completely relaxed. The cramped little room at the centre where she talked, with its crumpled divan bed and unwashed tea-making equipment, seemed strangely reminiscent of a student's bedsitter.

'Although this is a university city, I wouldn't say we get a particularly high number of students as callers,' she said. 'In fact, we don't get very many students at all. I think they have their own help lines within the university. We tend to get more students as volunteers than as callers, and quite a lot of volunteers from the local Roman Catholic theological college, just outside the city, but they tend to leave when they've passed their exams, and they also create problems for the rota when they go on holiday.

'I know I was very young when I became a volunteer but I think I've always been an old woman at heart! When I was interviewed I never felt I was being questioned about my age. Not at all. I think that half the people on my training course were about my age. There weren't a lot of people who seemed a lot older than me, although of course we have got volunteers in the branch of seventy. I don't feel as if I'm too young to be a Samaritan. Callers who meet me face to face don't seem to react in any way on account of my age. And of course a lot of people round about my age like to talk to someone of their own age. We get a lot of people who are gay, and have problems at home with their families. There's a great range of problems. We've just lost a steel works in the town, for a start.

'The boredom of unemployment is a great problem for people. They become depressed because of it. They've no motivation. I think if people had work there wouldn't be half so much depression. We'll always have people who are unhappy, but there wouldn't be so many. I'm a fairly happy person. I would say so, yes. You have to be able to take the depressing part of the work and care about it and then forget about it. You can't take it home with you or you'll worry yourself silly. You can get too involved. No one that I've ever befriended has ever died, that I know of. But you can't know, you see. You might just lose contact with them, and you don't know if it's because they've died or they don't want to be befriended any more because they're all right now. You never know how high your success rate is.

'Outside the Samaritans I haven't known anybody who has killed themselves, but apparently my grandfather committed suicide. I didn't know him, but I think I knew how it affected my family, because he disappeared, and they found him in a river, about four days later. My mother's told me about it, and I think I must have taken that in. It must have made an impression on me when I was young, hearing about that. I don't know whether it contributed to me ending up being a Samaritan. I think I just had a feeling I could help people who felt depressed, maybe because I'm the sort of person who gets depressed myself, at times. But if I feel depressed I just think there's somebody worse off than myself. I have friends I can talk to. A lot of people who end up phoning the Samaritans don't have anyone they can turn to.

'I think everything I heard when we were trained came as something I would have expected Samaritans to be involved with apart from the sex calls. The telephone masturbators. When we heard the tape of a mock-up call, I thought, "Oh, heck, can I cope with this?" But the tape was highly exaggerated, to make you realize what you would be up against, so that when you actually got one it wouldn't be as bad as you expected. Though some of them are pretty bad. I thought, "I can't cope with somebody saying things like that to me, I will feel as if I am being used like a prostitute over the phone." Then I went away and thought, well, all the other things I've heard about I can cope with, I must just try to cope with the M-calls too and not take it all too much to heart, and think to myself, he's just a caller, he doesn't know who I am, he just wants someone to get his frustration out on, I suppose. When it actually happened it wasn't anywhere near as bad as I expected it to be. I just took it in my stride.

'And I've had to take a lot of testing calls from teenagers. It tends to be a bit of a joke. You know, let's phone the Samaritans, Mum's out, we've got nothing to do. Our practice is to encourage them to phone again. You don't say, "Don't be a silly little boy, go away," you try to be nice to them and encourage them to phone again in case in the future they really do have a problem. You don't say, "Oh, get lost you silly little child, I'm busy," you say, "What's your name? Have you really got a problem or are you just having a bit of fun?" and they usually admit it and put the phone down.'

John Eldrid summed up his views on young volunteers by saying, 'If they've got a reasonably good life going for them outside the centre they are not very likely to succumb to other people's depression. A lot depends on whether they are using the Samaritans as a kind of escape. Obviously one tries to check this out. My son joined the Samaritans at seventeen, in the Festival branch, and it certainly never had any adverse effect on him. I think a lot depends on the person's own lifestyle. But of course if a young person is befriending someone, and gets quite close to them, and they kill themselves, then obviously this will be quite traumatic and the volunteer will need a lot of support.'

While the Samaritans in the United Kingdom have no plans to lower their minimum age for volunteers to sixteen, as the Samaritans have done in Boston, Massachusetts, where volunteers between sixteen and twenty, recruited specifically to befriend other 'teenagers', have been named, all too predictably, Samariteens, it *is* possible to serve as a Samaritan while still at school. Lucinda, who is now nineteen, applied to the central London branch to train as a volunteer when she was only sixteen, and was told they preferred not to consider recruits below the age of about nineteen (although central London have in the past accepted volunteers of seventeen). So a year later she contacted her local branch, and became a volunteer at the age of eighteen, while she was still a schoolgirl. After one year as a Samaritan, she spoke about her limited and youthful experience.

'I didn't know a great deal about the Samaritans before I read Monica Dickens's book at the age of sixteen.[1] That really did make me very fascinated about the whole idea. I read it actually simply because I like reading Monica Dickens's fiction. From quite a young age I'd been interested in voluntary work, cubs and things like that, and I think I was looking for something I could do, without quite knowing what. I wrote to the central London branch. I was terrified of ringing them up because I didn't want to be treated as a caller. They put me off temporarily, until a friend, interested in being a social worker, suggested we both contact our local branch. We made separate appointments. We didn't like to reveal the fact that we knew one another, we thought it might look as though we weren't serious.

'At the start I was totally unprepared for the sex calls. I didn't know they existed or ever happened. Or not to the extent they do happen. I may have been asked at my interview if it would bother me, but I didn't realize how much it would affect me. Or at least, how often it would occur. I think I just assumed it would be every now and again, like you get at home. After a year, I would say the sex calls are basically boring, because you feel you really want to be there for other people. I know a lot of Samaritans come off the phone after taking a sex call and they say, "Oh, how disgusting, why can't they just leave us alone," but inside I feel sympathy for people who have to make calls like this. I must admit I feel very upset about them. Invariably they are unemployed, between about fifteen and twenty-five, perhaps a little older, usually sitting at home doing nothing. I

[1] *The Listeners* (Heinemann, 1970).

find it very difficult just to write these people off as being boring or revolting, they've got many more problems than we realize. At the beginning I was very shocked and very upset, and found it very difficult to cope with. After a while you build up some sort of immunity. Often they slam the phone down when you try to talk about anything else.

'I didn't mention joining the Samaritans to my parents at all. I told them some time during the training course, when I knew that I did want to go through with it. I think they'd have liked to have been told earlier, but I didn't tell them because I didn't know how serious I was about it. You really don't know what you're facing at the beginning, and I really didn't know what my parents' reaction would be. They know I have a certain number of sex calls to deal with, but to be honest, I don't know what their reaction is. I don't discuss the Samaritans very much with them. And I never told any teachers at school that I was a Samaritan. The school itself didn't know.

'The first call I took was from a regular caller who calls us all the time, a bit of a madman, actually. But I didn't know that at the time, so I tried to be very serious and helpful. Someone soon rescued me by putting a note in front of me telling me what to do. Being supported like that I found a very great help. The general response to me, from other Samaritans, being so young, has been absolutely fine. I find sometimes if a caller comes to the door I tend to be pushed into the background a bit, because they feel that somebody older ought to be doing the interviews, but not always, I have done plenty of interviews. Once a lady at the door saw me and asked if she could speak to an older woman. It didn't bother me. Sometimes if a young person comes to the door I'll be asked to see them on the assumption they will relate better to me, but I'm not sure that's actually true. I think if I was a caller I might prefer to talk to somebody older. But generally it doesn't seem to matter.

'My positive lack of experience of life is irrelevant because I'm not there to give advice, whether it's about something I know about or not. But being a Samaritan has certainly made me much more aware of what goes on in the world. How many people out there are unemployed, unhappy, lonely. But I don't think it's changed my attitude to people, except for my sympathy towards people who make sex calls. Before, like any member of the public, I would have looked on them as being wicked and vile and disgusting, whereas now I know their problem goes much deeper than that.

'I'm not sure Samaritans should stay in the movement thirty years. I can see a situation where I could get very stale. In the way you can build up an immunity to sex callers, I think after a certain number of years you might find you didn't react to anything. So I don't think I could be a Samaritan for thirty years. But I wouldn't leave now. I feel a great sense of responsibility, now I've been trained, and the drop-out rate is so high. In my branch we've got eighty volunteers and we really need 110. I like night duties best because I feel I'm doing much more positive work at night. You get some very sad stories at night. I have been upset sometimes and rung other Samaritans to talk about it. I find it difficult talking to very lonely callers, people who are very, very lonely, and have very little to look forward to. People who have been bereaved call at night because they can't sleep, and they tend to go on for a very long time.

'I often speak to callers of my own age who have such terrible lives compared to what I've got. When I was worrying about my school exams and waking up in the morning in a terrible state I went down to the centre, and spoke to a girl of nineteen whose mother had committed suicide, and she'd had two miscarriages, and then I thought, what am I worrying about? I don't look forward to going to the centre. I'm not a born Samaritan who wants to submerge themselves in every aspect of the Samaritans. I couldn't do that. But I certainly have no immediate plans to leave. Ten people started on my training course, six got through and now there are four. And one of those is on leave of absence. So after only one year there are just three active volunteers left out of my intake. And I'm one of them!'

·8·
PUBLIC PERCEPTIONS

In 1985, Audience Selection conducted a survey among 1,532 people to try to discover something about the public's perception of the Samaritans. Asked initially to name just one charity, 287 people came up with Cancer Research. Five people – the same number to whom the National Trust immediately sprang to mind – named the Samaritans. Eventually a total of 728 people – forty-eight per cent of the sample – named Cancer Research as a charity known to them, forty-two per cent Oxfam and thirty-one per cent Save the Children. Even the Royal National Institute for the Deaf rustled up six per cent. On four per cent, representing a total of sixty-four mentions altogether, and on equal pegging with the National Wildlife Fund, came the Samaritans. Asked how desperate they thought the Samaritans were for money from the general public in comparison to the others, ten per cent said they thought the Samaritans were extremely desperate, fifteen per cent said very desperate and fourteen per cent did not know. To the question, 'Do you personally think the Samaritans are a deserving charity to give money to in comparison with other charities?' twenty-eight per cent said they thought they were very deserving, forty-seven per cent only fairly deserving, ten per cent not very deserving and five per cent not deserving at all.

The previous year, a National Opinion Poll had revealed 'a lot of uncertainty' as to whether local government or even Westminster funded the Samaritans, an organization seen largely as only providing a telephone service. It was found that 'virtually everyone had heard of the Samaritans' but that about one in ten aged between fifteen and seventeen, and one in six over the age of seventy or currently unemployed, could not say what the Samaritans did. Some confusion with the Voluntary Euthanasia Society seems to have existed for two per cent, who believed that the Samaritans would tell you how to kill yourself if you wanted them to, but a major muddle revolved around the question of befriending; thirty per cent said the Samaritans went out to people who had cut their wrists or taken an overdose, twenty-three per cent did not know whether this was so or not, and forty-seven per cent maintained that the Samaritans never went out on such occasions. Perhaps rather more alarmingly, ten per cent of those in the sample of 1,896 people over fifteen thought the Samaritans decorated old people's homes, and twenty-three per cent thought they took bread and soup to down-and-outs. Asked why some people might be put off calling the Samaritans, thirty-five per cent mentioned a concern about confidentiality, more perhaps a reflection upon a world that practices deception as a matter of course than upon the reliability of the Samaritans themselves.

So when it comes to attaining public awareness of its existence and purpose, what has Cancer Research – or Oxfam or Save the Children, or even Mencap or the Salvation Army, for that matter – got that the Samaritans have not? Fund-raising and public relations are intimately linked – it is on the strength of the projection, by whatever method, of a charity's image that income from the public depends – and for four and a half years (she left in 1986) Barbara Lynch, a professional fund-raiser, took on the task of producing, for what is known as the National Appeal, an annual income of £1.75 millions. Her job inevitably necessitated some very clear-headed thinking about the related topics of advertising and press relations. Reflecting on her experience of the Samaritans as an outsider, she said: 'I think it's quite difficult for the Samaritans to raise funds because of the sort of charity it is. People tend to want to give money to something very specific, and the money the Samaritans spend tends to be on what other charities hide under overheads. Take the case of the phone bill. No other charity would advertise the fact that they spent £275,000 a year on telephones. Children's charities, for example, can actually portray the victims they help, and that of course is something the Samaritans can't do. When we talk in terms of statistics we find it very hard to put a human face on them. People like to buy something specific with their money, whereas we want them to give towards a service, and it often isn't specific enough.

'I don't think the general public gives nearly as much to the Samaritans as it could, but big companies are pretty generous, and charitable trusts are particularly generous. I think the image of the organization as far as the public is concerned – and research has proved this – is of rather an old-fashioned, possibly government-funded, set-up. They can't see why it has any need for money. They think, "Samaritans are volunteers, people ring *them* up." People react emotionally to charity. Not very many react rationally. When we give to a charity we give because we are giving to people less fortunate than we are, and we want them to be victims. There is still a very strong feeling in this country that if you are depressed, and certainly depressed enough to kill yourself, it's because you're weak, and that by funding a service that helps people like that you're perhaps not doing the individuals themselves very much good.

'People don't want to know about despair. It's something we tend to experience individually, and although that could be said of cancer, cancer is now a much more open subject than it used to be. We all know someone who's had cancer, or died of it. But there's been a tremendous turn around. Not so many years ago people wouldn't even mention the word. There was a fear that if you talked about cancer, somehow you'd get it. And perhaps that attitude still exists with depression. It is probably something people want to forget about rather than do something that will help. And of course, we can't promise, as we can with cancer research, that if you give us money we might be able to make things go away. There isn't an overall cure for unhappiness. There isn't going to be a drug for it.

'People see the Samaritans as an extension of the welfare service. Very much so. They think of the Samaritans as they do the Citizens Advice Bureaux. Lots of people think the Samaritans give a wonderful service, but while very few people actually think the volunteers are paid, they certainly think the Samaritans are funded by the government. And the other problem is that the Samaritans themselves don't like fund-raising very much. They're always very worried that if they do go out and fund-raise they will be giving away the fact that they are Samaritans. And anyway, I think the sort of people who make good Samaritans don't make good fund-raisers, because the fund-raiser's mentality is a bit like the salesman's, it's quite pushy, whereas volunteers are selected for their ability to be passive. And so in many ways we deselect potentially good fund-raisers when we're recruiting Samaritans. There are many charities whose primary aim is fund-raising. I'm thinking of War on Want and Help the Aged. Mainly they raise money and then they spend it to alleviate the problem. That's not how the Samaritans see themselves. They see themselves as providing a service which is essentially run by volunteers, and the fact that there are costs is something they have only recently begun to realize. I imagine most branches would be very relieved to draft on to the branch committee an outsider with expertise in fund-raising.'

The £1.75 millions raised every year from an office in the same building as the central London branch goes towards paying telephone bills, national publicity, financing the general office at Slough and paying the salaries of full-time staff. Because central London's running costs are exceptionally high and the branch could never be expected to become self-financing, fifty per cent of the national appeal is allocated to central London. A government grant currently set (and fixed for a three-year period) at £131,500 is made by the Department of Health and Social Security. Every branch has to raise locally enough to meet their domestic expenses, and they presently send seven and a half per cent of their income to Slough as a contribution to the cost of the services the general office provides, like running conferences and arranging inspections by Visitors, and to supplying grants, currently amounting to £71,000, to the regions. There is a recommendation that a certain proportion of funds raised locally should be spent on publicity, and branches are asked to resist approaching national firms with local offices due to be canvassed by the appeals director. If a branch incurs high costs it is because it is receiving a lot of calls, which will mean it is situated in a densely populated area where in fact fund-raising ought to be relatively easy. Those branches that find it hardest to meet their target are usually in rural areas, and particularly depressed rural areas, where potential supporters are scattered.

Barbara Lynch's job was to approach major companies and charitable trusts, to organize concerts, balls and highly publicized auctions, and to try to inculcate in branches an understanding that fund-raising needs to be high on their agenda. 'What the national fund-raiser has to do,' she says, 'is act as an interpreter between the Samaritans, who have their own language and their own customs and beliefs, and the outside world, which wants thumb-nail sketches of the organization in terms they can understand. I don't think the Samaritans in general understood the need for money at first, but they're getting much, much better about this now. I think over the last four years they have come to realize you can't have total privacy if you want people to give you money. They tended to want absolute secrecy about their organization. They didn't want to speak to journalists, whereas now they do, but they want to speak to them at length so that they can really explain what they are doing. And I think that has been greatly helped by the national appeal, because I couldn't do things quietly, in a vacuum, if I was going to raise the money they needed. I think they have realized that. And I also think the Samaritans are unique. The only other charities that have similar problems are the mental health charities, but they don't have the same problems that we have about actually portraying sufferers. There isn't the same stigma attached to mental disability as there is to depression.'

In one year, Miss Lynch doubled the income from the national appeal. But like so many outsiders working conscientiously for an organization traditionally deeply suspicious of the 'media', she has sometimes wondered whose side she was meant to be on. The answer, of course, as with any good press officer, is both. 'The branches,' she says, 'resent what they see as a growing professionalism in the Samaritans. It's a dirty word to them, professionalism. They want things done well but they don't like the idea of professionals, whose motives they suspect, working for them. In some ways, the fund-raising is no different than for any other charity, but the organization can be quite difficult to get through to! A major problem which other charities don't have is this idea of appointing people to posts like branch director for a maximum of three years. I've had to try and indoctrinate Samaritans into the rules of fund-raising, and as soon as I get one lot sorted out, they change. There are a whole lot of new faces at the top and you have to start all over again. There doesn't seem to be any hand-over in the branches at all. That's frustrating. I understand the idea behind rotation, you can get people who stay in jobs too long, but continuity is desperately important when you're building for the future, which is what we're trying to do. The Samaritans are still going to expand, and they're going to need more and more money.'

In April 1984 clashes occurred which presented a nice example of a public relations exercise requiring expert handling on behalf of a jittery client. Permission had previously been granted to the Samaritans by the Bank of England, custodians, apparently, of the nation's image of its currency as well as its expenditure, to feature a crumpled £5 note in press advertisements; a stark headline 'Suicide Notes' was backed up with copy stating that it cost £2.66 a minute to run the Samaritans, and asking readers to 'spare a few minutes'. Because the Samaritans wanted to make use of the same motif as the central feature of a national fund-raising campaign, aimed at raising £150,000, by adapting it to a poster, they were obliged to resubmit the idea to the Bank of England, who now refused permission, on the grounds that 'designs which might be seen by the public as lowering the dignity or prestige of the currency will not be permitted.' All Barbara Lynch's instincts as a professional were to capitalize on misfortune, for she, like her colleagues in Fleet Street, had been trained to spot a good story when she saw one. 'From a fund-raising point of view, it was a wonderful thing to have happened, because it got a lot of attention, and a lot of sympathy, and also some money.' Prompted by a press release sent out by Barbara Lynch, the *Guardian* ran a front-page story; there were editorials and the inevitable follow-up radio and television interviews. 'We got a tremendous amount of publicity, far beyond what we could have afforded. It was a very fortuitous thing to have happened, but the organization was slightly anxious about it because it seemed to be the Samaritans making a fuss. It was not something I would have courted, but when it came it was useful.'

Alerted by the findings of the National Opinion Poll, which had highlighted widely divergent perceptions of the role of the Samaritans, and in particular the failure of the public to recognize them as a charity, a public relations agency was hired and Saatchi & Saatchi were commissioned to dramatize the Samaritans' public image. One result was a poster that won three campaign press awards. It featured a photograph (using a model, of course) of a girl with straggly hair, aged perhaps eighteen, with tears discernible on her cheeks, a telephone receiver to her ear and a couple of bottles of pills, some red, some white, strewn on a table in front of her. Utilized in different contexts, the photograph has appeared with a variety of captions. One reads, 'The only thing holding her back is a thin piece of cord with you on the end of it.' The award-winning poster carried a lot of advertising copy, designed to attract new volunteers, and the words 'I'm about to kill myself. Can you talk me out of it?' made up a double-column headline. It won the *Guardian* silver award for the best-written advertisement, but no doubt its merits had been judged by *Guardian* staff who were not themselves Samaritans. Its apparent flouting of Samaritan practice by seeming to suggest pat answers to specific problems aroused the indignation of *Samaritan* readers. A member of the Winchester branch wrote to the magazine to complain that the nature of the copy 'seemed to be quite alien to anything a Samaritan would say to a distressed and suicidal caller.' He went on, 'For potential volunteers, at whom the poster is directed, to be led to think this is how we respond to callers, or worse still for any potential caller to believe this is the kind of response they may receive, seems to me appalling and likely to do incalculable harm.' He hoped the poster would be withdrawn, as it was 'totally inappropriate.'

Another volunteer, also 'appalled' by the poster, was the recruitment officer from the branch in Hove, who wrote to say, 'I'm afraid that if anything this poster, with its melodramatic headline, is more likely to scare away than to encourage potential applicants.' The burden of her complaint, like that of her colleague's from Winchester, was that, whereas the Samaritans are trained not to supply ready-made and specific responses, as though every problem had a 'correct' answer, the advertisement did just that. She thought that, 'would you like to tell me about it?' should have been included as an option in every issue raised.

These complaints bring sharply into focus the possibly irreconcilable dichotomy between the intimate knowledge of its own mode of operation possessed and prized by a non-professional organization (in the case of the Samaritans, one dealing in highly sensitive areas of human activity) and the necessity an advertising agency considers essential to translate that private understanding into an instantly assimilated message. These problems scarcely exist when it comes to selling food. No matter how disgusting someone's sausages may be, the aim of the manufacturer is to sell them, and if a television commercial succeeds in that endeavour, the agency can say and do whatever it pleases. But the truth is, a literal telephone conversation between a volunteer and a caller would make pretty disastrous advertising copy, and Samaritans individually are bound to react sensitively to translations of their almost sacred principles and practices into the language of the vulgar mob. Of course, Saatchi & Saatchi's copy must have been approved by the executive committee, so perhaps it is even more pertinent to note that the mixed reception to this attempt to modernize and clarify the Samaritans' image may reflect a divergence of attitudes within the movement, between the hierarchy and the shop floor.

Perhaps also the Samaritans have become too accustomed to the never changing format of their own magazine. One of the *Samaritan's* purposes is to act as a sounding board for complaints and as a forum for the exchange of news and ideas, and these functions it performs openly and usefully. But no one could ever accuse it of sensationalism. After fourteen years the layout and contents remain utterly predictable, a perfectly preserved fossilized memento of 1972. As a mirror-image of the movement, it seems quite out of tune with any professed attempt to enliven the Samaritans' public persona or conception of themselves. The quality of the movement's throw-away leaflets, too, can sometimes be indifferent. There is a dreadful air of unreality about leaflets designed as strip cartoons with characters called Mandy, told to scram because she's boring and a creep, and Scott, 'who has never had a girlfriend.' By comparison, a headline like 'Why you should think more seriously about killing yourself' over a clearly laid-out poster aimed at potential callers jolts one with a pleasant, professional shock.

When it comes to receiving beneficial publicity, the Samaritans are inevitably in the fortunate position of being able to see it generate almost at will. Women's magazines, the women's pages of national newspapers and a good many feature radio programmes soak up articles and interviews concerned with Samaritan activity, and the assistant general secretary, one of whose tasks is to handle public relations, happens to possess a natural and unaffected flair for talking to reporters and responding to interviews. But there is always a danger, as there is in any organization which does not employ a full-time press officer with experience as a journalist, that certain stories initiated outside the office, with potentially damaging consequences, will tend to acquire an unquenchable life and momentum of their own. Because of what many Samaritans see as a high-handed and insensitive approach adopted by some directors to the whole question of the care and sacking of volunteers, the movement is particularly vulnerable to former Samaritans airing their grievances in public. This happened when, on 30 July 1986, the *Guardian* published an account by an anonymous Samaritan of her reactions to the voluntary work she undertook, those reactions being mainly a sense of total inadequacy in relation to the depth of some of the misery and despair she tried to relieve. It proved too much of an irritant for one former Samaritan, who unleashed in the letters column a fairly extreme mixture of disillusionment, bitterness and criticism, based to a large extent on the way in which she claimed she had been cold-shouldered when herself in serious need of emotional support.

'I am sure now,' the *Guardian's* disaffected correspondent wrote from Harrow, without in any serious way attempting to substantiate her devastating charge, 'that the good done by the Samaritans is counterbalanced, or perhaps outweighed, by the damage to both volunteer and client.' She went on to say she had written a much milder letter than she had intended. Mild, too, was Simon Armson's reaction when challenged in a radio interview to confront these unpalatable accusations. His more forthright view of the matter, expressed off the air, was that the former Samaritan would have been quite entitled to express her opinions in the movement's own magazine, but that she had been remiss to do so in a national newspaper. However, the fact that theoretically the *Samaritan's* print run of 13,500 circulates mainly among Samaritans is no guarantee that copies will not fall into the hands of journalists, just as parish magazines may do. Publication is publication. And in any case, there seems no valid reason in principle why criticism of the Samaritans should not be voiced in the correspondence column of a national newspaper. Presumably criticism expressed in a feature or leading article would be taken on board. This is no more than a natural hazard faced by any organization striving to do good in a world which enjoys seeing people with a 'moral' line to plug – clergymen, politicians, Samaritans – come to grief.

The way in which individual Samaritans take care of their organization's reputation outside the centre where they function as volunteers is always another potential source of damaging publicity, and no more startling *cause célèbre* has hit the headlines since the Samaritans were founded than the case, in 1983, of the writer Charlotte Hough, at that time working at the Canterbury branch. Mrs Hough had homes in Canterbury and in London, where, quite unconnected with her Samaritan duties in Canterbury, she befriended a lonely old lady, Miss Annetta Harding. Mrs Hough recalls: 'Miss Harding had already determined to end her own life, and now, four years later, blind and ailing, she named the day. Unable to dissuade her, I offered to be with her, and I calmed her fears of resuscitation by assuring her, in all good faith, that she could not survive, considering the massive dose of drugs she had arranged to take. But I also promised that if necessary I would apply the plastic bag that Miss Harding had laid ready. In the event, Miss Harding, happy and serene, slipped into a deep coma and remained just breathing, probably dying but possibly not. After two and a half hours I realized there was no alternative but to keep my promise, which at the time I made it seemed like nothing more than soothing words. After it was all over I yielded to the Canterbury Samaritans's suggestion that I tell them this story, and as a result I was charged with murder.'

An anonymous tip-off had already been made by a man to the *Standard*, who alerted the police. The press had a field day, and for two reasons. They managed to associate Mrs Hough, essentially an author of children's books, with a book about murder ('Crime Writer Charged with Murder' could hardly have been a more damaging headline), and they identified her as a Samaritan, without in any way attempting to differentiate between her duties as a volunteer in Canterbury and her private life in London, the implication being that assisting someone to commit suicide, if that was what Mrs Hough had done, might be something a Samaritan would do *as* a Samaritan. Here was a classic public relations scenario concerning a clash between public and private conduct.

In fact, a three-day trial at the Old Bailey was largely taken up with semantics as to whether the old lady had died from the effects of the pills she had voluntarily swallowed or from the effects of having the bag placed over her head by Mrs Hough (or both), and eventually Mrs Hough was advised to change her plea of not guilty to murder to one of guilty to attempted murder, as a result of which she was sentenced to nine months in prison – but not before the judge had somewhat fatuously told her, 'I have no desire to punish you but I must deter others less altruistic than yourself.'

The *Sunday Times* made the point that Charlotte Hough's only crime had been compassion, and that the case served to underline once more the need for better legislation governing voluntary euthanasia, and the dangers of being without it. Meanwhile, the Samaritans were faced with the question whether Mrs Hough's private conduct in agreeing to stay with someone while they died, never mind assisting them to die (which is what the jury decided by their verdict that she had done), had so prejudiced her credibility as a Samaritan that it was not possible for her to continue serving as a probationary volunteer. She says, 'I was taken off the list immediately, without my knowledge and without being given any explanation.'

Undoubtedly the last lingering recollections left with the public was of a connection between Charlotte Hough's 'attempted murder' and her membership of the Samaritans. It was a public relations exercise impossible to win, and the long-term effect impossible to assess, although, as Miss Harding had been a member of what was at that time calling itself Exit, the case may possibly have accounted for the two per cent discovered by NOP in their survey the following year who seemed to be confusing the modes of operation of the Samaritans with those of the Voluntary Euthanasia Society.

Mrs Hough served her sentence, and was released to resume her vivacious and creative life. The one consolation for every organization when things go wrong from a public relations point of view is that round every corner lurks another banana skin lying in wait for another hapless victim, and that ultimately all newspapers are written, printed and distributed to wrap up the fish and chips.

·9·

NOT LIKE AN ORDINARY DEATH

Attitudes towards suicide have altered radically over the centuries, and have differed fundamentally between different races and cultures. People have been condemned to death for attempting to commit suicide and ostracized for failing to do so. Shifts in reaction to suicide may have had something to do with differing views about death itself. Epicurus, who did not believe in any sort of afterlife, saw no evil in death whatsoever. Sir Thomas More, who was to become a saint, departed from his medieval roots so far as to commend euthanasia. One modern definition of suicide, quoted in James Rachels's *The End of Life: Euthanasia and Morality*,[1] suggests that a person commits suicide if he intentionally brings about his own death, others do not coerce him, and death is caused by conditions arranged by the person for the purpose of bringing about his death. Such a definition may serve as a useful departure point for discussion, but it fails to take account of the successful suicide of someone who in effect has been playing Russian roulette, whether with a revolver or with drugs. Just to confuse the issue even further, it is worth bearing in mind that the Church of Rome condemns suicide, yet in order to qualify for martyrdom it is necessary to seek death.

In the second half of the twentieth century the Samaritans almost certainly reflect society's current feelings, that while

[1] Oxford University Press, 1986.

those driven by despair to suicide, or indeed those who take their own lives quite deliberately, in cold blood, so to speak, are not automatically condemned to hell fire, suicide nevertheless is somehow 'wrong' and ought, at almost all costs, to be avoided and prevented. It is a kind of instinctive reaction. Beating people is wrong; suicide is wrong. Of course, some people enjoy being beaten, and some people who kill themselves do so with the clearest possible desire to die and intention to succeed. Yet they still leave an uncomfortable feeling behind. Even when someone who we know to have been in excruciating pain with no hope of recovery from an incurable illness ends their life with dignity in a rational frame of mind we feel guilty that they should have been brought to such a lonely and dramatic course of action. We feel that death ought to be taken out of our hands, that, in a perfect world, after which we all still hanker, death would come naturally and peacefully, preferably in our sleep.

Whatever their personal views on suicide, in the course of their duties Samaritans are only likely to encounter those people driven to thoughts of suicide by depression and who are still anxious to discuss their feelings, however obliquely, with another person. Someone like Captain Oates, whose 'heroic' death, intended to save the lives of his companions, was suicide in the strictest sense, is unlikely to telephone the Samaritans before walking into the snow, not because of the lack of a phone box but because he has quite deliberately determined to end his life and has no desire or need to be deflected. Someone like Dylan Thomas, who drank himself to death, might possibly ring the Samaritans from time to time, but he is very unlikely to do so because such a person's suicide by stealth is a way of killing yourself by self-deception. While in his cups, and probably not while sober, he would never admit that in the long run his actions were going to prove as lethal as if he were to inject himself with an overdose of morphia. Wilfred Owen's determined and morally quite unnecessary return to the front in 1918, after telling his mother of his need to go back and be with the soldiers he had known and who were now dead, was an act of suicide in the event, and one he would not have wished to be talked out of nor one that anyone regards with other than a sense of the loss to literature which resulted from his death.

The historical role-call of those who, for whatever reason and by whatever means, have committed suicide amounts to an exclusive volume of *Who Was Who*. Dora Carrington, Cato, Thomas Chatterton, Cleopatra, Hart Crane, Mark Gertler, Van Gogh, Tony Hancock, Hannibal, Ernest Hemingway, Judas Iscariot, Arthur Koestler, Malcolm Lowry, Jan Masalyk, David Munrow, Sylvia Plath, Seneca, Socrates, Alan Turing, Virginia Woolf – these are but a fraction of the best or most tormented minds ever born who ended their lives by their own hands. Statistics about suicide only began to be kept in 1860, but in many periods of history suicide has seemed to be so common as to be almost universal. In ancient Greece a man who wished to end his life could calmly seek permission from the senate. 'If your existence is hateful to you, die,' they were told. 'If you are overwhelmed by fate, drink the hemlock. If you are bowed with grief, abandon life.' The magistrates even conveniently kept a supply of poison for those who pleaded their case successfully. 'It is very provoking that people must always be hanging or drowning themselves or going mad,' was the tetchy Horace Walpole's verdict on the close of the seventeenth century. In the Middle Ages, as A. Alvarez has noted in his classic study of suicide,[2] men were preoccupied with death to the point of obsession, 'But for them it was an entrance to the afterlife; consequently, life itself seemed unimportant, devalued. The modern preoccupation – which began in the nineteenth century and has steadily intensified since – is with death without an afterlife. Thus how you die no longer decides how you will spend eternity; instead, it sums up and somehow passes judgement on how you have lived.'

Writing in 1971, Alvarez maintained that suicide was still suspect, but he thought that in the last eighty years a change of tone had taken place. 'The suicide prejudice continues,' he said, 'but the religious principles by which it was once dignified

[2] *The Savage God* (Penguin, 1974).

now seem altogether less self-evident. As a result, the note of righteous denunciation has been modified. What was once a mortal sin has now become a private vice, another "dirty little secret", something shameful to be avoided and tidied away, unmentionable and faintly salacious, less self-slaughter than self-abuse.' How true is this fifteen years on? Alvarez's current analogy with 'self-abuse' seems ironic, for as long ago as 1838 a French 'expert', one M. Jean Esquirel, was pronouncing masturbation to be a cause of suicide, a scaremongering tactic taken up in England fourteen years later by Sir William Ellis, superintendant of Hanwell Asylum, who decreed that the 'habit of solitary vice' gave rise not only to suicide but to asthma and epilepsy as well. What these hypocritical oafs (they had, after all, presumably masturbated when boys themselves without coming to any harm) were trying to establish was that all suicides were mad, and if masturbation could be established as a cause of both madness and suicide it might be possible to frighten people out of a habit at that time mistakenly thought to be prescribed in the Bible by Onan's rudimentary attempts at contraception. At least their cock-eyed theories were some sort of advance on previously held notions that all suicides were the outcome of wilful wickedness. Those who had succeeded were sometimes placed in a cask and thrown into the river; others were buried at the crossroads with a stone over their face and a stake through their heart. In some instances they were parcelled off to a school of anatomy. As recently as the middle of the nineteenth century, people who failed in a suicide attempt were hanged.

Today, suicides may well be 'forgiven' under the guise of being 'understood' if the person killing himself has established a heroic or romantic role before his death, an echo perhaps of the Romantic movement itself, inhabited by people like Byron and Keats, who dreamed of suicide morning, noon and night, thus in many cases very probably preventing them from committing the act itself. When, in 1986, a young and very handsome police officer, who had been paralysed six years previously after tackling two gunmen, committed suicide, the caption to a photograph of his funeral in a national newspaper read, 'Hero's farewell'. The feelings of his family were not recorded. He had been at risk because of his appalling loss of independence. Others who seem particularly to be at risk are men and women with above average intelligence to whom the intellectually perceived horrors of life outweigh the simple pleasures, and also creative artists, people who tend to experience everything around them with a heightened expectation and hence, no matter how successful or famous they may appear in other people's eyes, often regard their creative endeavours, and hence themselves, as a failure. For them, possession of creative powers is their *raison d'être*, and any loss of these powers can never be compensated for by the normal trimmings of old age, by cultivating a garden, playing bowls, enjoying grandchildren or just sitting around chatting.

Irrespective of innate intelligence, people engaged in certain professions have always been regarded as more prone than others to commit suicide. Statistics compiled some years ago purported to show a wide cross-section of professional men and women in England and Wales to be outstanding suicide risks. They included doctors, solicitors, teachers, civil servants, bank clerks, insurance agents and commercial travellers. The stress of daily contact with death and disease, together with the ready availability of medical knowledge and lethal drugs, might have accounted for the successful suicide bids among the doctors; stress again, and perhaps the temptation to embezzlement, could have accounted for solicitors taking their own lives; teachers, of course, are always prone to charges of paederasty; perhaps the civil servants felt frustrated by a lack of public recognition of their role in government, and by a general antagonism towards them if they happened to work in the Inland Revenue; bank clerks, too, may have been tempted to place their hand in the till, bearing in mind how notoriously underpaid they were compared to bank managers; insurance agents perhaps succumbed to depression doling out cheques to the bereaved, and commercial travellers doubtless pined for their loved ones in lonely hotel bedrooms. It will come as no surprise to discover that the highest rates of suicide among tradesmen at this time reclined among innkeepers, surrounded as they would have been by alcohol. Shopkeepers, farmers, garage proprietors, dock workers, cotton spinners, boiler makers, tailors, electricians and bankers were others whom the statisticians found to have an unusual disposition to suicide, and that must have taken care of almost everyone – washer-women excepted. The truth of the matter is that since the publication in 1897 of Emile Durkheim's seminal work *Suicide: A Study in Sociology*[3] suicide has become a subject of intensive research resulting in far more theories than scientific results, each new conclusion tending either to refute some other conclusion or obstinately declining to yield up any objective cause. As Alvarez has caustically commented, the Samaritans, in their practical way, probably do more in a month to prevent suicide than the scientists manage in a decade, but it is interesting to note that in his generous appraisal of the work of the Samaritans he felt constrained to insert the word 'probably'.

Just as there is no single cause of crime, there is no single cause of suicide; and just as crime statistics fluctuate, often for no apparent reason, so do those for suicide. Sometimes they seem measurable in a meaningful way against other sociological factors. Sometimes there appears to be no recognizable cause whatsoever. The British are generally regarded as unflappable and tolerant, and this may in part account for the relatively low suicide rate in England and Wales of 8.2 per 100,000 of the population. But how does one account for the astonishing, and over the years seemingly consistent, rate of 40.3 in Hungary? Not surely by national characteristics alone, nor by depression caused by living under a communist regime; the rate for Poland is only 12.1. We have long been told that the Swedes went in for suicide in a big way because they lived in such a materialistic society (President Eisenhower began this extraordinary rumour), yet as Alvarez has pointed out, the suicide rate in Sweden (at present 19.7) has remained about the same since

[3] Routledge, 1952.

1910, long before the welfare state had been invented. Switzerland, with all its affluence, and, like Sweden, its traditional neutrality, has a rate of 23.9. Do mountains induce suicidal impulses? Or cuckoo-clocks? Mediterranean nations who tend to let their hair down and shout and shriek a lot seldom, if ever, kill themselves, it seems. The suicide rate for Greece, 2.8, is the lowest recorded for any country, and Spain only admits to 3.9, but Spain's figures may well be massaged on behalf of the Church. So may Northern Ireland's, whose rate, despite the tensions under which the people have lived for so long, is mysteriously just half that for England and Wales. Some variations in the suicide rate between different countries can possibly be accounted for by the adoption of different procedures for recording the causes of deaths, for there are even countries where suicide is presumed in the absence of evidence to the contrary.

Thanks to the cult of hara-kiri we have come to believe that the Japanese commit suicide at a word of command from their Emperor, but the rate in Japan is 17.9, far lower than that for both East and West Germany, Austria, Denmark and Finland. However, it probably is true to say the Japanese are an imitative race, and well-publicized suicides in that country, by a schoolboy unhappy with his exam results, for instance, tend to set off fairly spectacular chains of similar suicides. In 1986 Yukiko Okada, an eighteen-year-old pop singer, killed herself after being jilted by an actor, as a result of which twenty-eight teenagers committed suicide, five of them in one day. But this is not an exclusively Japanese phenomenon. Following the suicide in London in 1770 of the seventeen-year-old genius Thomas Chatterton, Alfred de Vigny's play *Chatterton*, written at the height of the Romantic movement, was credited, between 1830–40, with doubling the annual suicide rate in France.[4]

[4] The largest mass suicide ever recorded occurred on 18 November 1978 when 910 followers of the San Franciscan leader of the People's Temple Cult, Jim Jones, took cyanide at a gathering in Guyana. Seven women, all members of one of the 183,345 religious organizations currently registered in Japan, committed suicide together in 1986 when their cult leader died.

We know that at present more men than women kill themselves, but we do not know why. Perhaps it is because men are more aggressive and less resilient (women tend, on the whole, to cope with widowhood better than men). But the ratio of men to women who take their own lives varies widely across the world. In Poland it is five to one, in Finland and Iceland four to one, in Norther Ireland it is almost equal. And these variations in ratio do not remain static; they seem to shift around like the grinding of the continents. In 1901 it was discovered that in England and Wales the ratio of men to women committing suicide was 3–1. Forty-four years later, that ratio had been reduced to 2–1. By 1974 the gap had narrowed to fewer than three men taking their own life to two women. But since 1983 the ratio has returned to 2–1. Within these national shifts there are further puzzling phenomena. In Newcastle, for example, a relatively prosperous northern city, the suicide rate is almost twice the national average, the rate for women being slightly above that for men (at a national level, 10.7 suicides are male and 6.5 are female). In fact, in Newcastle the rate for women is nearly three times the national average. But in Cumbria, the rate for women is only 2.5. The range of the male/female ratio varies from 4.4 in Cumbria to 0.4 in South Tyneside, which means that in Cumbria forty-four men kill themselves each year for every ten women; in South Tyneside the number is only four. But the general experience of more male suicides to female among the adult population holds very steady where children and teenagers are concerned. Both in the United Kingdom and in the United States, something like three times as many boys commit suicide as girls. So much for the myth of girls killing themselves every day because they have been jilted by their faithless boyfriends; in adolescence, most boys tend to retain the sensitivity they so tragically feel compelled to discard in later life. And other, more disturbing, relationships between adults and children appear to coincide. For someone who has survived a suicide attempt there is a much greater risk of succeeding a second time, and on 18 July 1986 *The Times* carried a report of an inquest on a boy of six who it was believed had died from a deliberate overdose of paracetamol, having been successfully treated for a similar overdose just fourteen days before. Incredible though it may seem, this child's death must almost certainly have been suicide; how many children of six, having undergone the distress of being revived, would carelessly have run the risk of hospital treatment again?

The only time when the number of suicides can be guaranteed to fall seems to be when a nation goes to war, for a country on a war-time footing can usually find a useful slot for the outsider. Many a maverick entrepreneur has dreaded the signing of the armistice. It is also confidently asserted that an excessive consumption of alcohol helps to increase the risk of suicide, but presumably it is also true to say that the more times you cross the road the more likely you are to be knocked down by a car. Often when a prominent politician or entertainer commits suicide we are educated by a hastily researched article in the press, explaining the causes, and the dangers he or she had run. The suicide in 1986 of Ted Moult, who was a farmer as well as a 'television personality', elicited the information in *The Times* that farming had headed the suicide list in the 1930s but that today the league table for suicides from all causes was led by hairdressers, followed by deck hands, general labourers, domestic staff and general managers. One marvels there are enough domestic staff left to find their way into any statistics. A hasty juggling act, however, revealed that 'when the figures are sorted into job-related categories a different picture emerges,' and sure enough, doctors were back at the top of the pile, followed by dentists, farmers and farm workers, pharmacists and therapists, judges and lawyers.

On a global scale, there are said to be 1,000 suicides a day, about a dozen of them occurring in England. Bad weather has been blamed for high suicide rates in the past, and one would not be surprised to discover the Samaritans rushed off their feet at Christmas, when the compulsory celebration of happiness hits particularly hard those who are alone and feel more excluded than ever. In fact, however, in the northern hemisphere suicides reach a peak in the spring, surely because the seasonal rebirth in nature serves as a reminder of the lack of a future an already depressed person may be feeling. For them, as Eliot has said, April is indeed the cruellest month, 'breeding lilacs out of the dead land.'[5] Again, although the Samaritans often report a preponderance of very lonely and severely depressed people calling them at night – as one might expect – the majority of suicides occur during the daytime, most commonly in the late morning and early afternoon. This may in fact be the time of day (the morning certainly) when most people have the most energy.

Explanations for changes in the methods used to commit suicide, and variations in the methods used as between different categories of people, seem far easier to offer than explanations for variations in suicide rates between countries or fluctuations in the numbers of suicides between the sexes. Not so long ago, suicide was almost synonymous in most people's minds with someone putting their head in the gas oven. With the introduction of North Sea gas, substantially free of carbon monoxide, that relatively simple, nearly always lethal, method had to be abandoned. Coincidentally, barbiturates became readily available, and they simply took the place of gas. In 1984, 4,315 suicides were recorded in England and Wales; it was estimated that in the same year some 100,000 people were admitted to hospital suffering from a drug overdose, and just over half the numbers of suicides for women are achieved by overdosing. But on the whole, people tend to choose a method of killing themselves that is readily to hand. A farmer is almost certain to have a gun. The chances are, he will use it, and so would other people if firearms in this country were freely available; in some American states the numbers of suicides by means of firearms is ninety per cent. People in high-rise flats are more likely to jump from a great height than people who live in bungalows, although of course anyone can climb over the top of a suspension bridge if they wish. On the other hand, only car owners will gas themselves in the garage or deliberately crash on the M1. On

[5] *The Waste Land* (New York, 1922).

the whole, men favour hanging. Twice as many women as men drown themselves. Fear of pain and possible injury rather than death does not seem to deter; in 1983, 263 people threw themselves under trains but only 212 were killed.

It has to be emphasized that no one knows exactly how many people commit suicide for the simple reason that not every suicide can be proven. Almost every hanging is self-evidently suicide, but not every overdose or drowning, and many coroners are extremely reluctant to bring in a verdict of suicide if the evidence can possibly be stretched to justify a verdict of death by misadventure. A coroner's court is seldom a scene of levity at the best of times; those who have been bereaved and are compelled to attend, often in the knowledge that a post mortem has been carried out on someone they loved, are often protected from the further anguish of a suicide verdict unless the evidence is overwhelming, even though the coroner has no doubt in his own mind that suicide has occurred. Dr Douglas Chambers sits as coroner for the Inner North District of Greater London, and his courtroom any day is fairly typical of coroners' courts throughout the country, with public benches taken up by two elderly ladies, a middle-aged couple, a small girl and two well-dressed men who turn out to be a pathologist and a surgeon waiting to give evidence. There is a police officer to swear in the witnesses; two press reporters disinterestedly scribble at a table below the coroner's chair, and ugly strip lighting harshly illuminates a scene of quietly and efficiently conducted gloom. Dr Chambers has some very definite and forthright views on suicide. 'It is a subject,' he says, 'more full of loopholes than any other. For example, the law insists on a standard of proof for suicide that is effectively the proof in homicide, because you are in fact trying a person after their death for committing what was a capital offence. So when relatives don't like a verdict of suicide, and the judges are concerned with an appeal, they are much given to telling coroners how stupid they are. Now, we're not stupid. You know damn well when a man's done himself in. But if he hasn't done it in a way approved by their lordships we dare not say so. So coroners are often reluctant to bring in a verdict of suicide because of the possibility of an appeal. Nobody wants to be taken apart by the divisional court. I would certainly agree with the assertion that there are more suicides than are recorded. Roughly speaking, in my area I return a verdict of suicide in about one-third of the cases where I am quite convinced it is suicide.

'I've done two inquests today and neither are going to figure in the suicide statistics. There was a chap dragged out of the Thames, rotting, so there's no diet left and we can't even establish a cause of death. It may just have been alcohol. But he'd lost his job, he'd been drinking too heavily, he hadn't any money, and he ends up in the river. No witnesses to his going in, and a cause of death that is unascertainable. Open verdict. The other was a chap, drink again, no previous threats, lots of history of illness, on blood pressure tablets, for some reason takes ten times the level of the drug prescribed. He was married and really his troubles were all due to drink. He's a chap with drink who's taken an overdose of tablets. If you return suicide in these circumstances the judges will just turn round and say, "Look, we would hold that his judgement was so clouded by alcohol that he couldn't know what he was doing, and thus could not hold the intent." So I said it was misadventure. That's an accident, so it goes down as an accidental death. Which it may well be. I don't believe it for one minute, but that's just a gut feeling. I've been challenged on this, but there's no doubt about it, all overdoses are suicidal. To be honest, the system is bizarre in the extreme, and that's a mild comment.'

With limited means at their disposal, it is, however, the prevention of suicide whenever possible rather than arguments about the number of suicides that take place in which the Samaritans are interested. They do not act entirely without personal experience. 'The suicide rate among volunteers is very high,' says David Evans. 'Certainly higher than the average for the population. It doesn't necessarily mean they are all very disturbed. It could mean they are more sensitive, and more aware, and a lot of people who tend to get depressed are people who are very good at giving support to others. I don't say you have to be suicidal to be a Samaritan but it isn't a bar. Any person can be suicidal, given the right situation and circumstances. Suicides are not a peculiar group of people. Suicide is endemic in the human condition. It is the one thing we have. We can do it.'

In May 1982 a volunteer in the Canterbury branch committed suicide. 'Those of you who have experienced a similar unhappy experience will understand the feelings of incredulity, guilt, shock, grief and anger which affected every volunteer in varying degrees,' one of his friends wrote in the *Samaritan* a few months later. She said that the kind of questions being asked were, 'Why didn't somebody notice?' 'Why didn't he talk to me?' 'What's the use of calling ourselves Samaritans if this sort of thing happens in our midst?' Many were trying to come to terms with their own feelings of failure at not 'interpreting the signs which, in retrospect, were so obvious.' She ended her article by saying, 'Some of us feel he will not have died in vain if as a result we all become more sensitive and caring Samaritans, in so far as we ask those who come to us in a crisis about suicide. But even in our branch this is still not being done on every occasion. How many more people have to take their own lives before we all ask that vital question which always opens up the possibility of talking about suicidal feelings?'

On Good Friday in 1984 a former director of a Samaritan branch (he was also a former parish priest) slit his throat. He had frequently spoken of his wish to die, and was discovered by his son, a volunteer at central London, who commented afterwards, 'He was not the first Samaritan to kill himself and it is unfortunately unlikely that he will be the last.' And he went on to echo the words of the general secretary: 'Those of us who kill ourselves do not do it because we are Samaritans, nor are the rest of us to blame, although inevitably it sometimes seems like that at the time. It is just that those whose nature is sensitive and caring are more likely to become Samaritans, and because of their nature they are more at risk from depression. This does not make them bad Samaritans when they are not depressed. One of the many supportive letters my mother received was from a former client who said my father had saved his life by giving him love, and empathizing with him in his depression.'

A questionnaire presented at a regional conference in 1986 produced some fairly startling results. Out of 181 volunteers from branches throughout the South West who were asked if they had at any time felt suicidal, twenty-one men and fifty-three women said they had. All but one of the men said it would have helped if someone had asked them, but only thirty-two of the women thought it would. Three of the men admitted they had made a suicide attempt, as opposed to twenty of the women. In percentage terms, 40.9 had felt suicidal, of whom 12.7 had attempted suicide. There is no reason to believe that such a questionnaire would not produce similar results in other regions, and they certainly seem to indicate that Samaritans are far more vulnerable to suicide than the population as a whole. They also illuminate most interestingly the disparity between successful male and female suicides. Two and a half times more female Samaritans than male had felt suicidal, while nationally, twice as many men as women commit suicide, suggesting perhaps that women somehow get on top of their problems more successfully than men. Again, far fewer women than men thought they needed to talk about their problems, a further indication, perhaps, of their superior ability to cope.

When on duty, Samaritan volunteers have at their elbow a check-list of signs that indicate a person may be in danger of committing suicide. Some people of course give no hint at all, committing suicide almost on the spur of the moment. A teenager, on the other hand, although many act on impulse, may well start giving away treasured possessions. If everyone who suffered from depression, bereavement, addiction to the bottle, loneliness, financial worries and insomnia committed suicide there would hardly be anyone left alive, but any suicidal indicators taken in conjunction with a call to the Samaritans, in itself a cry for help, need to be taken seriously. If people want to die badly enough they will succeed; an entire cargo of slaves managed to strangle themselves in the hold of a Spanish galleon despite the fact that space was so limited they were compelled to hang themselves squatting. But a great many suicides succeed almost by chance, and enough people who recover from a suicide attempt eventually express a preference for being alive rather than dead to make a continual attempt to save life worth while. In many ways it is the failed suicide who suffers more than anyone, having 'failed' in life and again in ending it. There is a feeling they have somehow come back from the dead, a ghoulish thought in itself, and often they themselves feel they have come back to face not sympathy but judgement. What many were seeking, usually through overdosing or gassing, was a temporary escape from intolerable pressures, a way of being dead without dying, the bliss of a long, deep sleep without emotional pain. Their first conscious realization on recovering may well be that after all nothing has really changed, that the emotional pain will recur, that because the attempt was a failure it needs to be repeated successfully; and many people who survive a suicide attempt will tell you that after falling at the first hurdle, the worst is somehow over and after that it feels much, much easier. Young people who have not yet learned to cope with anger and frustration, who have no experience of adult freedom by which to judge what they sense to be the ensnared, claustrophobic and pointless world of the adolescent, are particularly prone to carry out what John Eldrid has described as 'an aggressive act against Mother-Father'. However, he says, 'the rejected boy or girl remains deeply emotionally involved with the parent. If this love and affection over the years is not accepted, they feel despair leading to depression. Behind depression there is lot of anger. Freud would say when you attack yourself you are attacking the bad parent. There is a lot of anger around and more interest in death than sleep. Death is seen as a kind of mystical deliverance. Many suicide attempts follow a row with the parents. Mistakenly it may seem the bad feelings can be patched up, sorted out, when in actual fact the row confirms the prolonged feelings of rejection.'

At the best of times, the death of a child is almost unbearable; to lose a child by suicide scarcely bears thinking about. Not surprisingly, for on the whole young people do not die, the most common cause of death among the young after accidents and cancer is suicide. Following a television programme *The Shadow of Suicide* shown on BBC 2 on 20 January 1986, in which three families who had each lost a child by suicide talked of their experience, 258 people who had also been bereaved through suicide rang in, of whom fifty-nine had lost a child. The parents of boys and girls who kill themselves must rate as the most distressing victims of all. Many others, like the drivers of locomotives and underground trains, are totally innocent victims, whose experience of being used in a suicide is one that often leaves a scar for life.[6] We also tend to employ people to pick up the pieces on our behalf, sometimes quite literally. The young police officer called to the scene when someone has jumped from a window, possibly impaling themselves on a row of spikes, has the gruesome task of inspecting the body, calling an ambulance and perhaps even breaking the news to relatives. Then he is usually expected to go straight back on the beat and be cheerful to everyone. Someone who deals with suicide every day, far more frequently in fact than any Samaritan, is a coroner's officer. One such, who volunteered for the job after eighteen years in the police force, and has been attached to his present coroner's court for the past seven years, explains his motives and his work:

'The reason I volunteered was because it gives me a social life I hadn't had for eighteen years. Now I work basically from nine to five. I think most of us get fed up with shift work. Apart from that, it's interesting. It's terrible to say that death is interesting, but it is. Over the years you are asked to do what we call death messages, to inform next of kin, and I suppose over the years you acquire an ability to talk to people. If a policeman can't talk to people he can't do the job. I mean, if you're in an alley with a big lout, if you can't talk your way out of trouble then you've had it. Last year I dealt with 356 deaths, of which fifty-eight

[6] Some train drivers claim to have been involved in as many as a dozen suicides, but in 1983 the Criminal Injuries Compensation Board ceased to consider compensation claims from train drivers arising from suicide incidents. The matter is currently under review.

resulted in inquests. That means almost all of those were suicides. I get very few road traffic accidents. I would guess that the youngest was about twenty-two. When I go to talk to the family I get the impression they know it was suicide. There's not many times it comes as a shock. The lifestyle has given them an indication. But they'd rather there wasn't a suicide verdict. Certainly in the Jewish community there's a stigma attached to suicide.

'My wife has said that I'm bloody miserable since I've done this job, that I've changed. I always think that the average copper, the ordinary bloke on the beat, hasn't got a great deal of brain, and if I thought very carefully about these cases then I think I'd probably commit suicide myself. So really I think we become very cynical, don't we? We laugh at death, policemen do. There's the old police joke about going round with the death message. You know, you've got to go round and do this death message, and you knock at the door and say, "Are you the widow Brown?" I mean, that's a policeman's joke. You're going to break the news to a wife that her husband's dead and you knock at the door and say, "Are you the widow Brown?" Now, this is funny to a policeman, but it certainly wouldn't be funny to an outsider.

'Nothing really bothers me. I don't think it does. I'm not bothered going into a post mortem room and seeing a chap being carved about. I'm not bothered when a woman comes in here and says her three-month-old baby's died. It doesn't bother me. I don't lose any sleep. But I think the one thing that upsets me is when I get an old girl or an old boy come in here, and they've sold up and they're going to move to Suffolk for their retirement. Now that does get to me.

'Don't get me wrong, we do give the public sympathy. We've got letters here saying thanks, and a couple of women have sent me a pen with my name on. I think we can appreciate how they feel, and I like to think that we do our best to console them. We are concerned. But if you ask, do I take it home with me, No. Once they've walked out of the door, then that's it.

'There's one case I did get upset over. One of our undertakers that we deal with, he phoned me up one morning and he was obviously distressed on the phone, and I thought he was having a bit of a joke at first, and then I realized he was crying, and he apologized for the state he was in. Then he said, "My son's committed suicide." It was the son I was concerned about. He was such a smashing fellow. It was out of the blue, but he had been a bit of a depressed lad at times, although he held down a job. He had a girl. The girl threw him up, so the son went out, hired a garage, got all the equipment needed, a professional job. Now that really upset me.

'I always think we're actors here. You always say to people, "I appreciate how you feel, dear", but we don't have a clue. And when Brian phoned and he was in tears we hadn't a clue what he must have been feeling. On many occasions we tell people what they've got to do, and you think, I'm wasting my time telling you because it isn't going to register, is it?'

If one excludes unofficial cases of euthanasia practised by some doctors, amounting in most cases to no more than a controlled withdrawal of life-supporting drugs in cases of terminal illness where a peaceful death, perhaps from pneumonia or some other natural cause, would normally ensue in the absence of 'scientific progress', few people in our day have ever actively assisted in a planned and deliberate suicide, and fewer still have been prepared to record their experience. But Betty Rollin was actually recruited to help her own mother to die. At the age of seventy-six Ida Rollin had developed inoperable ovarian cancer. She endured two horrific courses of chemotherapy, as a result of which her hair fell out, she lost control of her bowels and she started vomiting so much she could not even retain medication. She gained one year's remission. When the tumour and the pain recurred, Mrs Rollin decided that she wished to die while she still had the strength to swallow. She asked her daughter to investigate how best to end her life and to acquire the necessary drugs.

'The kind of suicide I experienced is very unusual', Betty Rollin explains. 'I was there. I can imagine how people must feel when someone they care about kills themselves and was alone at that moment. So that for me it was so different. We shared it. There was no shock. Well, there was, because I never really imagined this could happen. It was amazing. My mother acted in death as she had done in life. That's what makes my memory of it so good, she died in exactly the same spirit as she had done everything. She was organized. She knew that she had to be calm. She was extremely rational. It wasn't that she was a brilliant woman or an extremely intellectual woman, but she was very rational, and that was her guiding strength. One reason I think she felt so calm was because she knew she was going to be able to escape. When she knew she was going to be able to do this thing she almost physically changed. It was such a tremendous relief to her to know she wasn't trapped any longer. Just knowing that the pills were there, that this was going to happen, gave her such a sense of relief. And she felt confident because my husband and I were with her.

'She didn't want us to be there at first, but we insisted, and she was awfully careful about saying we mustn't touch this and we mustn't touch that. No one ever thought there would be a book[7] describing all this, and we all felt, well, who will ever know? And she had a lot of confidence in us. She knew we weren't stupid.

'Suicide is a word that has come to mean something really ghastly. When you say the word suicide you think of depressed people who do violence to themselves. It has every connotation of something really awful. So in a sense there should be another word for what my mother did. But I do think of it as suicide because there's no other word. There is a fancy word that somebody thought up which I think is rather pretentious, "self-deliverance", and I don't like that either, so I'm stuck with the word suicide. But then, I have to say quickly that I do think my mother's suicide was a good suicide. I think there is such a thing. And I think this death of hers illustrates that about as well as anything could possibly illustrate it. She had a good

[7] *Last Wish* by Betty Rollin (Viking, 1986).

life, she appreciated her life, she felt that it was over and she escaped at a moment, looking back on it, which seemed just the right moment, before once again she would be unable to ingest anything. She escaped as herself, and moreover, because of my own – dare I say it – good research, the medication she took afforded her this release painlessly, swiftly.

'I get hundreds and hundreds of letters – I almost dread the mail – about these ghastly deaths. Oh, do I hear about these deaths people go through! You can't imagine what people go through. The tone is always, "I wouldn't have believed it could be like this. My mother was such a strong person, such a vital person . . ." And when I think of *my* mother, I feel so good about it. People often say to me – well, like this woman on the breakfast show yesterday – "You *must* feel guilty." On the contrary, I would feel guilty if I had not stood by her.

'What I did was legally just over the line, that is to say, my mother was in fact able to take the pills herself, and mostly what I did was just stand by her. I didn't actually assist her. The assistance I gave her was really research, emotional support and that sort of thing. And of course I did have to purchase the pills. My mother was bedridden. The other reason I didn't get prosecuted when my book was first published in the States was that the district attorney in New York obviously didn't want to prosecute me. It was the sort of thing where an individual running for office might have tried to pursue this if pressure were brought to bear, but that didn't happen. The prosecutors don't like these cases. I mean, they don't like to come after people like me. There are a lot of bad people in New York, where I live, there are dope peddlars and criminals of all sorts and they don't want a case like that.

'I do have a certain sympathy with the law, you may be surprised to hear, because I don't think we can have a society in which people kill other people. That's not a good way to do it. You will have sons and daughters pretending to be kind when they really want the inheritance. I think the law has a real problem here. And yet something has to be done. In Holland a patient like my mother could have asked a physician for a shot.[8] This idea that painkillers do it all is just baloney. It's not true. If the pain can be arrested, fine, but if not, I think suicide should be an option. But I don't think most people would do it. I think the tendency in life is to live. But my mother had the option. To be in a room with a door – and this was my mother's own metaphor – that's locked from the outside, that's imprisonment. And that's a terrible feeling. Can you imagine what it would be like to be locked in and not to know where the key is? It must be just hell. If you know where the key is you don't necessarily use it, but think what it does for your state of mind to know that you *can* use it.

'I know about depressed people, and there's all the difference in the world between their sort of suicide and what my mother did. My mother wasn't depressed at all. And I did not need to write a book as some kind of therapy. I never had a bad moment about it. I needed to write it because I was so proud of her. I felt that what she had done was so remarkable. I couldn't get it out of my head. I just thought, my God, I'm so glad I'm a writer, because I can write the story, and what a thing she did, my little mother. But as it turned out it was horrible to write, because I had to live through the whole business of her sickness again, which was not enjoyable.

'It was a sad thing, and I wish she hadn't suffered as much as she did, but her death was a great death. Her suffering was over. It worked. She just went to sleep. So she had the kind of death that cancer patients of that kind don't usually have. And when I think what might have been! Once I was convinced this really was what she wanted, to me that was what mattered – that the person gets what the person wants. Would I want to be master of my own fate? Of course I would. There was no doubt in my mind that she wanted it. So it was a question of going along with her wish, her last wish. And that really had nothing to do with

[8] Euthanasia has not in fact yet been legalized in Holland, although it is known to be carried out and a blind eye is generally turned. It was to a doctor in Holland that Betty Rollin was obliged to telephone from the States for advice about appropriate lethal drugs for her mother.

what my opinion was. But it made perfect sense to me. And you see, she never wavered. It wasn't as if it was a bad day. There could be no doubt. And another thing; our relationship was so good. If our relationship hadn't been so good I think I might have doubted myself.'

After nineteen years as a volunteer, a Samaritan who lives in Kent experienced the ultimate horror, the death by suicide of her own son. 'My whole life,' she says, 'had gone by without knowing of anyone killing themselves apart from suicides in the Samaritan movement, and one then has a different picture altogether. Christopher would have been twenty-three the day after he died. He was a very clever boy – adopted. Caroline, his adopted sister, was then twenty. As a boy he read books on chess when he went to bed instead of story books. Much to my husband's annoyance, he could beat him at chess when he was seven. He had a mathematical brain, and did extremely well. He took the 11+, and went to grammar school. He was the sort of boy who only had to be told something once, and he knew it. If anyone repeated it, he didn't want to listen. So at about the age of fifteen he started to opt out altogether. Being so clever, he must have been very frustrated, and I think it was partly our fault for not realizing what was going on.

'Eventually he met a girl and all I can say is they loved each other very dearly but they couldn't live with one another. They would have the most terrific fights, and you'd think that must be the end, but the next day one of them would be ringing the other. It was a little bit wearing at home! One night Christopher and the girl had a terrific row, and then they were back together. But then they talked together very seriously, and agreed that although they loved each other they would have to part because quite frankly they were tearing each other into little pieces. And so they parted in love rather than hate. And that final parting was something I don't think he could stand. It was a rejection that he couldn't take.

'If I can go back to when he was adopted, at nine weeks, although most children want to know where they came from, Christopher could never bear to be told that he was adopted.

We did tell him, of course, but he didn't want to know anything about it. And I can only think, that night, he felt that was the end because he'd been completely rejected. He did say to one or two of his friends that he wanted to die, and what was the quickest way, but quite frankly they took no notice.

'We'd gone to bed. Christopher came home, and I heard him come up to his room and shut the door. Normally I never need to get up in the night, but for some unknown reason, I needed to that particular night. This was only a few minutes after Christopher had gone into his room, and passing the door I heard a sound that I thought was sobbing. I knocked, and there was no reply. I went in, and he was already unconscious, which didn't seem right as he'd only just that moment shut the door. He was fully clothed on the bed but he had removed his shoes. It's silly how you think of these things afterwards. No shoes.

'I called my husband, Peter, and we got an ambulance and they took him to the hospital, with Peter. Because of my Samaritan experience I thought, well, in a moment they're going to ring up and say he'll be home in so many hours, he'd have been pumped out and all the rest of it. But they phoned to say it was more serious than perhaps I realized, his heart had stopped. They put him on a life machine and a few minutes later Peter phoned to say could I come. They tried all sorts of things. They worked terribly hard for about five hours, and then told us that he'd died. It was cyanide poisoning.

'Although people say you bite on cyanide and you're dead at once, you're not. That was something else I learned. This really caused my husband great heartbreak, because he's a very keen amateur photographer, and in his cupboard was a bottle of cyanide. We handed it straight over, of course, but the police said it was very old and hadn't been used for years. They didn't think the bottle had been opened, so we didn't know where he had got it from.

'You are devastated at the time. You have to leave the hospital and go home. And then I got terribly angry! I was furious! Peter wasn't, and still isn't, but I am. Christopher knew that I would be the one to find him, if it was not that night then the next morning, but of course one also realizes that when a person is at that pitch of wanting to die they can't think of anyone else but themselves. I've heard Samaritans say to a caller, "Have you got a family? What would they feel like if you died?" But it's useless to say that, absolutely useless. But I didn't know that before. I thought, give them any little thing to hold them back. But that's one thing I would never say to anyone now. If they want to live they have to live for themselves.

'The next thing I heard was that the girlfriend was saying, "Oh, isn't it dreadful, he died for me." My daughter was absolutely wonderful. She supported the girlfriend, because I couldn't. I did at the hospital, at the time. I rang her, because I thought she should be there, but I couldn't support her after that. Caroline still sees her, but I'm not nice enough to take her under my wing. I suppose I've got to have someone to blame, and my son's not here, so I can blame her.

'Whether I shall ever be able to forgive my son I don't know. I can't see it at the moment, because I look at the hurt that's been done to other people, to Peter, and to Caroline, who was away at the time, which was even worse. And that's when the Samaritans were so superb, because they got in touch with her for me, so that she wouldn't suddenly get a policeman knocking on the door. She was in London, in digs, without a telephone. I phoned central London and this dear man who I'd never spoken to before went on and on and on. "Now, are you sure you're all right. Now, is everything going to be all right?" And afterwards I said to Peter, "He bloody well befriended me!" Which was awful because he did everything he should have done, but I was dying to get off the phone. That's another bitter lesson I've learned. If people really do want to go, let them get off the phone.

'Then of course there was the awful wait for the inquest. You just sit and wait. The first thing I remember was the number of bouquets of flowers that kept coming, and I said, "It's like a perishing funeral parlour in here," and it was, but people were so kind. We had over 200 letters and these had to be answered.

My own branch was superb, even down to ordinary things like someone bringing a bag of scones with jam and cream, so that I didn't have to bake. One character made the most gorgeous soup. Things like that helped. Endless telephone calls, endless letters. Then I think the hardest thing was to go back on duty, which I did after about six weeks. I went back on duty first of all with a very special friend, so that was good, but at first it was hard meeting people. Then I thought, what if there's a youngster on the line saying, "I want to die", that sort of thing? It didn't happen straight away but it has since. Being able to talk to my fellow Samaritans was an absolute bonus, because people will cross the street rather than talk to you. And they do. I couldn't believe it. People I had known for years were actually crossing the road rather than speak to me.

'Before this happened I thought I had learned it all off pat, from a book. Oh golly! I've changed my mind about suicide, in a way. I always thought, oh God, how dreadful, those poor people, but I think I feel a little now how selfish they are, but that's just me. I know in my mind they can't think about others, but I still feel it's a cowardly act. In preparation classes years ago we used to talk about Captain Oates walking off into the snow and how brave, the others were suffering and they needed the food and all the rest of it, but that's not true, he went because he bloody well couldn't face it any more. It wasn't an act of bravery. It was quicker to go that way. But my ideas have changed on so many things. I took a Samaritan call only this morning, about a seventeen-year-old boy who *will* stay in bed all day and doesn't do this and won't do that, and I couldn't help thinking – in fact, I did actually say – "Of course, he may be staying in bed because he can't face the outside, it may not just be laziness, and so he does need help," and before, I may have thought, it's time he got out of bed.

'I think it's made me a little more tolerant, although I did say I would never grumble at Caroline again, and within a week I was shouting my head off. You wonder, could you have helped? Then there's the guilt. If only one of his friends had phoned and said Christopher is in a bit of a state tonight. And then I think, one can only say it was his choice. This is very much a Samaritan thing. If he had waited until the next day it might have been better. But it may not have been. So he may not have had a choice. But if it was something he decided to do, who am I to say he shouldn't have? And we say that about our callers. It's their choice. But it's not something I would wish on anyone else. It's not the same as any other bereavement. One person came up to me not very long ago and asked, "Are you beginning to live it down?" The stigma is still there. It's not like an ordinary death. If Christopher had died from a disease people's attitudes would have been quite different.'

It seems appropriate that the last word should rest with someone who attempted to commit suicide and failed. Pat is thirty-one, married, with a six-year-old son. She lives in a rural town in Surrey and works, as anonymously as she can, in London. She finds it hard to articulate her thoughts, and harder still to come to terms with her inherent dislike of sex, the reason for the failure of her first, unconsummated, marriage and the cause of inevitable tensions in her second. Born in Canada, she was brought up in Ireland, being readmitted to the Catholic Church at her mother's request when she was sixteen, after her parents' divorce.

'When I was sixteen and living in Belfast I was going out with a paratrooper, so the IRA rang my place of work and said if I didn't leave I'd be shot. So the next day I got transferred to England. I didn't know anybody. I was living in a hostel, and I was really very, very lonely. So I went to see the Samaritans, although at first I hardly said anything. I found it really difficult to talk about things. Eventually I began to see the same person once a week, and she's now my son's godmother. Then I got married, when I was eighteen. My husband was twenty-four and very devoted to his mother. We were married for about three years but we never went to bed together. I know now I got married purely because I was lonely.

'Then I took up psychiatric nursing. I left my husband and moved into a nurses' home, but he came back and beat me up and everything. Four or five months after I'd walked out, well, I didn't ring the Samaritans, I just did it. I broke a milk bottle. I didn't even think about it. Now I've got this massive scar. I actually cut tendons and everything. It was lunch-time, in the nurses' home. I felt that nobody wanted me. I was terribly, terribly lonely. I mean, it was all right going to work and putting on an act, but I'd been thinking about it for a long time. I'd done various things like taking tablets but I never really took enough, but that day I didn't even think about it, I just slashed my wrist. Somebody found me and got me to hospital. When I came round I couldn't believe what I'd actually done to myself. It was a massive cut, and I'd fallen on top of the milk bottle afterwards and managed to do my knee as well! I was in hospital for four weeks, in a psychiatric unit.

'Anyway, I got married a second time. It's quite a happy marriage, but Christmas before last I really, really got depressed. I couldn't figure out why. But I always have this problem with sex, you see. I was getting depressed because we kept rowing, over sex, and I'd taken an overdose and I just slept and slept and slept. It wasn't a serious suicide attempt. If I'd wanted to I'd have done what I did before. That's when I went back to the Samaritans. I just don't like sex, but I've since discovered why. It's because of my father. He abused me when I was eight, and again when I was fifteen. I couldn't figure out why it was that every time he came to see me, which he did every three years or so, I absolutely dreaded it. I just couldn't stand being anywhere near him. It was my mother who said, "Well, it's because of what he did to you." She knew. He's been married five times. I've got one real sister and I've got a *lot* of step-brothers and step-sisters! My real sister was actually raped by my father's brother, when she was fourteen. Another uncle, when I was fourteen and he was fifteen, did the same thing to me. I remember all of it. My sister was in the other room. I don't think my father sees anything wrong with what he did. He's got no moral attitude towards anything. His wife rang me the other day and told me he's sleeping with two other women now. He just couldn't care less about women. When I was about eight we lived in one room, in a slum, frankly, and my father would take me shopping at Harrods. He's very well-off. He's a heart surgeon.

'With my father, I can remember what happened before, and after. I can't remember what actually happened at the time.

'When I first saw my present Samaritan befriender I couldn't talk about anything. It takes a long time to trust somebody anyway. The things that have happened to me, I wouldn't tell to anyone. I can understand it, but I don't think I've really come to terms with it. I keep thinking, maybe he didn't do it. But I know he did. There's no point in trying to make excuses. My husband finds it very hard to believe. I've been accepted by his family but they don't know anything about me. Nobody knows anything about me. I don't like people to know. I just wish I could take away the first twenty-four years of my life. In the summer I have to wear long sleeves, because people can see my scar, and people have said to me, "What's that?" and of course I'm not going to tell anybody what it is. It will never go.

'I always think, if people knew about me they wouldn't want to know me. There's a stigma attached, particularly to suicide. When I left nursing I went to the Department of Health and Social Security and the man actually said I should be registered disabled. I'll never forget that. I walked out, and I thought, never again will I go back. I'll find a job some other way. But incest isn't such a stigma because people don't believe it anyway. But there'd be no point in me making it up. If you met my father you'd understand.

'I couldn't have gone through it all without the Samaritans. They were the only people. There wasn't anybody else.'

SAMARITAN PRINCIPLES AND PRACTICES

Principles

1 The primary aim of the Samaritans is to be available at any hour of the day or night to befriend those passing through personal crisis and in imminent danger of taking their own lives.
2 The Samaritans also seek to alleviate human misery, loneliness, despair and depression by listening to and befriending those who feel that they have no one else to turn to who would understand and accept them.
3 A caller does not lose the freedom to make his own decisions, including the decision to take his own life, and is free to break contact at any time.
4 The fact that a person has asked the help of the Samaritans, together with everything he has said, is completely confidential within the organization unless permission is freely given by the caller for all or a part of such information to be communicated to someone outside the organization. A Samaritan volunteer is not permitted to accept confidences if a condition is made that not even the director should be informed of them.
5 Samaritan volunteers, in befriending callers, will be guided and actively supported by experienced leaders who will have the advice, when required, of professional consultants.
6 In appropriate cases, the caller will also be invited to

consider seeking professional help in such fields as medical and social work, and material help from other agencies.

7 Samaritan volunteers are forbidden to impose their own convictions or to influence callers in regard to politics, philosophy or religion.

Practices

1 Samaritan volunteers are carefully selected and prepared by the local branch in which they are to serve.

2 The Samaritans are available at all hours to callers, and may be contacted (anonymously, if desired) by telephone or personal visit or by letter.

3 When a caller is believed to be in danger of suicidal action, the Samaritan is particularly encouraged to ask the caller's permission for contact to be maintained during the crisis.

4 Samaritans offer longer-term befriending of callers when appropriate, while recognizing that the branch may from time to time have to set limits.

5 Samaritans listen to those concerned about the welfare of another person and, if satisfied that the third person is despairing, depressed or suicidal, may discreetly offer befriending.

6 Samaritans are normally known to callers only by a forename, and contacts by callers made only through the branch centre.

7 Samaritan branches are banded together in a legally constituted Association whose Council of Management represents all the branches, and reserves to itself the appointment of the person in charge of each branch.

INDEX

Also available in Fount Paperbacks

BOOKS BY C. S. LEWIS

Reflections on the Psalms

'Absolutely packed with wisdom. It is clearly the fruit of very much reflection . . . upon one's own darkness of spirit, one's own fumbling and grasping in the shadows of prayer or of penitence.'

Trevor Huddleston

Miracles

'This is a brilliant book, abounding in lucid exposition and illuminating metaphor.'

Charles Davey, The Observer

The Problem of Pain

'Written with clarity and force, and out of much knowledge and experience.'

Times Literary Supplement

Surprised by Joy

'His outstanding gift is clarity. You can take it at two levels, as straight autobiography, or as a kind of spiritual thriller, a detective's probing of clue and motive . . .'

Isabel Quigley, Sunday Times

Also available in Fount Paperbacks

Half Way

Jim Thompson

We all have to face the changes that middle age brings. Jim Thompson shows how this can be a time of growth, development and change for the better in all areas of our life.

". . . a warm, stimulating book . . ."

John King, Church of England Newspaper

Now and For Ever

Anne Townsend

"A well-researched, highly relevant book on all aspects of marriage today . . . Amidst the current spate of books on marriage, this one stands apart, deserving a place on the best sellers list."

Susan Rimmer, Church of England Newspaper

Mother Teresa: Contemplative in the Heart of the World

Angelo Devananda

This book focuses upon the spirituality which has inspired the wonderful work of Mother Teresa among the poor and dying, consisting mainly of long passages of her own words.

Also available in Fount Paperbacks

A Gift for God
MOTHER TERESA OF CALCUTTA

'The force of her words is very great . . . the message is always the same, yet always fresh and striking.'

Malcolm Muggeridge

Strength to Love
MARTIN LUTHER KING

'The sermons . . . read easily and reveal a man of great purpose, humility and wisdom . . . in the turbulent context of the American race conflict, Dr King's statements have the ring of social as well as spiritual truth . . .'

Steven Kroll
The Listener

A Book of Comfort
ELIZABETH GOUDGE

'The contents are worth ten of the title: this is a careful, sensitive anthology of the illuminations in prose and verse that have prevented the world from going wholly dark over the centuries.'

Sunday Times

The Desert in the City
CARLO CARRETTO

'. . . we have been in the hands of one of the finest of modern spiritual writers, who helps us on the road of love in Christ.'

Philip Cauvin, the Universe